P9-ASJ-944

DATE DUE

GAYLORD	PRINTED IN U.S.A.

Banking and Monetary Policy in Eastern Europe

Studies in Economic Transition

General Editors: **Jens Hölscher**, Senior Lecturer in Economics, University of Brighton; and **Horst Tomann**, Professor of Economics, Free University Berlin

This new series has been established in response to a growing demand for a greater understanding of the transformation of economic systems. It brings together theoretical and empirical studies on economic transition and economic development. The post-communist transition from planned to market economies is one of the main areas of applied theory because in this field the most dramatic examples of change and economic dynamics can be found. The series aims to contribute to the understanding of specific major economic changes as well as to advance the theory of economic development. The implications of economic policy will be a major point of focus.

Titles include:

Irwin Collier, Herwig Roggemann, Oliver Scholz and Horst Tomann (*editors*)
WELFARE STATES IN TRANSITION
East and West

Hella Engerer
PRIVATIZATION AND ITS LIMITS IN CENTRAL AND EASTERN EUROPE
Property Rights in Transition

Hubert Gabrisch and Rüdiger Pohl (*editors*)
EU ENLARGEMENT AND ITS MACROECONOMIC EFFECTS IN
EASTERN EUROPE
Currencies, Prices, Investment and Competitiveness

Jens Hölscher (*editor*)
FINANCIAL TURBULENCE AND CAPITAL MARKETS IN TRANSITION
COUNTRIES

Jens Hölscher and Anja Hochberg (*editors*)
EAST GERMANY'S ECONOMIC DEVELOPMENT SINCE UNIFICATION
Domestic and Global Aspects

Emil J. Kirchner (*editor*)
DECENTRALIZATION AND TRANSITION IN THE VISEGRAD
Poland, Hungary, the Czech Republic and Slovakia

Julie Pellegrin
THE POLITICAL ECONOMY OF COMPETITIVENESS IN AN ENLARGED
EUROPE

Gregg S. Robins
BANKING IN TRANSITION
East Germany after Unification

Johannes Stephan
ECONOMIC TRANSITION IN HUNGARY AND EAST GERMANY
Gradualism and Shock Therapy in Catch-up Development

Hans van Zon
THE POLITICAL ECONOMY OF INDEPENDENT UKRAINE

Adalbert Winkler (*editor*)
BANKING AND MONETARY POLICY IN EASTERN EUROPE

Studies in Economic Transition
Series Standing Order ISBN 0–333–73353–3
(*outside North America only*)

You can receive future titles in this series as they are published by placing a standing order. Please contact your bookseller or, in case of difficulty, write to us at the address below with your name and address, the title of the series and the ISBN quoted above.

Customer Services Department, Macmillan Distribution Ltd, Houndmills, Basingstoke, Hampshire RG21 6XS, England

Banking and Monetary Policy in Eastern Europe

The First Ten Years

Edited by

Adalbert Winkler
Head of Economics Department, Internationale Projekt Consult, Frankfurt am Main and Senior Lecturer, University of Würzburg

First published 2002 by
PALGRAVE
Houndmills, Basingstoke, Hampshire RG21 6XS and
175 Fifth Avenue, New York, N.Y. 10010
Companies and representatives throughout the world

PALGRAVE is the new global academic imprint of
St Martin's Press LLC Scholarly and Reference Division and
Palgrave Publishers Ltd (formerly Macmillan Press Ltd).

ISBN 0–333–97718–1 hardback

This book is printed on paper suitable for recycling and
made from fully managed and sustained forest sources.

A catalogue record for this book is available
from the British Library.

Library of Congress Cataloging-in-Publication Data
Banking and monetary policy in Eastern Europe : the first ten years /
  edited by Adalbert Winkler.
    p. cm. — (Studies in economic transition)
  This book is based on papers submitted and discussions held at a
conference which took place at Wasserschloss Klaffenbach near
Chemnitz, Germany in February 2000.
  Includes bibliographical references and index.
  ISBN 0–333–97718–1 (cloth)
  1. Banks and banking—Europe, Eastern. 2. Monetary policy—Europe,
Eastern. I. Winkler, Adalbert, 1962– II. Series.

HG2980.7.A6 B364 2001
332.1'0947—dc21
                                                              2001040650

10 9 8 7 6 5 4 3 2 1
11 10 09 08 07 06 05 04 03 02

Printed and bound in Great Britain by
Antony Rowe Ltd, Chippenham, Wiltshire

Contents

List of Tables

List of Figures

Acknowledgements

This book is based on papers submitted and discussions held at a conference which took place at Wasserschloss Klaffenbach near Chemnitz, Germany, in February 2000. The generous financial support of the Commerzbank Foundation is gratefully acknowledged. All my colleagues in the Economics Faculty at Chemnitz University of Technology gave their active support to this conference, but I owe special thanks to Bernhard Eckwert and Andreas Szczutkowski, who were always ready to help in preparing and organizing the event. Of course, the conference could not have taken place without the assistance of Brigitte Becker, Sylvana Möbius and Pavel Kroha. Carsten Roth and Karsten Bänder provided invaluable assistance in the production of the typescript.

Finally, I would like to extend my sincere thanks to the management of IPC GmbH, Frankfurt am Main, and to the senior editors of the Studies in Economic Transition series, Jens Hölscher and Horst Tomann, for their support.

Adalbert Winkler
Frankfurt am Main

Notes on the Contributors

Zsófia Árvai, born 1973, works for the Economics and Research Department of the National Bank of Hungary. Her publications have dealt with foreign exchange policy, currency crises and the monetary transmission mechanism. Her current areas of research are interest rate transmission and the consumption and savings behaviour of Hungarian households.

Gerwin Bell, born 1962, is Senior Economist in the International Monetary Fund's European I department. He has been extensively involved in IMF-supported adjustment lending operations in Africa, the Middle East and Eastern Europe. He was educated at University of Trier, Germany, and Yale University, where he also lectured. Publications are on unemployment theory, labour markets and macroeconomic policies. Currently, his main interest of research concerns the macroeconomic and especially monetary policy dimension of financial sector issues.

Peter Bofinger, born 1954, has been a professor of economics at the University of Würzburg since 1992. Previously he worked as a lecturer at the Universities of Kaiserslautern and Constance, and as an assistant to the German Council of Economic Experts and the Regional Central Bank of Baden-Württemberg. Now a research fellow at the Centre for Economic Policy Research, he is the author of numerous publications in the areas of monetary policy, international financial markets, transition economics and pension systems. He is currently working on a book on monetary policy which is expected to be published at the end of 2001.

Lajos Bokros, born 1954, is Director of Financial Advisory Services, Europe and Central Asia at the World Bank. After receiving his PhD in economics in 1980 and working as a research fellow at the Financial Research Institute of the Hungarian Ministry of Finance, he headed several departments at the National Bank of Hungary between 1987 and 1991 and was Director of the State Property Agency from 1990 to 1991. From 1990 to 1995 he was chairman of the Budapest Stock Exchange, and from 1991 to 1995 chairman and CEO of Budapest Bank. Before joining the World Bank he served as Hungary's Minister of Finance in 1995 and 1996.

Claudia Buch, born 1966, is head of the research group 'Financial Markets' at the Kiel Institute of World Economics, and has published extensively on issues such as financial market integration, banking and financial market reform in transition economies, international capital flows and economic reforms in transition economies. She holds a Masters in Economics from the University of Bonn, an MBA from the University of Wisconsin, and a PhD from Kiel University. Dr Buch has been a visiting scholar at the Salomon Centre for the Study of Financial Institutions (New York University), the University of Michigan (Ann Arbor), and the National Bureau of Economic Research (NBER) (Cambridge, MA). Her main area of research is financial market integration with a focus on Europe and the role of banks in intermediating capital flows.

Christa Hainz received her degree in economics from Ludwig-Maximilians-University in Munich. Since 1997 she has been working on her thesis on problems of corporate finance and corporate control in transition economies.

Werner Neuhauss, born 1950, is a Senior Project Manager and Financial Sector Specialist with Kreditanstalt für Wiederaufbau (KfW), Germany's development bank, in Frankfurt am Main. He has been active for many years in international cooperation, and German financial cooperation in particular. Among other activities, he also served as an adviser to a well-known microfinance institution in the Dominican Republic from 1991 to 1993. After four years with KfW's financial sector department, he has been involved since 1998 in designing and conducting several of KfW's credit programmes in South-eastern Europe.

Zbigniew Polanski, born 1958, is Professor of Money and Banking at the Warsaw School of Economics (Chair of Monetary Policy). He is also Adviser to the President of the National Bank of Poland and head of the Money and Banking Unit at its Research Department. From 1990 to 1991 he was Fulbright Professor at the University of Maryland (US) and from 1992 to 1993 Visiting Professor at Carleton University (Canada). He has authored and co-authored many publications (papers and books) both in Poland and abroad, and has won several awards in Poland. His main areas of interest are monetary policy and issues of financial system development, particularly in the context of post-socialist transition.

Monika Schnitzer, born 1961, did her post-doctoral thesis in economics at the University of Bonn after completing her PhD in the European Doctoral Programme (EDP). Since 1996 she has been a full professor of economics at Ludwig-Maximilians-University in Munich, where she has a chair in comparative economics. Her current research is on banking, barter and foreign direct investment in transition countries.

János Vincze, born 1958, is an adviser in the Research and Economics Department of the National Bank of Hungary. He was Visiting Professor at the Budapest University of Economic Sciences, and at the Central European University. He worked as a consultant at the OECD from 1992 to 1993. His publications include macroeconomic subjects such as inflation, monetary transmission policy and vulnerability to financial crises, as well as microeconomic topics such as corporate finance. His main research interest at present is the general equilibrium modelling of open economies.

Adalbert Winkler, born 1962, studied economics at the University of Trier and at Clark University, Worcester, Massachusetts. He obtained his doctorate from Trier University in 1992, and then worked as a research assistant in the university's Department of Money, Credit and Finance. Since 1994 he has been head of the Economics Department at Internationale Projekt Consult (IPC), analysing economic and financial sector developments in many Eastern European countries, focusing on the evolution of national financial systems and SME promotion. In addition, he is a lecturer at the University of Würzburg. From November 1999 to January 2000 he was Visiting Professor, Commerzbank Chair for Money and Finance, at the Chemnitz University of Technology.

Timo Wollmershäuser, born 1972, studied economics at the Universities of Paris (Panthéon-Sorbonne) and Würzburg. Since 1999 he has been employed as a research assistant and junior lecturer in the Department of Economics at the University of Würzburg. His main research interests are in the field of monetary and exchange rate policy.

Claus-Peter Zeitinger, born 1947, is the founder and managing director of Internationale Projekt Consult (IPC) GmbH, a Frankfurt-based firm which specializes in consultancy support for financial systems and financial institutions in developing countries and transition economies. He studied economics at the University of Frankfurt, where he earned a doctorate. He has acted as a consultant to several donor agencies and financial institutions in many countries, in particular Latin America and Eastern Europe, where IPC has gained experience in setting up micro banks from scratch, in upgrading target group-oriented financial institutions and downscaling commercial banks.

Introduction

Adalbert Winkler

Ten years ago, when the transition process in Central and Eastern Europe started, almost nowhere were the differences between the systems and the East–West divide manifested more starkly than in the financial sector. Whereas in market economies the financial sector plays a key role in the coordination of economic activities, central banks and state-owned commercial banks in Central and Eastern Europe had been merely responsible for passively accommodating and monitoring the payment flows between enterprises, as dictated by the central planners. In no way was the financial system actively involved in allocating resources to maximise the efficiency of their use. The task facing the transition economies was thus 'to create a functioning financial system where none had existed before' (EBRD 1998, p. 92).

Despite, or perhaps precisely because of this extreme contrast, it was believed at the start of the reform era that financial system development would be a major factor in the transition process. The banking sector, in particular, was to undergo reform: privatization and restructuring of the existing commercial banks, and the entry of newly founded private banks – in many cases induced by fairly liberal licensing regimes – were seen as appropriate policy measures to end the inefficient and wasteful allocation of resources under central planning and replace it with private sector-driven financial intermediation, the purpose of which would be to organize the investment of savings in the most productive enterprises. The international financial institutions and numerous bilateral development agencies supported this process by granting loans and providing technical assistance for banking sector restructuring, regulatory reform, financial institution building and credit lines for small and medium-sized enterprises on a large scale.

Judged against these expectations, and given the efforts to achieve them, the first decade of financial development has been extremely dis-appointing. In some Commonwealth of Independent States (CIS) countries, the banking sector has been weakened to such an extent that even its ability to carry out payment transactions – 'the "bread and butter" of a financial system' (Caprio 1995, p. 258) – is questionable. The degree of monetization and financial intermediation has dropped to a far lower level than in Western market-based economies, even allowing for lower income levels. In particular, credit to the new private sector is in very short supply. And instead of being 'agents of change' (Van Wijnbergen 1993), banks and financial institutions, because of their governance problems, have often acted as agents of the *status quo ante* by granting bad loans to prop up ailing (former) state enterprises or the companies of the banks' owners. In some countries it turned out that as much as 40 per cent of the total assets of the banking system were worthless. Banking supervision and regulation largely proved incapable of dealing with these problem banks, and in the end almost all of the reforming countries were confronted with financial crises: banks and entire banking sectors collapsed, currencies tumbled and the value of money and financial assets vanished in hyperinflationary episodes, leaving the financial sector almost completely marginalized.

There can therefore be no doubt that this is an appropriate time to take stock of financial development in the region, to draw together the 'lessons learned' and seek insights that will help to address the question, 'Where do we go from here?' This is precisely what this volume seeks to do. It brings together a range of contributions authored by academics engaged in research into the economics of transition and by practitioners who, from different angles, have shaped the process of financial development in the countries of transition over the last decade. Thus, this volume has two objectives: first, to provide an analytical account of some of the key issues of financial development in the region; and second, to present and discuss the various ideas and activities of the institutions that are accompanying the transition process in Central and Eastern Europe.

The chapters in this volume are organized as follows. Following an introductory survey of the current state of financial development and perspectives for the future, the volume centres on three topics: (I) the governance of banks in emerging financial systems; (II) the spread of financial crisis; and (III) perspectives for monetary policy and banking sector development in the coming, second decade of transition.

Chapter 1 by Lajos Bokros, comprising Part I, sets the stage by describing the political economy of financial sector development in the first decade of the transition process. His central themes, which are taken up in more detail by other contributions, are: financial intermediation by banks and capital markets; privatization and governance in banking; foreign participation; corporate finance and the lack of access to credit for small and medium-sized enterprises; the relationship between macroeconomic stabilization and financial development; and the opening up of cross-border capital flows. These topics provide a framework to account for Bokros' categorization of the ten transition countries he analyses: Poland and Hungary are advanced reformers; the Czech Republic and Slovenia are reluctant modernizers; Slovakia and Croatia are struggling with a double legacy; Romania and Bulgaria are desperate reformers; and Russia and Ukraine are prolonged crisis cases. At the same time, Bokros draws lessons from the first decade of financial development in Eastern Europe, and argues that financial sector development in the region will have to be built on three pillars: corporate governance, competition, and prudential regulation and supervision.

Following this introduction, the theme of Part II is the governance of banks in emerging financial markets. Chapter 2 explores one of the few clear tendencies in financial development in Central and Eastern Europe over the first decade: the increasing participation of foreign, Western banks, particularly in the more advanced Central European states. Seeing that the banking sectors of these countries are comparatively stable, Claudia Buch raises the question of whether foreign ownership is a kind of panacea, ensuring the smooth development of local financial systems. The empirical evidence she presents can be summarized as follows:

1. There is no support for the claim that the entry of foreign banks caused large-scale failure of domestic banks. This is explained by the fact that, at least initially, foreign banks tend to follow their corporate clients abroad, and they tend to occupy relatively small market niches. Competitive pressure on the incumbent banks thus increases only gradually, which gives them time to adjust.
2. The market entry of foreign banks, in particular the acquisition of domestic banks through foreign banks, has had the intended effect of improving the efficiency of the domestic banking systems.
3. With regard to the activities of foreign banks the evidence from the countries under review shows that foreign banks find it more difficult to obtain market shares in the deposit business than in the lending business. For other transition countries, notably most of the successor states of the former Soviet Union, Buch suggests that they may find it useful to adopt a more liberal approach to the market entry of foreign banks.

In Chapter 3, Werner Neuhauss discusses, with reference to the example of the German Development Bank Kreditanstalt für Wiederaufbau (KfW), the problems created by the present unstable financial environment for bilateral and multilateral financial institutions that are providing funds to local commercial banks in order to promote lending to private small and medium-sized enterprises. After a brief description of KfW's activities in this field, Neuhauss identifies three instruments that can be applied in these circumstances, and illustrates how they are being used in the context of the German–Ukrainian Fund. Those instruments are:

1. a very intensive, in-depth analysis of potential partner banks
2. imposition of certain limits to exposure and limitation of the volume of funds released at any one time
3. a substantial amount of technical assistance funding for training and monitoring to overcome the institutional deficiencies and the lack of know-how at the partner banks

If these instruments are used proficiently, Neuhauss concludes, it is possible to contain the level of risk involved and, despite financial fragility, to make a significant contribution to expanding the frontier of finance to include micro, small and medium-sized enterprises in the countries of transition.

In the first decade of transition, the financing of economic activity through commercial banks and capital markets was frequently impeded, or even halted altogether, by financial crises. This phenomenon is the central theme of Part III and is addressed by three contributions. In Chapter 4, Zsófia Árvai and János Vincze seek to discover what causes financial crises in transition countries by looking first at theoretical models for explanations. They distinguish between currency attack and escape clause models. However, applying these categories to a characterization of the crises observed in transition countries turns out to be problematic: several of the transition country cases suggest that both crisis regimes may have been relevant in the sense that, in order to avoid an attack on the currency and the attendant costs, central banks opted for the escape clause when in fact at that time they could have kept their commitment to a stable exchange rate. Interestingly, the authors found that scenarios like this took place not only when devaluations loomed, but also when revaluations – i.e. reverse attacks – seemed imminent. With regard to policy issues, Árvai and Vincze find that financial market liberalization may add to the vulnerability of the countries in question, implying that capital controls may indeed be useful to avoid crises. The accompanying lack of capital market discipline, however, can reduce the willingness to undertake reforms, which in turn can cause serious output losses. As financial crises were not a really devastating experience for most transition countries, the authors conclude that financial market liberalization, even if it entails accepting some concomitant pains, is wiser than insisting on avoiding financial market turmoil at all costs.

The boom in financial crises in transition analysed by Árvai and Vincze creates the impression that financial crises are an inevitable feature of the transition process. However, reforming countries do exist that have been able to avoid financial crisis. One of these countries is Poland, which has also recorded the largest economic growth of all the transition countries since 1989. Both of these facts indicate that the Polish experience of financial development is worthy of detailed analysis and that there may be some valuable lessons to be learned. Such an analysis is provided by Zbigniew Polanski in Chapter 5. He sketches the evolution of the Polish financial system and links financial issues with economic development, stressing both the methods adopted to solve problems inherited from the socialist economy in the first half of the 1990s and measures taken to prevent currency crisis during the second half of the decade. According to Polanski the main ingredients of Poland's success story were the following:

1. correct sequencing of reforms
2. assuring financial stability by correctly designing economic agents' incentive structures
3. sound macroeconomic policies, in particular exchange rate flexibility, in order to absorb external shocks and to discourage speculative capital inflows (an issue which is also taken up by Bofinger and Wollmershäuser in Chapter 7)

The Polish example notwithstanding, the crisis-ridden development of the financial system in most of the transition countries is increasingly shaping the advice and policies of the multilateral financial institutions in and for these economies. Against the background of evidence compiled by Árvai and Vincze, Gerwin Bell, in Chapter 6, takes up questions that are relevant to many policymakers:

1. how to develop financial markets without running the risk of creating macroeconomic imbalances
2. how to develop a macroeconomic adjustment programme which would minimize the adverse impact on financial intermediation

His answer consists of three parts: first, macroeconomic policies have to assure that open and hidden fundamental weaknesses, like the contingent liabilities borne by governments, including explicit and implicit loan guarantees, are minimised; second, financial sector policies should foster positive competition, notably through permitting foreign entry into the financial system and by ensuring transparent and rules-based regulation; third, in the case of severe macroeconomic imbalances, whether triggered by a financial crisis or not, an appropriate design of macroeconomic adjustment policies calls for a policy mix which does not rely solely on tight monetary policies. All the same, macroeconomic adjustment still has to be carried out, even if it temporarily holds back financial sector development. However, in the longer run, Bell concludes, there is no contradiction between macroeconomic stability and a properly functioning financial system.

In Part IV the focus shifts to the future development of the financial systems in the transition countries. Here, two aspects stand out that are central to the analysis offered by many of the other contributors: the connection between exchange rate policy, capital account opening and financial/currency crisis; and the role of foreign institutions and capital, including the international donor community, in improving governance in the financial systems of the region. In Chapter 7, Peter Bofinger and Timo Wollmershäuser consider the relevance of monetary policy and exchange rate policy to financial system development in transition economies, and in particular the EU accession countries. Specifically, they ask whether these countries can follow exchange rate targets on their path to EMU without incurring the risk of excessive capital inflows which sooner or later would lead to a collapse of their currencies and severe economic disruption. Pivotal to their contribution is therefore an analysis of the mechanics of exchange rate targeting under the specific conditions of a disinflationary phase. It is shown that under an arrangement involving a fixed nominal exchange rate target central banks are inclined to follow interest rate policies that are inconsistent with an equilibrium on international financial markets. A strategy of permanently fixed exchange rates is advisable only for very small countries and for countries with a relatively small inflation differential *vis-à-vis* the anchor currency. For all other countries, flexible exchange rate targeting is recommended. Given that in the two-year period preceding final EMU entry (stage III) the chosen parity constitutes a ceiling for the final conversion rate, Bofinger and Wollmershäuser finally recommend that the accession countries should carefully analyse at a very early stage whether a pre-cautionary devaluation *vis-à-vis* the euro is required.

In Chapter 8, Claus-Peter Zeitinger summarizes the experience gathered in introducing the idea of 'New Development Finance' to the countries of transition in Central and Eastern Europe. Based on an analysis of some key characteristics of financial institutions in transition economies, he first highlights the need for financial institution-building in general, before explaining the rationale for a particular approach which has been chosen by the international donor community for a number of countries: the establishment of a new target group-oriented financial institution. As examples, he describes the FEFAD Bank in Albania, the Micro Enterprise Bank (MEB) in Bosnia-Herzegovina and the Microfinance Bank of Georgia (MBG). Based on various financial indicators, Zeitinger demonstrates the impact that the three institutions have already made on their respective financial sectors in the short time since they were established. He concludes by noting that at least in countries with extremely underdeveloped financial systems, the contribution of financial institution-building can be far more than the proverbial drop in the ocean.

In Chapter 9, Christa Hainz and Monika Schnitzer round off the volume by offering an outlook for the development of the banking system in transition economies over the next decade. They focus on the question of whether policymakers in the transition countries have to choose between stability and competition when designing measures to improve the development of their local financial systems. Hainz and Schnitzer answer this question by first reviewing the theoretical literature on the subject. They reach two conclusions: in a static context, there is a trade-off between competition and stability. In a dynamic, long-run perspective, however, conditions can be specified which suggest that instead of a trade-off, intensive competition can go hand in hand with banking sector stability. However, based on an investigation of how the initial conditions and the reform strategies chosen in different countries have shaped the banking sector in Eastern Europe, Hainz and Schnitzer argue that neither the trade-off scenario nor the positive dynamic perspective suggested by the theoretical literature is applicable to the transition countries. Rather, given the institutional deficiencies, governance problems, poor regulation and the specific market structures that exist in these countries, it appears likely that more banks will engender not more competition but more instability. What, then, needs to be done in order to build strong and efficient banking sectors? The authors suggest that the answer lies in the tendency which can already be observed in many countries: further consolidation – shaking out inefficiently small, undercapitalized and poorly trained banks – and the entry of foreign banks into the local banking markets on an increasing scale.

References

Caprio, G. (1995) 'The role of financial intermediaries in transitional economies', in *Carnegie-Rochester Conference Series on Public Policy*, Vol. 42, pp. 257–302.
EBRD (1998) *Transition Report 1998 – Financial Sector in Transition*, London.
Van Wijnbergen, S. (1993) 'Enterprise reform in Eastern Europe', in *The Economics of Transition*, Vol. 1, No. 1, pp. 21–38.

Part I
Keynote Address

1
Financial Sector Development in Central and Eastern Europe

Lajos Bokros

Introduction

Financial sector development in Central and Eastern Europe has proved to be a very dramatic process characterized by some well-trumpeted success stories, but even more so by many unexpected collapses of seemingly decent institutions and some systemic meltdown as well. The overall record of transition in the area of financial sector development is much less impressive than achievements in macroeconomic stabilization, economic liberalization and privatization of formerly state-owned enterprises. There are several reasons for this. Among others I would highlight the specific complexities of the financial business and the intense political as well as emotional sensitiveness attached to any major move in this area. Influential stakeholders such as politicians, government officials, business and media people tend to overestimate the real value of particular institutions and at the same time overemphasize their importance to the national economy. In the absence of strong external and internal governance structures managers and at times also owners of banks, brokerages and insurance companies abuse this situation to increase their own influence and perceived importance. The story and history of financial sector development in most countries of Central and Eastern Europe in the first decade of transition ending 1999, therefore, has been an uphill struggle to restore reliable channels and prudent practices of financial intermediation – to create a new culture of trust and confidence against all odds of a dire legacy sometimes characterized by crime and corruption, cronyism and collusion.

Trust based on culture and tradition

It is of course of crucial importance that financial intermediation be re-established in a credible way since there is no economic growth without channelling effectively and efficiently the financial savings of the enterprise and household sectors into investment. This is precisely what is lacking in the transition world after the devastating experience of communism where reallocation of funds was carried out by orders rather than voluntary action based on calculated risk-taking. This has clearly created a different culture and tradition, one which did not require the involvement of trust. To change this culture and tradition back again to a market-oriented one takes a long time even if the political class understands what it takes to re-create this trust and behaves accordingly. But the first decade of transition shows that the constituting elements of this trust have not been fully understood and even less so promoted in practice. In most countries there has been some abuse of the incipient public trust and in some countries – notably Russia – public trust has been systematically destroyed by consecutive abusive degradation of the financial system. In Russia, for example, those who put their money into licensed banks may have lost it at least twice: first, when hyperinflation in the first half of the 1990s wiped out most savings; and second, when the banking sector collapsed in August 1998. Those who kept their savings in foreign currency either under the mattress or abroad still have it. (This means that capital flight is not only a phenomenon reflecting illegal and massive exportation of funds by some wealthy businessmen and a few criminals, but it is also a well-established everyday practice, even for ordinary people, reinforced by hard ways of learning.)

Initial conditions

Some countries started to reform their financial system – first and foremost banking – even before the political changes. Hungary and Poland had established a two-tier banking structure as early as 1987 and 1988, respectively. Yugoslavia, having always had a formal two-tier arrangement throughout the socialist period, started to liberalize banking regulation gradually in the second half of the 1980s. Czechoslovakia, Romania, Bulgaria and member states of the Soviet Union were much less fortunate; financial sector reform could start only after the rather tumultuous political events and under the auspices of the first democratic governments. It is interesting to note, however, that in all countries regulation for the establishment and operation of banks and other intermediaries was quite liberal – sometimes even too liberal – which unleashed substantial initiatives leading to rapid growth in the number and size of these institutions. The good news was that, apart from initially restricting banks' ability to collect household deposits and/or engage in foreign exchange related transactions, there were no significant administrative restrictions in attracting clients, setting fees and interest rates. Competition was not restricted by administrative limitations on client range, lines of business or product pricing. The bad news was that prudential regulation did not exist either – minimum capital standards, liquidity ratios, the concept of solvency and capital adequacy, requirements for asset classification and provisioning, adequate tax rules, etc., were all missing at the beginning of transition. This created a somewhat 'wild east' type of environment for liberal capitalism where clients and managers of still state-owned financial institutions, as well as owners and managers of newly established private ones, could use and sometimes abuse many of the legal and regulatory loopholes for their personal advantage and at the expense of depositors, creditors and ultimately taxpayers as well.

Common features in 2000

After ten years of transition the financial sector in Central and Eastern Europe is characterized by

- a low level of financial intermediation (5–40 per cent of GDP only)
- relatively poor asset quality and serious undercapitalization
- still quite narrow range of services, especially in non-banking
- largely immature governance structures, external and internal
- increasingly sophisticated legal and regulatory framework
- a shallow implementation and enforcement capacity

Compared to either the developed industrialized countries or even some of the fast-growing Asian or Latin American ones, financial intermediation in Central and Eastern Europe is still very shallow. The level of savings channelled through the banking and insurance systems lags behind mature economies, and the amount of funds directly injected into the real sector in the form of loans, corporate bonds, secondary share issues, etc., seems to be well below comparative standards and genuine demand. Even the most advanced Central European economies – Poland, Hungary and the Czech Republic – show a large deficit in corporate lending; the outstanding amount of loans to the real economy does not exceed 40 per cent of GDP. This marked shortfall is the direct result of quite a few factors: in all countries we have seen excessive and generous lending for some years followed by a credit crunch and extreme risk-aversion after the collapse of some banks and brokerages and the tightening of both monetary policy and prudential rules applicable to asset classification, valuation of collateral, provisioning, etc. While the expansion in the first period was clearly assisted by directed and insider lending promoted by influential members of parliaments, government officials and well-connected businessmen, the backlash to this lavish and sometimes imprudent behaviour has resulted in the starving of even the most creditworthy and viable ventures. Many banks in the transition world continue to act like brokerages in money and capital markets by trying to link their business partners directly and offering them fee-generating services rather than taking any risk in their own balance sheets by properly intermediating available funds.

Consecutive attempts to clean up the mess and improve the quality of assets by government intervention have also proved to be a double-edged sword. While rehabilitation of the largest state-owned banks (SOBs) was clearly inevitable given the sizeable amount of inherited bad loans, state-orchestrated programmes of bank recapitalization and restructuring were too generous, too broad, too many and too costly. Managers of SOBs were inclined to understate the true size of their losses before it was too late and then rushed to overstate it once a programme of rehabilitation had been announced. Since it was very difficult to distinguish between bad assets truly inherited from the past and generated after the political changes and it was almost impossible to establish who was responsible for the sharp deterioration of the loan portfolio in light of the collapse of a good number of corporate clients, governments had no choice but to admit defeat and proceed with pumping fiscal funds into ailing flagships of the banking sector. This was not a good excuse, however, for the lack of serious efforts to define and enforce an adequate set of time-bound, quantifiable and monitorable performance criteria against which the achievements of old/new management should have been evaluated. For this reason and also for the rather loose design of other aspects of the rehabilitation plans, coupled with serious flaws in understanding and realizing the magnitude of implicit losses in the case of individual banks, quite a few governments were falling into the trap of being forced to repeat bank and insurance consolidation, thus spending a disproportionately large amount of fiscal resources on an economically unavoidable but politically very painful process. Even Hungary, which is considered to have achieved the best results in financial sector development by now, spent more than 10 per cent of its GDP in more than three rounds of banking sector rehabilitation. In Romania, the flagship bank Bancorex, the former foreign trade bank, had been recapitalized five times before the government finally decided to liquidate it. In other countries – most notably in Croatia – governments felt obliged to rehabilitate large private banks as well in order to avoid a systemic collapse. But in countries where private commercial banks had not played any significant role in collecting household deposits and channelling them to the real sector, even a systemic collapse did not necessarily trigger any meaningful governmental action for banking sector rehabilitation. Russia is obviously the best-known example for this quite rational inaction.

'Banks have much money but all that belongs to other people.'

There is terrible confusion about the nature and role of banking business in the transition world. People tend to have rather distorted views about the essence of banking especially if they make judgements while having only a very superficial understanding of what financial intermediation is all about. In the early period of the evolution of banking it was quite common and publicly accepted to demand that banks should pay high interest on deposits, charge low interest on loans and still remain profitable in order to maximize dividends after corporatization. Managing risks and liquidity in a prudent manner while keeping growth in check and optimizing the costs for gaining maximum productivity were concepts largely unheard of or clearly misunderstood. Private businessmen, local governments, even some churches wanted to establish their own banks in order to attract other people's money to finance their own particular businesses and other activities. In the name of promoting the establishment, expansion and proliferation of new firms, banks, private and public alike, were expected to accumulate a largely illiquid investment portfolio of corporate equity. SOBs were openly criticized by government people for not bailing out important enterprises and placing too much money into risk-free government debentures. Those few managers who wished to set aside more reserves to cover eventual losses of their banks were raided by the tax police. There was no consistent set of behavioural guidelines established by governments to be followed by the managers of SOBs.

Representatives of various state institutions sitting in boards and supervisory boards of SOBs were following either the narrow interest of their respective government department at best or their own personal interests at worst. These representatives were replaced very frequently and in many cases were sent there to promote openly specific political interests of their own constituencies. There were no prudential rules guiding their activity either. Modern banking legislation was introduced late and changed quite frequently. Regulatory and supervisory agencies have remained weak and overpoliticized even in the most advanced economies. In sum, the structures of both internal and external governance have remained largely inadequate except for those financial institutions which were finally privatized to strong and prudent investors, in most cases to first rate and reputable foreign strategic partners.

Increasing differences among countries in financial sector development

Behind this generally opaque picture there are huge and growing differences in financial sector development among countries, explained mainly by the varying degree of government policies and reforms implemented for modernization. Since these divergences are gaining increasing importance by the day and greatly contribute to the ever-growing differences in mid-term development potential as well, it is necessary to highlight them more in detail.

In this short study I will compare the experience of ten Central and Eastern European countries which in the year 2000 could be characterized as belonging to five groups:

1. Advanced reformers: Poland and Hungary
2. Reluctant modernizers: Czech Republic and Slovenia
3. Struggling with double legacy: Slovakia and Croatia
4. Desperate reformers: Romania and Bulgaria
5. Prolonged crisis cases: Russia and Ukraine

It needs to be emphasized, however, that the above classification reflects the achieved level of progress made in financial sector modernization only and may not necessarily imply that the countries in question have reached similar degrees of development in other areas of structural reform. In contrast to macro reforms, where shock therapy and comprehensive packages of adjustment can occur and be successfully implemented all at once, in case of structural and institutional reforms at the micro level there is only gradual progress in a rather evolutionary path which shows a cyclical pattern over time. Nevertheless, after the first ten years of transition one lesson is clear: the maturity and consistency of reforms aiming at financial sector modernization has proved to be the most important factor behind the sustainable and healthy growth of financial intermediation which, in turn, has greatly contributed to the rejuvenation and emergence of a competitive and fast expanding real economy producing sustainable growth.

One more caveat: other factors, such as initial conditions (e.g. the degree of freedom tolerated under the communist system, the relatively free flow of people and ideas, the openness of higher education, the level of private property and experience in entrepreneurship at large, etc.), geographic location (i.e. proximity to Western markets), political factors such as democratic stability and maturity, cultural attitudes like popular sentiments towards foreign investment, widespread and genuine desire to access NATO and the EU, etc. have also been playing a very important role in determining overall progress in economic adjustment and modernization of the ten countries in question. No doubt all these factors have shaped policies and reforms targeted towards financial sector restructuring and the results and failures of these policies and reforms have modified the impact of all other factors as well.

Advanced reformers

Advanced reformers have the following characteristics:

- Most large banks are controlled by foreign strategic investors
- Foreign capital has a dominant role in overall banking
- Most banks have good portfolios, adequate reserves and capital
- Internal corporate governance is close to Western practices
- The quality of services is improving rapidly in corporate business
- There is fast development and a wide selection of services in retail banking
- There are fairly large and liquid capital markets (government bond and equity)
- There is advanced regulation with improving enforcement
- The environment is competitive, with well-regulated entry and exit
- Cross-border financial services have been almost completely liberalized
- There are pockets of resistance in privatization and regulation
- Pension reform and fund management is at an advanced stage

Poland and Hungary both had a very liberal approach in attracting foreign direct investment in their move to modernize the financial sector. Newly established foreign subsidiaries and joint ventures with SOBs and insurance companies appeared in the market even before the political changes. Interestingly enough, Hungary sold off the controlling stake in its two large state-owned insurance companies by 1993 just to avoid their bankruptcy and eventual liquidation. Moreover, all other newly established smaller ventures in the insurance business were acquired by foreign strategic investors in the first half of the 1990s. Poland, in turn, was much more cautious and somewhat timid in this area: its single state-owned insurance firm has never been restructured and still awaits privatization.

Banking was much more exposed to fast track modernization in Poland. Large SOBs, originally established to serve certain well-defined regions and partially modernized through twinning arrangements with experienced Western financial institutions, have now all been absorbed by foreign investors and are competing at the level of the national market. Interestingly enough, the only exception is by far the largest bank, part of the former specialized savings bank, PKO BP, which is still owned completely by the state treasury and keeps being overburdened with the unresolved stock of the non-performing housing loan portfolio. This is a primary example of the more sensitive and complex nature of savings bank restructuring; the political class tends to nurture the illusion that it is really a very special type of business, a crown jewel not to be sold to foreign investors.

Hungary also fell into the same trap to a certain extent when Postabank, a newly established and privately owned large spin-off emerging from the postal savings business, went bankrupt in 1998 as a consequence of brutal mismanagement and eventual fraud. The government felt obliged to rehabilitate this bank with a huge dose of taxpayers' money. There has been extensive debate ever since about whether to keep it in state ownership or privatize it again and, if so, whether to sell control to a wealthy and prudent strategic investor or to aim at an initial public offering only. The former special savings bank OTP is actually privatized in that manner. In Poland, Bank Handlowy was proud of having no controlling stakeholder for a long time, only to see itself being swallowed by Citibank almost completely after a not-so-disguised takeover bid from the German Commerzbank had been opposed by the Treasury. This example clearly shows that, despite political resentment and fierce debate, privatization by selling control to a reputable foreign strategic partner is by far the most successful way of stabilizing and modernizing ailing SOBs. If and when control is effectively kept, either by a government department or in the hands of a self-serving management, even in a case of majority private ownership it can easily lead to a sharp downturn in the fortunes of the bank. In turn, if and when management is prudent and supported by quality investors, the bank may fall prey to large strategic bidders in a fast consolidating market.

Foreign strategic investment in most leading banks has proved to be an unqualified success in both Poland and Hungary after several consecutive efforts of government orchestrated and financed consolidation of insolvent SOBs. Foreign strategic partners have been able and willing to provide not only much needed additional capital and management skills but contributed considerably to product development and innovation, modernization of risk management and treasury operations, internal audit and control, information technology, etc.

It is no coincidence that Poland and Hungary provide the best examples of capital market development as well. Both countries have a fairly large, well-capitalized and rather liquid equity market by regional standards. This regional leading position is a very significant achievement in light of either the absence (Hungary) or the very subordinated importance (Poland) of a mass scheme in privatization. Instead, governments and market participants decided to rely on two important factors: a gradual and by the mid-1990s complete liberalization of foreign portfolio investment (coupled with early capital account convertibility for this type of investment) and high levels of transparency by adopting and enforcing the latest Western standards on information dissemination, listing rules, price formation, clearing and settlement, etc. A high level of self-regulation has characterized both institutions all along which has helped tremendously to re-create the culture and trust needed for a steady growth of turnover in capital market transactions. Apart from trading in equity, the Warsaw Stock Exchange has developed a sizeable corporate bond market, while the Budapest Stock Exchange has become very active in trading government securities. Derivative instruments, such as options and futures, are also traded, albeit this market is still in an early stage in both countries. Poland and Hungary have already started a comprehensive overhaul of their pension system by establishing a three-pillar structure with fully funded and privately managed mandatory and voluntary schemes. These latter – together with the private insurance companies – are now providing the backbone of domestic institutional investment by channelling a growing amount of contractual savings through the recognized capital markets.

The depth of financial sector reform in these two countries is reflected by the high and sustainable level of economic growth achieved in the last three to four years. There is already a wide choice of financial services readily available for real sector firms on a competitive basis. Due to the broad liberalization of cross-border financial transactions at least in the longer end of the market the largest ventures – including the foreign ones – can easily finance themselves even from abroad. Mid-size companies have dozens of banks wooing them and also have access to the less heavily regulated segments of the private capital market. Small firms, however, still face certain difficulties – only a few banks have decided to serve this market segments. At the same time the difficulties of banks in keeping a track record of these small ventures, assessing their risk-return profile and foreclosing collateral in case of default has to be acknowledged as well.

Reluctant modernizers

Reluctant modernizers have the following characteristics:

- The largest banks are still under government control or just recently privatized
- There have been postponed and half-hearted moves to invite foreign strategic investors
- The rehabilitation of leading banks is under way or recently completed
- The portfolios of other, mostly midsize banks are relatively healthy
- Corporate governance is to be strengthened considerably
- The quality of services and retail banking is developing rapidly
- Smaller, quite fragmented and rather illiquid capital markets exist
- Regulation is improving, with few loopholes and uneven enforcement
- There is increasing competition in domestic financial services
- Non-bank financial intermediation is in need of further reforms
- There is some resentment and resistance against further liberalization
- Pension reform and fund management are still at an early stage

The Czech Republic and Slovenia are prime examples of countries where certain favourable initial conditions – especially high levels of per capita income based on rich industrial tradition and a sophisticated economic structure well developed by regional standards; new impetus provided by becoming liberated from being obliged to support less developed parts of the country as a consequence of the break-up of both Czechoslovakia and Yugoslavia – have turned out to be a mixed blessing. Both countries enjoyed unprecedented political stability and even a long honeymoon period with the same government or grand coalition until very recently. The tremendous success of early macrostabilization coupled with a successful shift of export orientation to Western markets has produced a sense of complacency and great reluctance to undertake more substantive and painful structural reforms such as financial sector modernization. Both countries undertook an early recapitalization of their largest financial firms and then decided to stop there. Governments were clearly and publicly against selling control of the flagship banks and insurance companies to any foreign investor. Quite the opposite; either they claimed that banks were already in private hands (in the case of the Czech Republic large banks were half-privatized as a consequence of the mass privatization) or decided that in the absence of strong domestic investors it is better to keep them under close state control (Slovenia).

Mass privatization does not seem to have helped financial sector modernization. In the Czech Republic at least two of the largest banks – Komercni Banka (KB) and Investicni a Postovni Banka (IPB) – felt obliged to continue financing many of their traditional and still unrestructured clients, a good number of which also became owned by them through the investment management companies they established. Increasing equity holdings of banks in their clients' capital was seen as copying the positive German practice of intimate relationship between banks and industrial enterprises without having the burden of German regulation and the German investors themselves. Slovenia used to have a similar aversion toward foreign investors. Even foreign financial investors have not always been welcome in large banks, brokerages and insurance companies. The Yugoslav way of mass privatization has created even more conflicts of interests because in this latter case banks were frequently owned by their less than fully creditworthy clients, rather than the other way around. This is clearly considered the most dangerous way of interlocking ownership representing a vicious cycle.

The cost of reluctance and complacency has proved to be high for the Czech Republic. This is clearly reflected by the recent forced renationalization and rapid sale of the falling IPB to Ceskoslovenska Obchodni Banka (CSOB), an unprecedented move in the history of bank consolidation and privatization. There are several lessons to be drawn from this case. First, there is no point in selling even a relative majority stake to any foreign entity if real management control and responsibility are not transferred. Second, not all respected foreign names represent trademarks of truly prudent strategic partners. Third, governments should prepare very carefully the legal documentation for all transactions making sure that after due diligence, the value of the assets is reasonably and realistically assessed and any remaining uncertainties regarding asset value and contingent liabilities are clearly identified and the assets involved clearly ring-fenced. None of these fundamental criteria seems to have been met when IPB was sold to Nomura. As a consequence, a textbook case of moral hazard has emerged where the private partners have been able and allowed to privatize all the gains and the (new) Czech government was finally obliged to socialize the losses. The cost of reha- bilitation for the three large Czech banks will finally also exceed 10 per cent of GDP, which could have been much lower had these banks been sold to reputable and prudent foreign strategic investors after the initial clean-up, which took place well before the break-up of Czechoslovakia, and eliminated all non-performing assets inherited from the communist period. Even though the Czech Republic can easily afford the resulting increase of its public domestic debt, this is a serious loss of opportunity in terms of lower growth and slower catching up with the EU.

Slovenia has been less complacent in policymaking and declarations but equally reluctant in inviting foreign stakeholders in financial sector institutions. The two largest banks, Nova Ljubljanska Banka (NLB) and Nova Kreditna Banka Maribor (NKBM), are still controlled by the treasury and no specific plans for their final privatization are in sight. Although some foreign banks established wholly owned subsidiaries and started to compete with the two large banks as well as the much smaller regional financial institutions, the small Slovene market has become so overcrowded that now there is a serious threat that the two large public banks will lose market share quickly, especially when free branching will be the name of the game by the time of EU accession. In addition, Slovenia imposed quite a few breaks on the flows of not only short term but also equity capital in an apparent move to defend the domestic currency, and has kept them in place until very recently. Even direct investment in non-financial firms has been sometimes discouraged, perpetuating the inefficiencies of enterprises caused by the flawed mass privatization programme, which in turn have effectively blocked any major restructuring by making it impossible to reduce excessive labour and by keeping salaries much higher than affordable, sustainable and reasonable.

Government policies did not facilitate quick adjustment and deep restructuring either. Payroll taxes are intolerably high just to support a very generous and hardly reformed pay-as-you-go pension system and overextended health care. Private initiative in managing pension funds as well as insurance premia and other contractual savings are at an early stage – only partially accessible to foreign players. In sum, it is a fair statement that the Slovene financial sector is clearly underperforming its potential because – apart from successful bank rehabilitation – it has not been exposed to any major fundamental reform so far.

It is also the irony of history that both the Czech and Slovene equity markets are much smaller and less liquid than the Polish and Hungarian ones; not so much despite but largely because of the unfavourable initial conditions created by the mass privatization schemes. Again, the Czech equity markets constitute a perfect example of what went wrong. At first sight mass privatization programmes seem to have provided a magnificent boost for the formal capitalization of open markets, especially in the absence of any meaningful criteria for listing and information dissemination on stocks. Ideological extremists have even praised the lack of requirements for entry in the name of unlimited liberalism to create markets first rather than kill them with burdensome regulation and heavy supervisory structures. But the lack of transparency and enforceable rules has proved to be an open invitation to abuse, finally resulting in a backlash as a result of the widespread disillusionment with and even hatred against stock markets.

Negative sentiments, especially among foreign portfolio investors, coupled with the heroic efforts of some enlightened officials of the otherwise weak and politically targeted supervisory agency, have recently resulted in tightening regulations to promote trust and confidence which has either been lost or was never there in the first place. The Prague SE has delisted hundreds of firms in the last couple of years but, despite introducing and enforcing tough rules for listing and continuous disclosure, its overall turnover, was still less than one-third of the Budapest SE in 1999. (Hungary constitutes by far the best comparator for the Czech Republic for having the same size economy, roughly GDP US$50 billion, and with the same population – 10 million people – shrinking and ageing quite rapidly.)

Struggling with a double legacy

This involves the following:

- The largest banks are or are about to be sold to foreign strategic investors
- There is a strong drive to privatize all banks after costly systemic rehabilitation
- A number of insolvent banks are still to be rehabilitated or finally liquidated
- Portfolio quality is largely poor except for some medium-sized banks
- Prudential behaviour is still marginal in corporate governance

- The quality of services and retail banking are slowly improving
- There are small and illiquid capital markets with low foreign participation
- There is improving regulation, but still timid and uneven enforcement
- There is weak competition with strong regional and sectoral segmentation
- Non-bank financial intermediation is largely in a pre-transition stage
- There is serious intention and efforts to liberalize cross-border transactions
- Deep fiscal problems exist; pension reform has been postponed

The political and economic development of Slovakia and Croatia during the first decade of transition are strikingly similar while they constitute a marked antidote to the Czech Republic and Slovenia with which they once had a common fate and history for almost 70 years, respectively. Both countries had nationalist and autocratic governments after (re)gaining independence in the early 1990s. Since Croatia was involved in a prolonged armed struggle for restoring its own territorial integrity and indirectly also in Bosnia, nationalist tendencies have become more deeply rooted and have caused more distortions in the weak economy and fragile social fabric than in Slovakia. Charismatic and populist political leaders attempted to create a domestic oligarchy in both countries which gained prominence quickly in insider transactions following the mass privatization programmes which had been started in Czechoslovakia and Yugoslavia.

Initial conditions were much less favourable for the development of financial institutions in many respects. Both countries have inherited a more inward or eastward oriented and less competitive real economy with disproportionately high emphasis on less than state-of-the-art heavy industries (shipbuilding in Croatia and armaments in Slovakia). Markets for these products have collapsed very quickly and neither of these countries has been able to regain sustainable export-led growth ever since. Overall real sector modernization has proved to be painstakingly slow. Relatively high growth in the mid-1990s was based on an artificial boost of demand fuelled by corporate borrowing in both countries and, in addition, by a reconstruction boom in Croatia as well. Since the inherited foreign debt of both countries was minimal, fiscal overspending made it possible to hide structural weaknesses and postpone serious reforms.

Major financial institutions became formally private almost by definition as a consequence of the mass privatization schemes. Croatia had experienced the least advantageous form of privatization because – as in Slovenia – when workers' self-management had formally been transformed into share ownership for insiders, banks immediately and almost automatically fell into the hands of their still unrestructured clients. In addition, the strong regionalization of Croatia – reflected also in the name of its banks – created local monopolies with little competition. Autocratic governments even promoted the sense of national unity by way of assisting the establishment of interlocking ownership between local firms and financial institutions blessed and sanctioned by local governments. An intimate web of mutual services and the lack of transparency created an extremely fertile ground for political abuse and corruption which finally resulted in the collapse of many sizeable banks. Bank rehabilitation has proved to be an unusually broad and expensive exercise in both countries and covered almost the whole sector, public and private financial institutions alike.

The legacy of this futile experiment with oligarchic development is as damaging as that of the communist system. Recently elected democratic governments in both countries are trying desperately to overcome the dire consequences of these distortions by implementing bold reforms aimed at catching up with the most advanced transition economies. In Slovakia, the government has cleaned up the portfolio of the three largest SOBs, Vseobecna Uverova Banka (VUB), Investicna a Rozvoja Banka (IRB) and Slovenska Sporitelna (SS), and has announced its deter-mination to sell controlling stakes in all of them to first-class foreign strategic partners as quickly as it is possible. Legal and regulatory mod-ernization as well as corrections of insider privatization deals take place at a rapid pace together with a strong drive to attract foreign direct investment in large non-financial firms. Sweeping financial liberaliza-tion made Slovakia eligible for OECD membership in 2000. Croatia, for its part, has successfully completed the privatization of its flagship bank, Privredna Banka Zagreb (PBZ), while continuing its serious efforts to attract strategic partners for a number of medium-sized banks. (The sale of control to strong foreign professional investors in Rijecka Banka (RB) and Splitska Banka (SB) is about to be finalized.) However, the liquidation of a number of deeply insolvent medium-sized banks needs to be completed in Croatia before good governance can become predominant in managing financial institutions. Insurance still remains largely unrestructured in both countries, while foreign players are gaining ground very quickly at the expense of the still largely state-owned former monopoly.

Again, the irony of history is that the Slovak and most likely the new Croat authorities will show more genuine desire to introduce the most advanced best practices of corporate restructuring, insolvency, liquidation, and at the same time spare no real effort to woo much-needed foreign direct investment (FDI) to compensate for the bad image their countries have acquired compared to the more favourable perceptions of international investors regarding the Czech Republic and Slovenia. Given their double legacy and their less developed economic structure, Slovakia and Croatia will likely encounter more difficulties in attracting a sizeable amount of FDI from truly reputable foreign firms. This is especially true in the case of direct investment in financial institutions: the prime motive of interest and action is not so much the present value of existing ventures but the future growth potential of the whole economy and the chances of the country gaining access quickly to the EU. Slovakia tends to be much more fortunate in this regard. It may even be able to catch up with the first-tier accession candidates, while Croatia has yet to start serious negotiations at all.

As far as capital market development is concerned, mass privatization coupled with the lack of adequate regulation and enforcement proved to be detrimental to substantive take-off. Within this bleak picture there are certain differences leading the observer to conclude that the Slovak equity market has more stocks and perhaps more liquidity, but the Croats have some larger, better-quality firms (Pliva, Podravka and Zagrebacka Banka are well-known names even in the international arena). Legislation and regulation have improved recently but enforcement still leaves much to be desired. Latecomers are struggling not only with the already mentioned dire legacy of oligarchic development, but also with the lack of enthusiasm for going and remain public. The small size of the domestic market coupled with the lack of institutional funds to be invested constitute additional impediments in the short run. Fiscal constraints and strong vested interests in maintaining generous pension privileges – especially in Croatia – will make any effort to provide a strong boost to contractual savings highly unlikely in the foreseeable future. Conversely, government bond markets have a better chance of expanding quickly due to the sizeable fiscal deficits and debt in both countries.

It is an interesting feature of the institutional arrangement in both countries that the respective central banks play a crucial role not only in overall banking regulation but also in supervision and oversight.

Since both institutions assumed the role of a proper central bank, and started issuing money and regulating money supply less than ten years ago, it is no surprise that there is a relatively weak institutional capacity to carry out these new functions. Both central banks have done a good job in implementing prudent monetary policies which has contributed significantly to the maintenance of macroeconomic stability throughout the 1990s. Banking supervision, in turn, has become a politically sensitive and controversial business where strong vested interests, at times working against prudent practices, have prevailed. It is not so much the weak intellectual capacity but the lack of political support which has prevented tough prudential regulation and supervision from being implemented.

Desperate reformers

Desperate reformers have the following characteristics:

- Few large insolvent banks are still in government hands
- Desperate attempts have been made to privatize sizeable banks
- Quite a number of insolvent banks are still to be rehabilitated or liquidated
- Portfolio quality is largely poor, except for some smaller banks
- Prudential behaviour is still marginal in corporate governance
- Quality of services and retail banking is slowly improving
- There are very small and illiquid capital markets with low foreign investment
- Regulation is improving with uneven and unpredictable enforcement
- Competition is weak, and foreign subsidiaries are playing only a marginal role
- Non-bank financial intermediation is in a pre-transition stage
- There is serious intention for further liberalization including cross-border transactions
- There is a lack of institutional investors, with no pension reform in sight

Except for Albania and the former members of the now defunct Soviet Union, Romania and Bulgaria have truly inherited nothing but the worst from the communist system in Eastern Europe. Both countries used to have extremely rigid, neo-Stalinist economic management systems, maybe with more tolerance toward small-scale auxiliary ventures in

Bulgarian agriculture but especially devastating autarchic tendencies in Romania. While preserving national statehood after World War II may have been an asset, public structures have proved to be very weak with a quite shallow implementation capacity ever since.

Political fragmentation, especially in Romania, has led to a further weakening of the reform drive which has not resulted in a critical mass of consistent measures to be introduced in almost any area of the transition agenda. Romania not only lost the first six years of transition in terms of postponing structural reforms; even the first two governments of the coalition which won the 1997 election were much paralysed by factional fighting. Bulgaria, in turn, has been more fortunate. After the deep crisis of 1996/7 an unusually strong and unified government has tried to make up for lost time by restoring not only macrofinancial stability but starting also corporate restructuring, privatization and financial sector modernization. Despite the additional negative impact of external factors, such as the Kosovo conflict and the disruption in trade and transportation links, Bulgaria has managed to distinguish itself as having an economy with the best mid-term perspectives in the whole of the Balkans. In the last months of the 1997–2000 election period Romania also started to catch up desperately and made progress under the leadership of its new technocratic prime minister. Nevertheless, both countries have a long way to go before they can truly satisfy the membership criteria for the EU and close the gap with others.

Banking sector development was started with the establishment of three or four large (typically a foreign trade, an industry and an agriculture oriented) SOBs without transforming the old savings bank into a universal financial institution. The left-leaning socialist governments in the first half of the 1990s did not consider bank privatization seriously. All they did was to allow the proliferation of new and small private commercial banks as a consequence of a quite liberal policy on entry which could also be interpreted as a lack of adequate regulation on minimum capital standards and prudential requirements of ownership. These small banks constituted a mixed blessing because most of them turned out to be almost like pyramid schemes and went bankrupt quickly, providing justification for those who opposed the privatization of banks altogether. However, the large SOBs did not perform better either and virtually all of them in both countries proved to be technically insolvent by the mid-1990s as well.

Reactions to this disappointing development were somewhat different in the two countries, mostly because of the diverging political solutions to the emerging crisis. In Bulgaria, the whole unreformed economy collapsed at the end of 1996 and the new authorities made a complete U-turn on policy. They decided to rehabilitate all SOBs by cleaning up their loan portfolios and announced an uncompromising and ambitious privatization programme involving foreign strategic investors. The Bulgarian government established a specific institution, the Bank Consolidation Company (BCC), to direct and harmonize efforts of both pre-privatization restructuring and individual transactions of selling control. Given the dire situation of the Bulgarian economy and the negative image of the country it has been extremely difficult to attract prudent foreign partners, but the steadfastness and perseverance of the government has paid off. The Bulgarian government has made wise decisions on timing and sequencing and has thus been able to build up momentum and gradually change the perception of the outside world regarding the prospects of the Bulgarian economy. The easiest target, Postbank, a newly established and hence relatively unspoiled small SOB, plus a spin-off of the large foreign trade monopoly, the United Bulgarian Bank (UBB) went off the hook first, followed by two somewhat larger, regionally important and but still more easily restructured SOBs (Expressbank and Hebrosbank). The privatization of the largest and by far the most important bank, the former foreign trade monopoly Bulbank, which covers almost 40 per cent of the economy, has been successfully completed despite the fierce and open resistance of the incumbent management to the sale of control to foreign strategic interests. Only two large SOBs remain to be sold – Biochim and Savings Bank – which may not be too difficult given the good momentum generated by recent transactions.

Romania has been able to make much less progress in both bank rehabilitation and privatization. While BancPost, a similarly newly established and healthy SOB, was quickly sold, together with the relatively clean and small Development Bank (BRpD), there has been no real progress on the large, truly systemic banks. On the contrary: the flagship bank, Bancorex, the former foreign trade monopoly, was recapitalized five times at a cost of more than US$1 billion to the Romanian taxpayer, only to be finally liquidated last year. Banca Agricola (BA) was subsequently rehabilitated and drastically cut in size and has in the meantime been privatized. Banca Comerciala Romana (BCR), which was perceived as the healthiest of the large three, is still in government hands. Given the volatile political environment and the excessive bargaining power of the managers of the SOBs – who were appointed on the basis of their political affiliation according to coalition agreements

– there seems to be no quick fix either for BCR or for the other SOB, the recently corporatized Savings Bank (CEC).

Given these circumstances, it is almost inconceivable to expect substantive improvements either in corporate governance and prudent behaviour or quality of services, quality of assets, internal audit, risk management, credit allocation, etc. While legislation has improved considerably in the second half of the 1990s in both countries, enforcement has remained uneven, unpredictable and sometimes politically conditioned, especially in Romania. Shallow implementation capacity constitutes a real bottleneck in both jurisdictions. Neither of the two central banks has ever been up to the requirements of crisis prevention and management.

The lack of confidence and confusion about rules and values to be upheld are clearly highlighted by the latest events in the series of mini banking crises hitting Romania. As a side-effect of the collapse of a sizeable investment fund, there was a run on BCR and at the same time three other medium-sized banks went into receivership. (One of them was the proudly named International Bank of Religion.) In the meantime courts finally rejected the request of the National Bank of Romania to declare bankrupt Dacia Felix Bank – precisely two years after it had originally been submitted.

Capital markets are very small and illiquid in Romania and Bulgaria despite or because of the flawed and botched mass privatization programmes which flooded the initially underregulated equity markets with hundreds – in the case of Romania, thousands – of low-quality stocks. While there have been heroic efforts in both countries to introduce serious confidence-building measures by creating all necessary infrastructure for trading, clearing and settlement as well as listing and information dissemination, neither domestic nor foreign participants have invested any meaningful amount of money in those two markets so far.

The underdeveloped nature of banking, insurance and capital markets in Romania and Bulgaria is strongly correlated with the early results in restructuring the real economy. It is clear that the severe distortions caused by inept and irresponsible communist megalomania render the legacy extremely difficult to deal with – again, especially in Romania. A very large number of sizeable industrial firms are not privatizable at all even after financial liquidation and dismemberment. In quite a few important cases only the physical closure of enterprises makes sense because markets are completely lost, the technology involved is outdated and harmful to health, there is immense ecological degradation and only financial liabilities rather than assets. The establishment of a market economy depends largely on new ventures, both domestic and foreign. Since foreign direct and portfolio investment have been quite negligible until very recently, both economies have depended mostly on the expansion and organic development of domestically owned small and medium-sized enterprises (SMEs). Due to the rapid contraction of the state sector the new and vibrant private sector has simply been unable to compensate for the losses in overall output. In addition, SMEs are much less bankable and have little access to open capital markets. The state of affairs in the financial sector is just a mirror image of the hardships in the real economy.

Apart from the growing arrears in certain enterprises, especially in public utilities and the ballooning intercorporate debt reflecting soft budget constraints and lack of strong market discipline which would involve credible threats of bankruptcy and liquidation, fiscal prudence has largely been maintained in the second half of the 1990s in both countries. Bulgaria was helped by the currency board arrangement (CBA) introduced in the summer of 1997, but Romania, which has been reported as being on the verge of a financial collapse from time to time, has been able to maintain fiscal discipline and has outperformed even Hungary in terms of general government balance. The sad irony here is that fiscal prudence alone is not a recipe for restarting economic growth, especially if there is no supply-side adjustment in the economy due to the lack of flexible micro structures able to respond to market signals. Postponing structural reforms time and again might render prudent macroeconomic policies largely useless or even harmful. Romania has proved to be almost a textbook case for this lesson.

Prolonged crisis cases

These have the following characteristics:

- Most banks are in private hands and the majority of them are insolvent
- Selective rehabilitation is coupled with a reluctance to invite foreign strategic partners
- Large numbers of banks are to be delicensed and liquidated
- Portfolio quality is very poor, with little sign of improving
- Corruption is rampant, along with crime and cronyism
- There is low service quality, and rudimentary retail banking
- Small, discredited and abused capital markets exist

- There is weak regulation and openly politicized enforcement
- Domestic markets are fragmented and subject to monopolization
- Non-banking financial intermediation is almost non-existent
- Attitudes towards financial liberalization are largely hostile
- There is permanent fiscal crisis, and pension reform is not on the agenda

Russia and Ukraine represent such peculiar cases that they hardly find their place in international comparison. Russia is unique in terms of sheer size and strategic importance while Ukraine is unique for its truly permanent crisis and apparent lack of opportunities. Russia could well afford not to implement any serious structural reform because its vast exportable natural resources coupled with its fine ability to extract unlimited amounts of financial assistance from the West have always helped it to survive the worst of its crises. Ukraine has given up its nuclear arsenal and does not posses any meaningful amount of natural wealth. Moreover, regaining full sovereignty after 300 years of Russian dominance is not an easy task. The Ukrainian state is particularly weak, became very fragmented and has fallen prey to the emerging local oligarchy. In Russia the ruling elite (the political class and the oligarchy) is largely unwilling while in Ukraine it is unable to introduce substantive market-oriented reforms.

Financial sector development was very similar until the mid-1990s. As in Romania and Bulgaria, three or four large SOBs were originally carved out of the mainframe of the former Central Bank of the Soviet Union. Saving banks which were operating throughout the communist period maintained their narrow focus for many years. There was also hyperinflation which eliminated not only the value of banking assets but also that of the liabilities as well, thus realizing a very special 'bank rehabilitation scheme' financed exclusively and involuntarily by depositors. This devastating crisis, however, created a window of opportunity to strengthen the hard core of the banking sector by privatizing the SOBs of systemic importance in a prudent and efficient way. Unfortunately this moment was lost because the political class in both countries remained at least very suspicious if not openly hostile to the idea of selling their perceived 'crown jewels' to foreign investors. Instead, they decided to create a domestically rooted echelon of large entrepreneurs by allowing some well-connected people to emerge as tycoons by acquiring immense chunks of former state property for a symbolic price. This artificially and deliberately accelerated 'original accumulation of capital' was first assisted by selective licensing of foreign trade transactions in a still largely closed economy, then by the mass privatization schemes which resulted in concentrating large amounts of wealth in the hands of insiders, and finally – at least in Russia – by the 'loans for shares' schemes when a handful of these previously privileged individuals were offered the chance to take over the controlling stakes in large chunks of the extractive industries. In Russia the emerging oligarchy was able to acquire control over the large SOBs as well, while in Ukraine most of them are still in government hands but have lost considerable market share to new and private financial institutions.

Another common feature of banking sector development in Russia and Ukraine was the rapid proliferation of small private financial houses in the first half of the 1990s. As in Romania and Bulgaria, this tendency was not so much the result of a genuine drive for liberal market reforms but rather due to the lack of meaningful and consistently applied legislation and regulation for a long time. Although banking laws and rules have improved considerably in the last two years in both countries, central banks are still struggling with the immense backlog of delicensing these small, frequently non-operative bank-like entities.

From a systemic point of view, however, it is more important to analyse the situation and health of the large banks operating nationwide. It is a common feature of banking in both countries that even the large banks play only a very marginal role in financial intermediation in general, and in financing the real sector in particular. This is one of the most important reasons why the collapse of the whole Russian financial system in August 1998 did not really trigger a serious downturn in the real economy. On the other hand, the insignificant role of banks in financing real sector activity did not prevent the same banks from accumulating huge losses in their loan and investment portfolios. Although it is true that the August 1998 meltdown was basically triggered by the collapse of the government debt market and further exacerbated by the devaluation of the Russian currency, this is not to conceal the fact that the crisis was only making illiquid already insolvent banks. At present the reverse is also true; the actual refloating of the Russian economy as a consequence of the exceptionally high export prices for oil and some other natural resources coupled with newly found fiscal discipline and real sector growth largely due to opportunities of import substitution, has restored liquidity for quite a few banks while in most cases their more fundamental problem of deep insolvency has not been addressed at all.

There are at least two more reasons why financial intermediation has not developed in a more satisfactory manner. First, real sector decline was dramatic in both countries. Russia has already lost almost half of its former output, while Ukraine lost more than 60 per cent. Unlike Romania and Bulgaria, even SMEs could not develop fast enough in these rapidly declining economies due to the other main factors worth mentioning here: self-serving bureaucratic bottlenecks, devastating criminalization of economic and social life and finally rampant corruption. Rent-seeking behaviour and public acceptance of corruption predominate. It cripples almost all economic activity, but first and foremost productive investment. As a consequence, except for firms in the export sector, creditworthy clients are few and far between while opportunities to make money in corporate lending are scarce and profitability is much higher in other areas.

Retail banking is even less lucrative under these dire circumstances, therefore banks did not put a high emphasis on developing these services. Rather, banks were and have remained much more interested in acting as brokerage firms in the new, but at least in Russia at one stage, fast expanding, capital markets.

Capital market developments are very different in the two countries concerned. Russia was a real magnet for foreign portfolio investors at least before the crisis even though legislation and regulation concerning property rights, transfer of title, minority protection, clearing and settlement, foreign exchange controls, etc. are still far from perfect even today. This exceptional appeal for investments in Russia was explained by the sheer size of the potential rather than actual market, the overall attractiveness of the export-oriented extractive industries, the marked liberalization of foreign portfolio investment and finally the significant amount of public borrowing which created a speculative market for state debentures. In Ukraine only the last of these factors was present, but it proved to be insufficient in light of political instability and lack of strategic importance.

Things have changed considerably after the outbreak of the Russian crisis. Since influential people – including reputable foreign firms – lost a fortune when capital and foreign exchange markets collapsed, it is very unlikely that the same enthusiastic rush for Russian equity and government paper will materialize in the foreseeable future. Russia is not keen to step into the same river either. Recent efforts to keep tight budget controls and at the same time implement fundamental reforms in taxation suggest that the authorities do not intend to restart massive foreign borrowing even after the oil bonanza. There is more hope of seeing a gradual revitalization of the equity markets in the long run if and when much needed changes in basic legislation and corporate behaviour take place.

While clearly there is opportunity if not certainty for the Russian real economy to take off, Ukraine is likely to prolong further its permanent crisis. The political class is more fragmented than ever and the government does not seem to have either the impetus or the political support to undertake some desperately needed basic reforms, such as public expenditure reshuffle, tax administration, legal environment and practice for corporate bankruptcy, bank rehabilitation and real privatization, as well as alleviating the burden on SMEs, reducing red tape, fighting corruption and crime, reorganizing agriculture, the energy sector, physical and human infrastructure, creating a favourable, appealing environment for foreign direct and portfolio investment, etc. Unfortunately, in terms of implementing efficient public policies and micro reforms, there is no one single bright spot on the horizon of Ukraine in the short and medium term.

If there are countries and cultures where the vast majority of the population has lost its trust almost entirely in public institutions and domestic financial firms, they are Russia and Ukraine – and without doubt, most other countries of the CIS. To change this still deteriorating trend will require heroic efforts and a sea change in behaviour on the part of the respective governments and the ruling oligarchies.

Three pillars of financial sector development

As is quite obvious even from a sketchy analysis of the political economy of financial sector development in the transition world, the formation and evolution of reliable channels of financial intermediation throughout the 1990s has been very different from one country to the next and there is no reason to believe that this trend of marked divergence will soon be replaced by strong convergence toward well-developed and mature structures. Some countries will join the dream land of the European common market within a very short period of time. Others will perhaps wait for another generation before getting in. There might be a tendency towards equalization in income-generating capacity among the transition economies after another decade of differentiation, but there will be no easy reversal of the culture and traditions which are so detrimental to the expansion of healthy financial intermediation fostered by efficiently managed and prudent institutions.

The emergence and dominance of local oligarchies, sometimes stronger than the state itself and characterized by rent-seeking behaviour, asset stripping, state capture, crime and corruption, could well become so embedded in the social fabric that it is no longer possible to get rid of them without a devastating, full-blown crisis of the economic and societal system.

Slovakia and Croatia have been very fortunate for having been able to change course early on; Bulgaria has every hope of following suit. Romania, however, is fast approaching an important historic crossroads since the results of the parliamentary elections in 2000 may well strengthen nationalist and populist elements and turn the clock back. Some other countries, most notably Russia and Ukraine, do not seem to have a historic chance of breaking the overarching influence of their local oligarchies in the short run. But the strongly appealing perspectives of EU accession and the genuine desire of the local electorate to achieve Western economic standards by embracing not only the values of an open and competitive market but also accepting its consequences can be crucial in a mid-term horizon. It is clearly in the interest and the moral obligation of people involved in the development business to facilitate the accumulation and strengthening of all creative elements which promote prudent civic culture and establish a tradition of individual integrity and honesty in business and civic life.

In the area of financial sector development there seem to be three fundamental pillars determining the scope, nature and quality of institutions emerging there and influencing the basic course of development these institutions embark upon:

1. Internal and external governance structures
2. Domestic and international competition
3. Prudential regulation and supervision

These three pillars are mutually complementary and overlapping: improvements in one area clearly help the modernization and strengthening in the others. Nevertheless, there is a critical mass in all three areas which must be achieved in order to reach maturity of the financial system and put it on a secure path of sustainable expansion and development while also maintaining a high level of trust and confidence. Unfortunately none of the transition countries has yet reached that stage of development; the regulatory and supervisory structures need to show considerable further progress even in Poland and Hungary.

Corporate governance

This would involve:

- once-and-for-all rehabilitation of viable SOBs of systemic importance
- recapitalization of private commercial banks only in exceptional cases
- the privatization of SOBs immediately after restoring minimum solvency by selling controlling stakes to reputable foreign strategic investors
- general depoliticization and professionalization of financial intermediation
- discontinuation of all directed and insider lending and investment practices
- management contracts with time-bound and monitorable performance criteria
- adequate representation of all stakeholders' interests in supervisory boards
- proper checks and balances in internal management, credit allocation, etc.
- implementation of management information systems and internal audits

In light of the growing tide of anti-foreign sentiment and fierce debate about the 'desirable and acceptable' level of foreign participation in the financial sector it seems impractical and unwise to advise governments that they should sell their largest and systemically most important financial institutions to foreign strategic investors. Even enlightened and pragmatic governments appear quite reluctant to offer management control to foreign professionals at least in the large saving banks and insurance firms no matter how prudent and reputable the prospective foreign buyers might be (PKO BP in Poland and OTP in Hungary are good cases in point). People might also find it strange that a kind of a 'universal panacea' is being offered to remedy most if not all fundamental weaknesses in the financial sector. Continental European experience does not seem to justify this peculiar type of sweeping privatization either; there are quite a few countries, such as Germany, France and Italy, where state – or at least local government – control as well as dispersed ownership of domestic non-financial institutions and individuals have characterized important segments of banking, insurance and capital markets without substantially deteriorating the quality of governance. Why is it not possible for Central and Eastern Europe to follow their example?

There are several reasons, some of them decisive. First, communism was too long and too successful in destroying trust in domestic private institutions and a tradition of prudent behaviour in economic and social life. Second, when the futile communist experience in economic management was finally over, world markets were already characterized by massive cross-border transactions and international competition was producing new and improved services at a scale never seen before. Third, the demonstrational impact of liberal capitalism – very much magnified by modern telecommunication – coupled with the strong desire to catch up with the most developed world produced the almost insatiable thirst of clients in Central and Eastern Europe for gaining immediate access to the latest and best services. The interplay of these and many other factors made it impossible that people finally free to choose should wait another 50 years before enjoying the same quality of services as their Western counterparts. But people demanding the best as customers are unfortunately unable to create them as producers. They demand that reliable and proven foreign products and services are clearly available to them immediately while simultaneously refusing to accept those structures – including those of foreign governance – which actually create and maintain the high level of quality of those products and services. (Communist deputies of the Russian parliament indicated privately that while they cannot accept foreign control in flagship domestic banks, they would also place their own money mostly in foreign banks domiciled in Russia or abroad. Nationalism and populism just perpetuate the rule of the oligarchy.)

Selling control in financial institutions to foreign strategic partners is the best way to bridge the huge gap between the very demanding and fully Westernized consumer mentality and the persistent ignorance of what it takes to be a prudent provider of the same quality products and services. Since there is no point in resisting or slowing down the influence of consumer capitalism the only way found is to accelerate the (re-)creation of the culture of confidence and the tradition of prudence inherent in an efficient, well-functioning market economy.

Competition

This would involve:

- equal opportunities for entry and exit with maximum transparency

- a decisive drive against all sectoral and regional market fragmentation
- the elimination of administrative limits on credits, interest rates and fees
- a gradual liberalization of cross-border transactions and capital flows
- simple, reasonable, transparent and equitably enforced rules for taxation
- a strong culture and regulation of creditors' protection in corporate life
- strict enforcement of insolvency across the whole spectrum of clients
- a level playing field in all areas of financial intermediation
- only temporary fiscal preferences to increase the creditworthiness of clients
- direct state involvement in building physical and human infrastructures

Managing transition is an art rather than a science; timing and sequencing are key. While fostering unlimited domestic competition is essential from the outset, international competition could be increased gradually but according to a well-established and publicly announced set of operational criteria. Countries preparing themselves for the single market of the EU will be able to catch up more quickly not only in terms of income and productivity but also of culture and tradition. Enhancing the creditworthiness of corporate and individual clients by introducing proper incentives for stimulating financial savings and investment could also multiply the growth and profit opportunities for financial intermediaries, thus creating a virtuous cycle of trust and prudence.

Competition, while being a strong incentive and disciplinary force to enhance quality and increase efficiency, should also be properly managed. Governments should focus on creating their own single market by eliminating all remaining administrative barriers, on the one hand, and helping disadvantaged clients like SMEs, on the other. Transparent, easily accessible guarantee schemes, one-time grants to cover initial costs, training and marketing subsidies, and infrastructure support make a lot of sense together with the strict and even enforcement of regulation on bankruptcy, liquidation, secured lending, foreclosure of collateral, title transfer, share and company registration, minority protection, taxation, etc.

Prudential regulation and supervision

This would involve:

- the implementation of the Basle core principles on banking
- even higher capital adequacy and solvency standards
- the strictest application of rules on portfolio classification
- only a gradual increase of provisioning requirements
- deposit insurance being extended only to reputable institutions
- the independent rating of leading financial intermediary firms
- the close cooperation or consolidation of supervisory agencies
- the political and financial independence of supervisory agencies
- strong cooperation between host and home country regulators
- a relentless fight against crime and corruption, cronyism and collusion

Finally, the weakest point. After ten years of transition there is no one single country in Central and Eastern Europe where the financial regulatory and supervisory agencies are really free from the sometimes very open and brutal political interference and thus able to apply the highest professional standards without compromise. It is less of a problem in those jurisdictions where governance in and competition among individual financial institutions is strong enough. Nevertheless, this is still a very dangerous situation because the accelerated pace of new financial products and services requires constant attention to market developments, frequent licensing and deep analysis of complex problems with increasing reliance on discretionary judgements. If the underlying values and mandates governing the behaviour of management and staff of these agencies are shaky or inconsistent then there is little hope of ensuring that public confidence prevails in these financial markets. Task number one for the next decade is to strengthen considerably the institutions of prudent regulation and supervision.

Part II
The Governance of Banks in Emerging Financial Systems

2
Governance and Restructuring of Commercial Banks

Claudia M. Buch[1]

Motivation

Banking reform in transition economies has been discussed controversially for the past decade and is likely to be a crucial policy issue for at least the next decade to come. Whereas some of the advanced reform countries have made substantial headway with regard to banking reform, some countries still have a long way to go. The recent currency crisis in Russia, for instance, has rendered almost the entire banking sector insolvent and has burdened policymakers with the task of creating an efficient financial system from scratch. The relevant policy issues are numerous: the problem of non-performing loans on the balance sheets of commercial banks has to be dealt with, the macroeconomic implications of banking reform need to be considered, an appropriate regulatory framework needs to be chosen and enforced, and the optimal sequence of internal and external financial liberalization must be selected. Eventually, reforms must solve the complicated issue of how to establish proper incentive, i.e. corporate governance mechanisms, in the banks and how to ensure an efficient intermediation between savers and investors.[2]

When and how to subject domestic banks to competitive pressure through foreign financial institutions is one of the key problems that needs to be solved. At least theoretically, market entry of foreign banks can be a double-edged sword: on the one hand, foreign competition can enhance the efficiency of the domestic banking sector, serve to improve know-how and technological skills, and provide access to foreign savings; on the other hand, domestic banks burdened with non-performing loans may not be able to withstand competitive pressure, which may result in bankruptcies, and valuable links between firms and enterprises may be destroyed. Consequently, policymakers have typically been cautious with respect to liberalizing fully the market access of foreign banks and have tried implicitly or explicitly to regulate entry.

Since the optimal sequence of banking reforms, in particular of internal and external financial liberalization, has been dealt with elsewhere (see, for instance, Cho and Khatkate 1989, Buch 1997), the purpose of this chapter is to review the experience of three of the more advanced transition economies of Central and Eastern Europe with regard to the market access of foreign banks. The cases of the Czech Republic, Hungary and Poland are chosen not only because data availability for these countries is much better than for less-advanced reform states; these countries also represent quite different strategies towards foreign banking. Whereas Hungary has had a relatively liberal attitude towards foreign banking from the onset of reforms, the Czech Republic and Poland have been more restrictive for a considerable amount of time. More recently, however, foreign banks have been involved more closely in the process of privatizing domestic financial institutions.

Ultimately, the experiences of these countries should help to answer the question of whether market entry of foreign banks, in particular the acquisition of domestic through foreign banks, has had the intended effect of improving the efficiency of the domestic banking systems. An empirical investigation of this question on the basis of aggregated data, however, is a difficult task, mainly because different causes of changes in the profitability of banks can hardly be disentangled. If foreign-owned banks were found to have a higher profitability than domestic banks, this could be the result of improved risk-management skills and corporate governance structures. It is equally conceivable, however, that foreign banks had better starting positions because they were not burdened by non-performing loans or because they enjoyed a better reputation than domestic banks, thus giving them some market power. Although this chapter will try to differentiate between these two interpretations, further microeconomic evidence to solve the issue will be needed.

At the same time, information will be provided concerning the scope of activities of foreign commercial banks. There has been an ongoing debate in the empirical literature on the determinants of foreign activities of commercial banks as to whether banks tend to follow their customers abroad (or vice versa). Whereas most of the earlier literature finds evidence for the follow-their-customers hypothesis, more recent evidence suggests that banks' foreign activities may increasingly be motivated by the intention to penetrate a foreign market (see Seth et al. 1998, Focarelli and Pozzolo 1999, Guillén and Tschoegl 1999). Obviously, the impact of foreign banks on the efficiency of the domestic banking system and on corporate governance mechanisms within banks is likely to be greater the more encompassing the activities of foreign banks are and the less they are confined to certain market niches.

This chapter also provides an overview of the theoretical literature on effects and determinants of the market entry of foreign banks and a summary of the available empirical evidence on these issues. It ends with a review of the experience of the transition economies under study.

Entry of foreign banks: the theoretical framework

The optimal sequence of internal and external financial liberalization has been discussed widely in the context of reforms in developing countries (Cho and Khatkhate 1989, Gelb and Sagari 1990, Mathieson 1980, Reisen and Fischer 1993), and the discussion has been revived after the recent financial crises of Asia, Latin America and Russia. When deriving policy implications for transition economies from this literature, it needs to be borne in mind that, in these countries, internal financial liberalization has been a much more encompassing task than in most other emerging markets. This is because, in transition economies, internal financial liberalization has implied the creation of a market-based financial system from their infancies: the monobank had to be abolished and to be replaced by a two-tier banking system. In addition, internal financial liberalization denoted the lifting of administrative controls on the activities of commercial banks, i.e., the abolition of interest rate and credit controls as well as the termination of subsidized lending programmes. As new commercial banks were typically carved out of the existing monobank structures, hereby inheriting the existing loan portfolios, the issue of how to deal with the non-performing loans on their balance sheets had to be solved.[3]

In discussing the optimal sequence between internal and external financial liberalization, this chapter will focus mainly on the market access of foreign banks and thus on foreign direct investment (FDI) in banking. Obviously, competitive pressure on domestic financial institutions can also come through liberalized and increased capital flows. Borrowing of domestic firms and households from abroad and the possibility of holding financial wealth in deposits abroad link domestic and foreign financial markets. Due to transactions costs involved in cross-border financial flows, however, competitive pressure is more indirect if only the capital account has been liberalized as compared with a situation in which foreign banks are allowed to enter the domestic market.

With regard to the optimal sequence of financial liberalization, most authors suggest that the capital account of the balance of payments should be liberalized only after the domestic financial system has been deregulated, and that the opening of markets for foreign competition in financial services should proceed only gradually. In fact, just as FDI in the non-financial sector can be immiserizing if domestic prices are distorted (Edwards and van Wijnbergen, 1987), FDI in banking may be detrimental to economic growth if the domestic banking system is highly regulated or even financially repressed. And, even if domestic financial markets have been liberalized formally, inherited institutional structures will proliferate for a considerable amount of time, which may weaken the competitiveness of incumbent financial institutions. However, arguments in favour of a reversed sequence or at least parallel reforms have been advanced as well. Lal (1987), for example, proposes to liberalize the capital account in parallel with the removal of restrictions on the trade in goods in order to remove distortions in the domestic financial markets. Similarly, Walter (1985) favours the national treatment in trade with financial services.

Market entry and non-performing loans

In a simple, static framework, the case against unrestricted market access of foreign banks can be made by noting that domestic banks in transition economies which struggle with a vast array of operational inefficiencies and with low-quality assets are unable to compete on equal terms with foreign rivals. The incumbent domestic banks have inherited loans from the former regime of central planning, and they typically lack both experienced personnel and reliable sources of information on enterprise performance needed to perform a reliable credit assessment. Substantial amounts of non-performing loans on the balance sheets of commercial banks have typically been the result. While cross-country comparisons of the scale of non-performing loans are complicated by different accounting standards, loan write-off regulations, or provisioning requirements, irregular assets have been substantial for quite some time into the reform process (Figure 2.1). In 1995, Hungarian and Polish commercial banks still reported about 15–20 per cent of their loans as being classified. Meanwhile, these shares have gone down to 10 per cent or less. In the Czech Republic, in contrast, about one-third of the banks' loan portfolio remains in a critical state.[4]

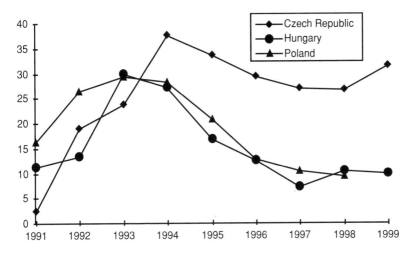

Sources: CNB (1999), NBH (1999a, 1999b), NBP (1999), Buch (1996b).

Figure 2.1   Share of classified credits as % of total credits, 1991–9

In the presence of non-performing assets, banks need to earn sufficiently high interest rate spreads on the profitable part of their operations in order to offset past losses and to maintain their operations (Buch 1997). High spreads, however, cannot be sustained if market access is liberalized: as the number of competitors rises, the equilibrium loan rate converges to the bank's marginal costs. This mechanism is the main rationale behind suggestions to postpone external financial liberalization until internal financial liberalization has taken place, and until domestic banks have recapitalized themselves through retained profits. The main concern against the market entry of *foreign* banks stems from the fact that they not only have a balance sheet which is clear from non-performing loans but that they also tend to have lower operating costs than domestic banks. Hence, their presence in the market may be even more detrimental to the incumbent banks than the emergence of new *domestic* financial institutions.

The market entry of foreign banks thus potentially forces existing banks out of the market, and it may hinder the market entry of new domestic banks. Bankruptcies of incumbent banks, in turn, have negative implications not only because (uninsured) depositors would lose their savings but also because banking failures might have spillover effects on other banks, and information capital might be destroyed.[5] Finally, the fact that market entry as such puts downward pressure on interest rate spreads may reduce the monitoring incentives of commercial banks, thus potentially increasing the riskiness of banks' assets (Aizenman 1998, Gehrig 1998). Hence, a government which assigns a high weight to domestic banks' profits would decide to postpone external financial liberalization until the efficiency of domestic banking has improved sufficiently.

Welfare gains of foreign entry

Obviously, the welfare costs of the market entry of foreign banks must be weighted against the welfare gains which arise from a more liberal regime. Generally, the case for international trade in financial services can be made in an analogy to international trade in goods.[6] Because the production of financial services is rather human capital intensive, countries which have a relative rich supply of skilled labour are likely to export financial services. Employing the principle of national treatment implies free trade in financial services to allow countries to exploit their comparative advantages. The analogy between trade in goods and in financial services is not complete, however. While trade in goods and factor movements can be viewed as close substitutes, the provision of financial services abroad is quite tightly linked to the actual presence of the financial intermediary in the foreign country. Because the provision of financial services is largely based on informational advantages that an intermediary has, personal contacts to customers are needed. Even though the need for a bank to be physically present in the market abroad diminishes as new communication technologies are developed, entry restrictions for foreign financial institutions remain quite effective in protecting the domestic financial sector from foreign competition. Capital account liberalization and FDI in banking are thus imperfect substitutes.

Apart from the utilization of comparative advantages in producing financial services, FDI in banking can contribute to a transfer of know-how into the domestic banking system and in improving its efficiency. This can be achieved directly through the acquisition of ownership stakes or, more indirectly, through the formation of twinning arrangements with domestic banks. These links could actually assist the domestic banks in better utilizing their information capital and provide the users of financial services with superior inputs. Hence, substantial gains from higher quality intermediation can be realized. In addition, foreign banks can improve the corporate governance of domestic banks if they acquire stakes in the privatized banks. Incidentally, this has been the main rationale behind the decisions of the authorities in most reform states to closely involve foreign banks into the process of bank privatization (see below, 'Strategies towards foreign banks'). Static models of market entry which ignore these positive spillover effects for the efficiency of domestic banks would thus significantly underestimate the welfare gains from external financial liberalization.

The extent to which these positive spillover effects can be utilized, however, depends crucially on the scope of activities of foreign banks and on their ability to penetrate different market segments. It is typically observed that, even if unrestricted market access of foreign banks is possible, these banks may choose not to enter into the traditional business of domestic banks but rather to restrict themselves to relatively small market segments. Export trade financing, investment banking and some areas of wholesale banking are the fields where foreign banks are most likely to be active. The restriction of foreign commercial banks to small market segments, in turn, implies that large segments of the domestic banking sector are effectively shielded from potentially positive spillover effects and that the transfer of know-how and good governance remains restricted. The experience of Germany is a prime example for the low penetration of the domestic market by foreign banks. Even though market entry of foreign banks has been handled quite liberally since the mid-1970s, foreign competition generally is meager with market shares of foreign banks hovering around 2–5 per cent in traditional commercial banking activities (Buch and Golder 1999). At the same time, foreign banks dominate the investment banking business in Germany.

The low degree of representation of foreign banks in the retail segment of the market is a phenomenon not only confined to Germany but also to many other European countries. Two explanations are conceivable. First, implicit (regulatory) entry barriers may prevent greater market access of foreign banks despite the formal abolition of explicit entry barriers. State-guarantees of deposits in domestic savings banks are one obvious candidate in this context. Second, the decision of banks to enter a new market, in particular one which requires the acquisition of an information base on customers and the build-up of a branch network, is more complex than the standard theory of (foreign) direct investment suggests. Traditional explanations of FDI in banking largely ignore the fact that investment decisions of banks are irreversible and are made under conditions of uncertainty. Hence, entry and exit into non-traditional markets are potentially subject to hysteresis. In banking, the issue of irreversibility of investment arises because access to a branch network is crucial for the attraction of deposits and because long-term customer relations are the basis for the lending business. When deciding whether to enter a new market, banks thus have to take three cost components into account (Chen and Mazumdar 1997):[7] fixed costs to enter the new market (which increase with the importance of legal entry barriers), fixed costs to leave the new market, and operating costs. The optimal investment policy of a representative bank must thus consider the value of the real investment option: as information about the economic environment improves over time, it pays to wait and to postpone investment. The presence of entry and exit costs thus creates a range of inaction: revenue has to increase sufficiently before banks move into the non-traditional market, but, having entered the new market, they do not leave unless revenues fall substantially.

In this context, the distinction between greenfield investments and acquisitions of domestic banks becomes crucial. With greenfield investments, new entrants need to build up reputation and a branch network from scratch, whereas they can potentially benefit from existing customer contacts when buying up an existing bank. Under perfect information about future business conditions, costs of the two modes of entry should be the same. Under uncertainty, however, greenfield investment is likely to entail higher costs. Viewed in this light, the decision of many authorities in transition economies to channel activities of foreign banks into acquiring domestic banks in the context of privatization might not have unduly restricted the choices of foreign banks.

Finally, an argument which is often voiced against the market entry of foreign banks is the fear that foreign banks pick only the 'best' clients, leaving the domestic banking sector with a pool of low-return, high-risk enterprises. A related fear is that foreign banks refrain from lending to domestic fines (see e.g. Weller and Scher 1999). Yet, these arguments do not justify shielding the transition economies from competition in financial services for two reasons.

First, *ex ante* and *ex post* knowledge about the quality of loan customers must be distinguished. *Ex ante* asymmetries in information are one main rationale for the existence of financial intermediaries in general and of banks in particular. Because the quality of prospective borrowers can typically not be assessed with certainty prior to the writing of a loan contract, screening and sorting mechanisms need to be designed which help to overcome informational asymmetries. The fact that foreign banks tend to operate with clients which *ex post* are revealed to have an above average profitability simply implies that these banks have developed better risk-assessment techniques than the domestic banks. These abilities cannot be utilized if markets are protected, and credit rationing may result (Stiglitz and Weiss, 1981).

Second, the fact that foreign banks in many cases merely follow their clients abroad and thus expand their home country business suggests that this type of business may not be available to the domestic banks. Foreign banks make use of the specific customer relationship that they have build up which cannot easily be replicated by a domestic bank. The relevant alternative to the presence of foreign banks abroad may thus be that they service their customers through the foreign bank's home country headquarters.

From a theoretical point of view, market entry of foreign banks can thus have positive and negative implications for the efficiency and profitability of the domestic banking system. While, on the one hand, potentially more efficient banks enter the market and allow for a transfer of skills and technology, domestic banks, on the other hand, may go bankrupt because of inferior cost and incentive structures. To the extent that domestic banks, which are in principle viable but which are burdened by non-performing loans from the past, are forced out of the market, the overall welfare implications of foreign entry may in fact be negative. Below, empirical evidence on these effects is provided from developing countries and emerging markets, and from transition economies.

Entry of foreign banks: the empirical record

A number of factors have been discussed in the literature which determine comparative advantages of international financial institutions (Goldberg and Johnson 1990, Grubel 1977, Sagari 1992, Walter 1985). Because one main reason for the existence of banks is their ability to process information more efficiently than other market participants, experience, prior customer relations and human resource endowments are driving forces behind the international expansion of banks. In addition, the regulatory environment of a host country, and diversification effects of international investments are important determinants of FDI in banking. The importance of existing customer relations implies that trade in goods and FDI in banking may be complements. The direction of causality is not clear, however. While banks may merely be following their customers into foreign countries, they may as well be present in foreign markets prior to their corporate clients and provide information about the new market.

Previous empirical work on the foreign activities of commercial banks has primarily focused on US banks.[8] FDI of banks has been shown to be positively related to FDI in the non-financial sector. This would support the hypothesis that banks follow their customers abroad although the direction of causality is typically not addressed explicitly. Likewise, it is conceivable that omitted factors are driving FDI in both sectors. Most studies thus control for market size (measured by gross domestic product (GDP) or the size of the population) and foreign trade activities. Typically, market size and foreign trade links exert a positive impact on the foreign direct investment of banks, while the individual impact of export activity may be positive or negative. Entry regulations have the expected negative sign.

Buch (2000) uses data on FDI of German banks in about 20 host countries. The results show a strong and positive correlation between foreign activities of banks and demand conditions as captured by (per capita) GDP and foreign activities of German firms, i.e. FDI in the non-banking sector or foreign trade activities. Exchange rate volatility seems to have a negative impact on FDI of banks. There is evidence that EU membership and the abolition of capital controls have promoted foreign lending but not FDI of banks, thus weakly supporting the hypothesis that the two are substitutes. Conditions on local banking markets such as returns and interest rate spreads, in contrast, have been much more difficult to single out as statistically significant determinants of foreign activities of German banks.

A priori, the statistically significant link between FDI in the non-banking sector or foreign trade activities, on the one hand, and FDI in banking, on the other hand, may be taken to support the claim that banks tend to follow their customers abroad. A study by Seth, Nolle and Mohanty (1998) uses data on the financial sources of affiliates of foreign firms in the US as well as data on the activities of foreign banks in the US to check the validity of this hypothesis.[9] Overall, the amount of loans granted by foreign banks exceeded the amount of loans received by foreign affiliates. This implies that foreign banks have granted loans to US firms as well, and that the motivation to 'follow their customers' has not been the sole reason to enter the foreign market. Moreover, there seems to have been a trend away from lending to companies from the home country over time. The finding that foreign banks are starting to penetrate the retail market in the host country is also supported by recent case studies summarized in Guillén and Tschoegl (1999) who study the investments of Spanish and Portuguese banks in Latin America.

Focarelli and Pozzolo (1999) analyse the foreign direct investment decisions of 2500 banks from OECD countries. They find that outward FDI in banking typically comes from countries with developed and relatively efficient banking markets. Host countries, in contrast, are those with relatively underdeveloped financial systems and a high scope for improvement in efficiency. Somewhat contrary to the earlier evidence, they find that the degree of openness of a host country or its degree of economic integration with the home country are of lesser importance.

Claessens, Demirgüç-Kunt and Huizinga (1998) have analysed the impact of foreign bank entry on the domestic banking sector in terms of efficiency, the range of operations or tax payments. Apart from earlier case study evidence, their analysis is one of the first which allows for a comparison of 80 countries (developing and industrialized) for a period of several years (1988–95). One of the findings is that foreign banks tend to have lower interest margins and profitability in developed countries as compared to domestic banks, while the reverse holds for developing countries. Econometric evidence furthermore reveals that while domestic banks indeed lost market shares and became less profitable as foreign banks entered, the overall welfare effect on the domestic economy is positive. Recent evidence for Argentina and Mexico additionally suggests increased stability of local banking markets precipitated by foreign entry (Goldberg et al. 1999). Using bank-level data for the 1990s, a positive impact on foreign entry on loans growth, coupled with a reduction in the volatility of loan growth is found.

Foreign banking in transition economies

Strategies towards foreign banking

Under socialism, market entry of foreign banks had been handled quite differently (Walter 1985). Former Czechoslovakia, at one extreme of the spectrum, had been virtually closed off for foreign banks, allowing not even – as had been the case in Poland – representative offices to be established. Hungary, in contrast, has had the most liberal regimes towards foreign banks. It prohibited foreign bank branches and foreign investment in domestic banks while generally allowing subsidiaries of foreign banks to be opened. Arguably, these differences in initial conditions have shaped attitudes towards foreign banks in the reform period (see e.g. Storf 1999). Also, countries have differed with regard to the amount of non-performing loans on the balance sheets of their banks and thus with regard to the potential threat stemming from foreign competition. Czechoslovak commercial banks appeared the most vulnerable since, in contrast to Poland, no correction hyperinflation had wiped out old loan portfolios.[10] Finally, the mode of privatization of the existing banks has had a significant impact on the timing and the mode of entry of foreign banks.

Notwithstanding these differences, all three countries had in principle lifted the barriers to the market entry of new domestic and foreign banks with the establishment of two-tier banking systems at the beginning of the reform process. Yet FDI in banking has not yet been fully liberalized, foreign banks can in principle be treated differently from domestic banks, and both domestic and foreign banks have at times been affected by moratoria on new banking licences.

In the *Czech Republic*, foreign banks have been allowed to establish subsidiaries and to buy stakes in domestic banks since 1990. However, branches have only been allowed to open since the beginning of 1992. The permission of the Czech National Bank is needed for the acquisition of domestic banks (CNB 1995). Yet, after the Czech banking sector experienced instabilities during 1993 and 1994, the issuance of new licences for domestic as well as foreign banks was stopped in mid-1994. Although foreign banks could still acquire stakes in existing domestic banks, the privatization process has not been speeded up for a considerable amount of time.

Generally, Czech commercial banks have been privatized in the context of the voucher privatization programme, which has resulted in complicated cross-holdings between banks and non-financial firms. Also, *de facto* state ownership in *de jure* privatized firms remained pervasive. Because of insufficient regulations of the financial sector it is also often asserted that the impact of this privatization scheme on corporate governance mechanisms has been detrimental.

The participation of foreign banks in domestic banks has been promoted on a larger scale only after the financial crisis of 1997 when it had been decided to speed up the privatization of the remaining stakes of the government in banks (IMF 1998). While an agreement to sell stakes in the third largest bank to foreign investors was reached in that same year, the privatization of the two largest banks was delayed until recently.

Also in *Poland*, the National Bank has generally limited the market entry of foreign banks to participation in the privatization of Polish banks and in troubled domestic banks. Licensing was quite liberal between 1990 and 1992. Foreign banks initially even enjoyed tax advantages during the first years of their operations, and they could keep part of their capital in foreign currency (Wachtel 1995). Between early 1992 and late 1994, however, the market entry for foreign banks was restricted. Despite several applications pending, no new licences to foreign banks were issued by the Polish National Bank during this time (PlanEcon, 1995). In parallel, cooperation in the banking sector has been promoted through twinning agreements between domestic and foreign banks. In 1993, Poland implemented a programme intended to solve the problem of inherited bad loans and to promote enterprise restructuring (Pawlowicz 1995). Under the programme, nine regional commercial banks, which had been carved out of the monobank in 1989, had to found loan work-out departments. At the same time, the banks were recapitalized for parts of their bad loan portfolios. With the technical assistance of foreign partner banks, the work-out departments had to develop and implement restructuring strategies for their corporate clients.

Reportedly, the twinning agreements have been fairly successful in improving banking skills (Storf 1999). Under the twinning programmes, ownership involvement of the foreign partners in the domestic banks, however, could not be promoted quite as much as had been envisaged. Rather, the main impetus for the market access of foreign banks came through the process of privatizing domestic banks (IMF 1997). In late 1996, a programme was passed under which some of the then state-owned banks would be consolidated first, while others would be sold to foreign investors directly. Three years later, substantial headway towards privatizing domestic banks has been made, and only two large banks, the savings and the agricultural bank, remain state-owned. Due to substantial structural problems, the privatization of these banks, however, is unlikely to take place soon (IMF 1999).

In *Hungary*, the market entry of foreign banks was already liberalized in 1987. The approval of the government is needed if foreigners wish to open a fully or partially foreign-owned bank, or if they wish to acquire stakes in an existing domestic bank (SBS 1994b). No approval is needed if these stakes are less than 10 per cent of the capital of the domestic bank. Although domestic commercial banks as in the Czech Republic or in Poland had to struggle with substantial amounts of non-performing loans initially, and although an effective solution to the problem had been put off for a considerable amount of time, there has been no explicit moratorium on the market access of foreign banks. Throughout the reform process, it has rather been the intention of the authorities to seek foreigners as strategic investors in the privatization of the existing banks. Meanwhile, foreign banks hold about 60 per cent of the capital in the Hungarian banking system, thus even exceeding the benchmark of 50 per cent set by the former government (Storf 1999).

Regulations towards the market access of foreign banks have been shaped not only by domestic policy considerations but also by the intention of the countries under study to join the EU and the OECD. As regards envisaged membership of the EU, the Visegrad countries signed Europe Agreements in 1991 which implied that the market entry of foreign banks had to be liberalized asymmetrically.[11] The reform states can maintain restrictions on the market entry of foreign banks until the end of a ten-year transition period. Because the Europe Agreements came into force after their ratification in February 1994 (Poland and Hungary) and in February 1995 (Czech Republic), the full transition period that applies to the financial sector ends only in the years 2004 and 2005, respectively. After five years, hence starting in the year 1999 (2000), remaining entry restrictions need to be phased out. Until full membership has been accomplished, restrictions to the market entry of foreign banks can generally be maintained for reasons of improved monetary control and prudential supervision of the banking system. The current members of the EU, in contrast, are not allowed to treat banks from the reform states any differently from banks from other EU states.

At its summit in Essen in December 1994, the EU went beyond the commitments laid down in the Europe Agreements and formulated an accession strategy for the new members. One essential part of this strategy was the White Book of May 1995 in which the EU outlined the prerequisites for accession to the Union (Table 2.1). Future members of the EU must accept the entire *acquis communautaire* and the regulations of the internal market. This implies, among other things, the acceptance of the principles of mutual recognition of banking licences, of minimum harmonization, and of home country control, which are enshrined in the Second Banking Directive of the EU of 1993.[12]

In March 1998, the process of enlargement reached its last stage for the time being. With the approval of so-called Accession Partnerships for ten applicant countries, the EU started the process of entry negotiations. In these Accession Partnerships, the EU's opinion on compliance with the requirements of the White Book was laid down (EU 1999). With regard to financial market reform, different policy areas were stressed. For the Czech Republic, emphasis was laid on reforms with regard to corporate governance and bank privatization. For Poland, the limited role of the financial sector with regard to financing the Polish

Table 2.1 Free movement of capital and of financial services in the EU

	Free movement of capital	*Free movement of services*
	Regulations of the White Book	
Stage I	Current account convertibility and liberalization of medium- and long-term capital flows.	First Banking Directive (freedom to provide services, the right of establishment, etc.); Own Funds Directive; Solvency Directive; Regulations concerning deposit insurance, securities markets, investment funds, money laundering.
Stage II	Full capital account convertibility, incl. liberalization of short-term capital flows.	Second Banking Directive (home-country control, single licence, mutual recognition), Annual Accounts and Consolidated Accounts Directive, Capital Adequacy Directive, Large Exposure Directive.
	Compliance of the Associated States	
Czech Republic	Restrictions retained on investment into real estate by non-residents and listing of foreign securities on domestic market. Liberalization envisaged within 3–5 years.	Conditions for operations of foreign banks largely in line with the First and Second Banking Directive; solvency and large exposure guidelines largely implemented; remaining restrictions with regard to deposit guarantees, capital adequacy, and consolidated supervision to be abolished in 1998. Mutual recognition from the year 2000.
Hungary	Restrictions retained on outward capital movements and investments of institutional investors. All medium- and long-term transactions planned to be liberalized within 1–2 years.	Rules for minimum capital, solvency, deposit guarantee, and provisions against money laundering are consistent with the acquis. First Banking, Own Funds, Large Exposure Directive, and most other directives have by and large been implemented. Capital adequacy regulations still based on credit risk alone (market risk to be covered as well within 1–2 years).
Poland	Restrictions on purchase of real estate by non-residents. Other remaining restrictions shall be abolished by the end of 1998 (medium- and long-term) and the end of 1999 (short-term capital).	Directives on solvency, deposit insurance, money laundering, and large exposure largely implemented. Capital adequacy only covers credit risk; consolidated supervision not fully implemented.

Source: EU (1995, 1997).

industry was mentioned, whereas for Hungary the need to fine-tune financial regulation and to enforce implementation was stressed.

Other external commitments are less binding and less comprehensive than EU membership. A partial exception is membership in the OECD which requires the adoption of the Code of Liberalization of Capital Movements. The deadline for the liberalization of foreign entry into the banking and financial sector under the Code has in some cases been set prior to the deadline envisaged under the Europe Agreements. In the case of Poland, for example, restrictions to the market entry of foreign banks had to be abolished by the end of 1998 under the Code.[13]

Market shares of foreign banks

Differences in the licensing practices towards foreign banks have clearly been reflected in the number of foreign banks present on local markets. In 1991, only 8 per cent and 16 per cent of the total number of banks operating in Poland and the Czech Republic, respectively, had a majority foreign owner (Table 2.2). In Hungary, one-third of all banks were already foreign-owned at this time. By 1998, the picture had changed quite considerably, as more than 50 per cent of the Czech and 45 per cent of Polish banks were foreign-owned.[14]

Table 2.2   Structure[a] of the banking systems by number of banks, 1989–99

	1989	1990	1991	1992	1993	1994	1995	1996	1997	1998	1999
Czech Republic[b]											
All banks	5	9	24	37	52	55	55	53	50	45	–
Foreign banks	–	–	4	8	11	12	12	13	14	13	–
Foreign branches	–	–	–	3	7	8	10	9	9	10	–
Hungary											
All banks	23	29	36	40	43	44	44	–	–	–	–
Foreign banks	7	8	13	16	20	21	22	–	–	–	–
Poland[c]											
All banks	20	52	74	84	87	82	81	81	83	83	80
Foreign banks	0	3	6	6	10	11	18	25	29	31	36

Notes:
[a] Classification according to the ownership status of the majority shareholders.
[b] Excluding building associations and banks under conservatorship.
[c] 1990 = June.

Sources: CNB (1999); Groszek (1995, p. 6); NBH (1991); Polanski (1994); SBS (1993); Wachtel (1995); NBP (1999).

Yet, the mere number of foreign banks that is operating in a country provides little information about the actual importance of their activities. At least initially, experience has confirmed prior assumptions that foreign banks concentrate on trade-related activities and wholesale banking. With a few exceptions, foreign banks had hardly expanded into the retail banking business in Central and Eastern Europe in the early reform years (Wachtel 1995), and early evidence for Poland even suggests that foreign entry has had a negative impact on overall corporate lending (Weller 1999). Generally, foreign banks can be expected to find it easier to acquire market shares in the credit market than in the deposit market, and they tend to focus their activities on the wholesale banking business. This strategic choice is influenced by the lack of a nationwide branch network which a retail banking strategy would require and which is rather costly to build up. The domestic banks, and in particular the traditional savings banks, in contrast, have access to a branch network which eases the accumulation of household savings. Since, at the same time, the privatization of savings banks has typically been last on the agenda, foreign banks' entry into the retail market has been constrained.

Evidence from the three countries under study indeed reveals that foreign banks have found it easier to penetrate the domestic loan rather than the deposit market. In *Poland*, market shares of foreigners in the loan market have been one-third the total in mid-1999; the share of majority foreign-owned banks in the deposit market has been only about 22 per cent (Table 2.3). To a large extent, this is due to the lack of access of foreign banks to a large branch network, as they account for only 10 per cent of all banking offices. It does, however, also reflect a focus of foreign banks on the wholesale segment of the banking market. Generally, the involvement of foreign banks in the privatization of domestic banks has had a key influence on foreign banks' market share. Whereas market penetration was below 10 per cent before 1996, it has risen sharply since then.

Overall, foreign banks in Poland held more than one-third of the capital of the banking system in mid-1999. As regards the countries of origin, the European Union clearly dominates (NBP 1999). Over 70 per cent of all foreign capital came from countries of the EU, Germany being the single largest source of inward FDI in banking with 35 per cent of the capital alone. US commercial banks were also relatively important, supplying 25 per cent of the total foreign capital in Poland's banking system.

Table 2.3   Indicators of foreign banks in Poland, 1993–9

	1993	1994	1995	1996	1997	1998	1999 (June)
Market share (% of total)							
Total net assets[a]	2.6	3.2	4.2	13.7	15.3	16.6	26.4
Net loans[b]	2.7	4.4	5.8	16.0	18.2	21.9	32.7
Deposits[c]	2.1	2.7	3.0	12.2	12.7	13.7	21.7
Total capital base[d]	2.2	3.7	7.6	20.9	24.0	24.7	34.9
Total employment[e]	0.6	0.8	1.5	10.5	11.1	11.9	21.0
Number of offices[f]	0.7	0.9	1.9	2.5	3.9	5.5	10.1
Profitability (%)							
Pre-tax earnings/total expenses							
Banking system	5.1	5.3	19.6	23.6	17.3	8.1	9.5
Foreign banks	47.6	38.7	26.3	24.5	15.7	9.9	8.0
Net earnings/total expenses							
Banking system	–2.2	0.5	11.9	16.3	11.7	3.3	6.3
Foreign banks	39.5	24.7	15.0	15.3	9.5	6.3	4.8
Total expense/total income							
Banking system	95.1	95.0	83.6	80.9	85.3	92.5	91.3
Foreign banks	67.7	72.1	79.2	80.3	86.5	91.0	92.6

Notes:
[a] Total assets less accumulated depreciation, specific provisions, and valuation allowances.
[b] Loans and advances (excluding purchased debt and funds disbursed under guarantees and endorsements, reported separately since 1996), less specific provisions.
[c] From non-financial sector only.
[d] Until year-end 1997 corresponding to 'gross own funds'.
[e] Equivalent to full-time posts.
[f] 1993–5 branch offices only.

Source: NBP (1999).

In terms of total assets, market shares of foreign banks in the *Czech Republic* are about 10 percentage points below those of foreign banks in Poland (Table 2.4). Also, foreign banks have made inroads into the loan and deposit market to a substantially lower degree. At the end of 1998, subsidiaries and branches of foreign banks held 22 per cent of the credit and about 15 per cent of the deposit market in the Czech Republic. Market shares in the securities market were below 10 per cent. In general, however, foreign banks seem to focus on the wholesale rather than the retail market. As in the case of Poland, foreign capital from EU countries dominates.

The acquisition of market shares by foreign banks in *Hungary* has been even more impressive (Table 2.5). By the end of 1998, foreign banks held about 60–70 per cent of total assets, registered capital, and receivables from customers of the banking system. Again, their market share in the deposit business (36 per cent) was substantially below average. In a sense, the high market share of foreign-owned banks in corporate loans shows that foreign banks have not confined themselves to small market segments only, or that they have shied away from financing domestic investment.

Table 2.4   Market share in the Czech Republic by banking groups, 1990–8

	1990	1991	1992	1993[a]	1994	1995	1996	1997	1998
Total assets[b] *(% of total market)*									
Domestic banks[c]	–	–	–	91.2	88.1	82.9	76.7	72.2	69.5
Large banks	–	–	–	82.3	79.3	73.7	72.4	68.2	66.0
Small banks	–	–	–	8.9	8.8	9.2	4.3	4.0	3.5
Foreign banks	–	–	–	7.2	11.3	15.9	20.0	23.3	25.1
Subsidiaries	–	–	–	5.7	7.2	9.9	11.7	13.7	15.6
Branches	–	–	–	1.5	4.1	6.0	8.3	9.6	9.5
Underwritten capital[b]									
Domestic banks[c]	–	–	–	81.5	83.5	81.6	–	–	–
Large banks	–	–	–	58.6	61.4	57.9	–	–	–
Small banks	–	–	–	22.9	22.1	23.7	–	–	–
Foreign subsidiaries	–	–	–	12.9	12.7	13.9	–	–	–
Credit market									
Domestic banks[c]	100.0	98.7	97.3	95.7	92.5	91.7	–	–	–
Foreign banks	0.0	1.2	2.7	4.3	7.5	8.3	–	–	–
Deposit market									
Domestic banks[c]	99.6	99.4	97.3	96.4	93.5	93.2	–	–	–
Foreign banks	0.4	0.6	2.3	3.6	6.5	6.8	–	–	–

Notes:
[a] 1993 = 1 January 1994.
[b] Data do not add up to 100 per cent because building societies are not considered.
[c] Domestic banks include banks with a foreign minority owner.

Sources: CNB, *Selected Indicators* (March 1996); CNB, *Annual Report* (1994, 1995, 1999); author's calculations.

On the contrary, a comparison of the balance sheet structure of domestic and foreign banks shows that the share of lending to firms has been consistently higher for the latter (Table 2.6). At the same time, lending to the government and the household sector has been less important than for the domestic banks. On the funding side, household deposits play a much smaller role for the foreign banks, who have a

Table 2.5   Market Share in Hungary by banking groups, 1993–8[a]

	1993 (% of total)	1994	1995[b]	1996	1997	1998
Total assets						
Domestic banks	84.8	80.3	60.5	53.4	38.2	37.4
Foreign banks[c]	15.4	19.7	39.5	46.6	61.8	62.6
Registered capital[d]						
Domestic banks	85.9	83.7	48.5	42.3	28.7	32.9
Foreign banks[c]	14.1	16.3	51.5	57.7	71.3	67.1
Corporate credits						
Domestic banks	84.5	79.1	47.8	41.9	29.4	23.7
Foreign banks[c]	15.5	20.9	52.2	58.1	70.6	76.3
Household deposits						
Domestic banks	87.0	84.6	90.4	83.3	68.6	64.0
Foreign banks[c]	13.0	15.4	9.6	16.7	31.4	36.0

Notes:
[a] Data for the years 1993–4 and 1995–8 are not fully comparable.
[b] June.
[c] Foreign banks = banks with a foreign majority owner.
[d] 1998 and 1999: including (excluding) other non-residents.

Sources: SBS (1993, 1994a, 1995), NBH (1999).

substantially higher share of foreign liabilities than their domestic counterparts.

Profitability of foreign banks

With regard to the profitability of domestic versus foreign banks in *Poland*, a quite interesting convergence process could be observed over time (Table 2.3). While, in 1993, foreign banks significantly outperformed domestic Polish banks on all counts, these differences had virtually disappeared by mid-1999. In contrast, foreign banks in the first half of 1999 were even slightly less profitable than domestic banks. By that time, the share of irregular claims in total bank portfolios was also in a comparable range for foreign (10.4 per cent) and domestic banks (12.6 per cent).

These figures, however, cannot be taken as evidence for the inferior performance of foreign as compared to Polish banks. This is because foreign banks have increased their share of the Polish banking market to a large extent through the acquisition of domestic banks. This implies that some of the changes that can be observed over time are merely due to a reclassification of banks. The degree to which foreign owners are

Table 2.6   Balance sheet structure of banks in Hungary, 1995–9 (June)

	Foreign banks				Domestic banks				
	1995	1996	1997	1998	1995	1996	1997	1998	1999
Assets									
Central budget	9.4	13.4	13.3	10.8	19.0	19.0	15.6	16.1	14.1
Corporate	37.3	35.9	35.1	37.7	28.3	28.8	30.7	30.9	31.8
Households	0.9	0.7	0.9	1.3	5.9	4.4	3.5	3.3	3.6
Foreign	7.5	8.9	9.1	11.8	3.5	5.7	8.1	10.0	10.9
Central Bank	28.0	22.8	18.8	17.6	21.9	23.2	19.3	17.5	15.9
Interbank	4.0	7.2	8.8	7.8	3.0	5.1	7.4	7.9	7.7
Securities, investments	3.4	4.1	4.2	4.1	4.7	4.3	4.9	5.6	5.5
Other assets	4.4	3.8	5.4	4.9	8.1	4.0	5.5	5.8	6.7
Others	5.0	3.2	4.4	3.9	5.8	5.5	4.9	2.8	3.7
Total	100.0	100.0	100.0	100.0	100.0	100.0	100.0	100.0	100.0
Liabilities									
Equity and subordinated loans	12.9	12.8	13.3	12.5	9.9	10.3	11.5	11.7	11.9
Central budget	1.4	1.8	1.5	1.6	4.2	3.9	3.7	3.2	2.8
Corporate	25.0	26.3	23.4	21.9	17.4	17.7	17.6	16.7	15.8
Households	6.9	10.3	14.1	18.7	28.4	28.8	27.7	32.5	33.3
Foreign	27.9	25.2	22.3	24.6	13.9	14.4	16.3	18.5	18.7
Central Bank	10.2	5.6	3.8	3.1	8.2	5.1	3.2	2.7	2.1
Interbank	7.3	10.0	12.2	11.0	4.9	7.1	9.3	8.7	8.1
Securities	1.4	3.1	4.4	2.0	7.3	7.9	6.3	1.7	1.7
Others	6.9	4.9	4.9	4.5	5.8	4.8	4.4	4.3	5.6
Total	100.0	100.0	100.0	100.0	100.0	100.0	100.0	100.0	100.0

Source: Unpublished data of the National Bank of Hungary.

able to improve the performance of their targets, in contrast, becomes visible only over time.

A similar observation can be made when comparing banks in *Hungary* (Table 2.7). Foreign banks were significantly more profitable than domestic banks during 1995–7. By 1998, profitability (measured in profit after tax relative to gross income) was about the same. Also with regard to the sources and uses of income, domestic and foreign banks had largely converged.

Unfortunately, a lack of comparable data for the *Czech Republic* prevents a cross-country comparison on bank profitability. One indirect indicator is interest rate spreads. Figure 2.2 shows that spreads in all three countries remained in the range of 4–10 per cent at the end of 1999.[15] Interestingly, there has been a significant downward trend only for Hungary since 1997. For the Czech Republic, this trend has been much more gradual since 1993, whereas spreads in Poland even seem to have

Table 2.7   Income statement analysis for banks in Hungary, 1995–8

	1995 Total	1995 Foreign	1996 Total	1996 Foreign	1997 Total	1997 Foreign	1998 Total	1998 Foreign
(% of total income)								
1. Interest revenue	443.0	261.6	320.7	281.3	307.7	296.0	277.7	269.0
2. Interest expenses	309.5	175.4	226.4	188.9	221.1	209.0	192.0	188.8
3. Net interest income	133.5	86.2	94.3	92.4	86.5	87.0	85.8	80.1
4. Other income	-33.5	13.8	5.7	7.6	13.5	13.0	14.2	19.9
(i) Fee and commission income	23.4	22.2	17.8	21.2	16.1	18.8	17.7	18.6
(ii) Fee revenue	38.6	30.6	24.4	27.4	24.0	25.5	23.9	24.3
(iii) Fee costs	-15.2	-8.3	-6.6	-6.2	7.9	6.8	6.2	5.8
5. Gross income	100.0	100.0	100.0	100.0	100.0	100.0	100.0	100.0
6. Operating expenses	90.5	45.5	71.4	53.5	75.6	70.7	70.4	70.8
(i) Personnel costs	41.3	19.5	32.3	24.8	31.9	29.6	29.2	28.4
7. Net income	9.5	54.5	28.6	46.5	24.4	29.3	29.6	29.2
8. Provisions changes	-49.7	-5.1	-11.6	-11.8	-1.3	-5.3	-9.5	-11.6
9. Net income of finance and investment services	0.0	0.0	0.0	0.0	25.7	34.6	20.1	17.6
10. Net income of non-finance and investment services	0.0	0.0	0.0	0.0	-0.1	0.1	0.2	0.3
11. Total income	59.2	59.6	40.3	58.3	25.6	34.7	20.3	18.0
12. Extraordinary profit	-19.9	-0.9	-2.9	-3.5	-0.1	-0.6	-2.3	-2.9
13. Profit before tax	39.3	58.7	37.4	54.8	25.5	34.1	18.0	15.1
14. Tax	8.7	10.8	7.8	11.0	5.9	6.5	4.2	3.9
15. Profit after tax	30.6	48.0	29.6	43.8	19.5	27.6	13.9	11.2

Source: Unpublished data of the National Bank of Hungary.

increased somewhat. Hence, this evidence would contradict the hypothesis that foreign entry reduces spreads, thereby eventually lowering the monitoring incentives of domestic banks. The hypothesis that foreign entry increases the riskiness of banks is also contradicted by the fact that in those countries which have opened up for foreign banks most decisively – Hungary and Poland – non-performing loans have come down much faster than in the Czech Republic (Figure 2.1). This evidence is in favour of an increased overall efficiency of the banking system through foreign entry, although the trend towards lower non-performing loans has already started prior to the progressive entry of foreign banks.

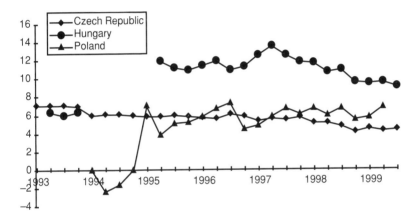

Notes: Czech Republic: Deposit and lending rate (IFS); Hungary: deposit rate for all banks on current account deposits (simple average), lending rate: all banks discounted bills, weighted average; Poland: lending rate working capital, commercial banks' deposit rate.

Source: Datastream.

Figure 2.2   Interest rate spreads, 1993–9

Conclusions

The purpose of this chapter has been mainly to review the experiences of the advanced transition economies of Central and Eastern Europe after opening up their banking sectors to foreign competition. Initially, there was a fear that domestic banks would be unable to withstand the competitive pressure of foreign banks, and hence that foreign entry would cause the failure of domestic financial institutions. This might have had negative implications for the stability of the financial system or for the preservation of information capital in the domestic banks.

It is, of course, difficult to link the failure of domestic banks to the market entry of foreign institutions. While there have certainly been liquidations of domestic banks, these were of a relatively modest scope and were typically restricted to small and medium-sized banks. The fact that large banks were found to be more stable than their often weak credit portfolios would suggest is certainly due to a combination of market power and government intervention, i.e., their being 'too big to fail'. While assessing the importance of these factors has been beyond the scope of this chapter, it seems nevertheless relatively clear that, overall, the entry of foreign banks has not caused large-scale banking failure. In fact, it seems as if the performance of the banking sector has been superior in those countries which have taken a relatively liberal approach towards foreign banks. This would confirm earlier studies on the impact of foreign bank entry on bank profitability which, overall, show that the positive effects of foreign banking outweigh the negative effects on the profits of domestic banks.

When assessing the competitive impact of foreign banks' entry on overall banking efficiency, the degree to which they make inroads into the retail banking sector is of special interest. The more foreign banks' activities are confined to certain market niches, the more leeway domestic banks have in extracting oligopolistic rents from their traditional markets. Evidence from the countries under study clearly shows that foreign banks find it more difficult to obtain market share in the deposit business as compared to the lending business. At the same time, market share in retail banking is very high in some countries, notably Hungary, suggesting that foreign banks not only apply a follow-the-customer strategy but also engage actively in lending to domestic firms. However, more case study evidence is certainly needed to evaluate this issue.

With regard to the future integration of banking markets and their envisaged EU accession, the countries under study have to fully implement the *acquis communautaire*, i.e., among other things the full implementation of free trade in financial services. Currently, FDI in banking in the countries of Central and Eastern Europe is still subject to a number of explicit and implicit entry barriers. Because of the reform progress that has already been made, abolishing entry barriers and allowing for home country control of foreign banks is unlikely to put the overall stability of the banking systems in the countries under review at risk. Yet, it would allow exploiting the benefits of open markets. In addition, entry of foreign banks can be considered to have positive spillover effects for the efficiency of banking supervision.

Many other reform states, notably most successor states of the former Soviet Union, may find it useful to study the experience of Central Europe with the market entry of foreign banks. At least initially, foreign banks tend to follow their corporate clients abroad, and they tend to occupy relatively small market niches. Competitive pressure on the incumbent banks thus increases only gradually, which gives them time to adjust. Liberalizing the market entry of foreign banks can, at the same time, have positive spillover effects for other reform areas.

The most important sequencing issue that arose from this study is that the incumbent banks should have received some compensation for their truly inherited bad loans before markets are opened up for foreign banks. Because the market entry of foreign banks can actually help to prevent new bad loans from emerging, there is no case for restricting market entry after recapitalization has taken place. On the contrary, foreign banks can contribute to improved efficiency in banking as a prerequisite for lasting stability of banking systems in transition economies. Finally, the strategy of involving closely foreign banks into the privatization of domestic banks has been sensible as it has often coincided with the banks' desire to acquire an existing customer base. However, there is relatively little reason to restrict foreign banks to this mode of entry.

Notes

1. The author would like to thank Marco Oestmann for most efficient research assistance as well as Endre Szelenyi of the National Bank of Hungary for the provision of data on the Hungarian banking system. Participants of the conference 'Financial Development in Eastern Europe: The First Ten Years', held at the Technical University of Chemnitz on 3–4 February 2000, provided helpful comments on an earlier draft. Of course, all remaining errors and inaccuracies are solely my own responsibility.
2. As regards corporate governance, not only the efficient governance of the banks themselves but also the role of banks in the corporate governance of non-financial firms is important. However, this issue is beyond the scope of this chapter.
3. Again, a full treatment of these problems and of the reform strategies being chosen is beyond the scope of this chapter. See Bonin et al. (1998) or Buch (1996) for surveys of the evidence.
4. Unless indicated otherwise, information on the structure and performance of the banking systems under study has been taken from the reports of the banking supervisors. See NBP (1999), CNB (1999) and NBH (1999).
5. In addition, the fear of foreign control in the banking industry and the eventual loss of monetary control can be voiced against the market entry of

foreign banks. See Grubel (1977) and Wachtel (1995) for an overview of the relevant arguments.
6. See Francois and Schuknecht (1999) for a more detailed treatment of the links between trade in financial services and economic growth.
7. Although Chen and Mazumdar (1997) discuss *inter alia* the need for the maintenance of firewalls between traditional and non-traditional banking activities, their main conclusions are applicable to the decision of banks to expand outside their home market as well. Their main assumption is that banks' revenues in the new market are stochastic and follow a geometric Brownian motion. In the context of international banking activities, this factor could be interpreted as exchange rate risk.
8. See Buch (2000) for a survey.
9. While suppliers and users of funds cannot be matched directly on the basis of these data, the authors compare the total amount of funds received by non-financial firms to the amount of loans granted by foreign banks in the US.
10. Note that this is not directly reflected in the official figures (Figure 2.1) as reporting systems were adjusted gradually only.
11. See EU (1993a, 1993b, 1994) and Kuschel (1992).
12. See Tirole (1994) for a discussion of the question whether the banking regulations of the EU would suit the needs of the transition economies.
13. See http://www.oecd.org//daf/cmis/country/poland.htm for details.
14. In all countries, foreigners have also acquired minority stakes in a quite substantial number of banks which might give them a controlling stake in the banks. The mere comparison of the number of banks with majority foreign owners may thus give a biased estimate of the actual role of foreigners in the corporate control of banks.
15. Due to different definitions of loans and deposits, the levels of the spreads cannot be compared directly across countries.

References

Aizenman, J. (1998) 'Capital Mobility in a Second Best World – Moral Hazard with Costly Financial Intermediation', National Bureau of Economic Research (NBER), Working Paper 6703 (Cambridge, MA).
Bonin, J. P., Mizsei, K., Székéley, I. P. and Wachtel, P. (1998) *Banking in Transition Economies – Developing Market Oriented Banking Sectors in Eastern Europe* (Cheltenham: Edward Elgar).
Buch, C. M. (1996a) *Creating Efficient Banking Systems – Theory and Evidence from Eastern Europe*, Kiel Institute of World Economics, Kiel Studies, 277 (Tübingen).
Buch, C. M. (1996b) 'Banken im Transformationsprozeß – eine Bestandsaufnahme für Polen, die Tschechische Republik und Ungarn', *Die Weltwirtschaft* 1 (Kiel): 70–102.
Buch, C. M. (1997) 'Opening up for Foreign Banks – Why Central and Eastern Europe can Benefit', *Economics of Transition* 5 (2): 339–66.
Buch, C. M. (2000) 'Why Do Banks Go Abroad? – Evidence from German Data'. Kiel Institute of World Economics, *Journal of Financial Markets, Instruments and Institutions* 9 (1).

Buch, C. M. and Golder, S. M. (1999) 'Foreign Competition and Disintermediation: No Threat to the German Banking System?', Kiel Working Paper 960 (Kiel).

Chen, A. H. and Mazumdar, S. C. (1997) 'A Dynamic Model of Firewalls and Non-traditional Banking', *Journal of Banking and Finance*, 21: 393–416.

Cho, Y.-J. and Khatkhate, D. (1989) 'Lessons of Financial Liberalization in Asia – A Comparative Study', The World Bank, Discussion Paper 50, (Washington DC).

Claessens, S., Demirgüç-Kunt, A. and Huizinga, H. (1998) 'How Does Foreign Entry Affect the Domestic Banking Market?', Policy Research Working Paper 1918, World Bank, (May).

Czech National Bank (CNB), *Vybrané Ukazatele Menoveho V[*]voje Ceské Republiky* (Selected Indicators of Monetary Development in the Czech Republic), various issues (Prague).

Czech National Bank (CNB), *Annual Report*, various issues (Prague).

Czech National Bank (CNB) (1995) *Devisengesetz*, Nr. 219/1995 der Gesetzessammlung vom 26 September 1995 (Prague).

Czech National Bank (1999) *Banking Supervision in the Czech Republic*, various issues (Prague).

Deyoung, R. and Nolle, D. E. (1996) 'Foreign-Owned Banks in the United States: Earning Market Share or Buying It?', *Journal of Money, Credit, and Banking* 28 (4): 622–36.

Dixit, A. K. and Pindyck, R. S. (1994) *Investment under Uncertainty* (Princeton).

Edwards, S. and van Wijnbergen, S. (1987) 'On the Appropriate Timing and Sequencing of Economic Liberalization in Developing Countries', in M. Connolly and C. González (eds), *Economic Reforms and Stabilization in Latin America* (New York), pp. 71–91.

Focarelli, D. and Pozzolo, A. F. (1999) 'The Determinants of Cross-Border Bank Shareholdings: An Analysis with Bank-Level Data from OECD Countries', Banca de Italia (Rome), mimeo.

Francois, J. F. and Schuhknecht, L. (1999) 'Trade in Financial Services: Procompetitive Effects and Growth Performance', Centre for Economic Policy Research, Discussion Paper 2144 (London).

Gehrig, T. (1998) 'Screening, Cross-Border Banking, and the Allocation of Credit', *Research in Economics* 52: 387–407.

Gelb, A. H. and Sagari, S. B. (1990) 'Banking', in P. A. Messerlin and K. P. Sauvant (eds), *The Uruguay Round – Services in the World Economy* (Washington DC), pp. 49–59.

Goldberg, L., Dages, G. and Kimney, D. (1999) 'Lending in Emerging Markets: Foreign and Domestic Banks Compared'. Federal Reserve Bank of New York and NBER, mimeo.

Goldberg, L. G. and Johnson, D. (1990) 'The determinants of US Banking Activity Abroad', *Journal of International Money and Finance*, Vol. 9, No. 2: 123–37.

Groszek, M. (1995) 'Role of Banks in Financing of Economic Development', Paper presented at the conference on 'The Role of the Banking System in the Economic Transformation of Central European Countries', Polish Economic Society (Warsaw: May), pp. 18–20.

Grubel, H. G. (1977) 'A Theory of Multinational Banking', *Banca Nazionale del Lavoro Quarterly Review* 123: 349–63.

Gullién, M. F. and Tschoegl, A. E. (1999) 'At Last the Internationalization of Retail Banking? The Case of the Spanish Banks in Latin America', The Wharton Financial Institutions Center, University of Pennsylvania, Working Paper 99–41.

International Monetary Fund (IMF), (1997) *Republic of Poland – Recent Economic Developments*, 21 February (Washington DC).

International Monetary Fund (IMF), (1998) *Czech Republic – Selected Issues*, 30 January (Washington DC).

International Monetary Fund (IMF), (1999) *Republic of Poland – Selected Issues*. IMF Staff Country Reports 99/32 (Washington DC).

Kommission der Europäischen Gemeinschaften (EU) (1993a) 'Europa-Abkommen zur Gründung einer Assoziation zwischen den Europäischen Gemeinschaften und ihren Mitgliedstaaten einerseits und der Republik Ungarn andererseits', *Amtsblatt der Europäischen Gemeinschaften*, L 347, 31 December: (Brussels), pp. 1–33.

Kommission der Europäischen Gemeinschaften (EU) (1993b) 'Europa-Abkommen zur Gründung einer Assoziation zwischen den Europäischen Gemeinschaften und ihren Mitgliedstaaten einerseits und der Republik Polen andererseits', *Amtsblatt der Europäischen Gemeinschaften*, L 348, 31 December (Brussels), pp. 1–32.

Kommission der Europäischen Gemeinschaften (EU) (1994) 'Beschluß des Rates und der Kommission vom 19. Dezember 1994 über den Abschluß des Europa-Abkommen zwischen den Europäischen Gemeinschaften und ihren Mitgliedstaaten einerseits und der Tschechischen Republik andererseits', *Amtsblatt der Europäischen Gemeinschaften*, L 360, 31 December (Brussels), pp. 1–34.

Kommission der Europäischen Gemeinschaften (EU) (1995) 'Weißbuch – Vorbereitung der Assoziierten Staaten Mittel- und Osteuropas auf die Integration in den Binnenmarkt der Union (Annexe)', KOM(95) 163 endg./2 (Brussels).

Kommission der Europäischen Gemeinschaften (EU) (1997) 'Agenda 2000 – Opinions concerning the Applications for Membership to the European Union' (Brussels).

Kommission der Europäischen Gemeinschaften (EU) (1999) 'Regular Report from the Commission on Progress towards Accession', http://europa.eu.int/comm/enlargement/ (downloaded 1 February 2000) (Brussels).

Kuschel, H.-D. (1992) 'Die Europaabkommen der EG mit Polen, Ungarn und der CSFR', *Wirtschaftsdienst*, 1992/II: 93–100.

Lal, D. (1987) 'The Political Economy of Economic Liberalization', *World Bank Economic Review*, Vol. 1, No. 2: 273–99.

Mathieson, D. J. (1980) 'Financial Reform and Stabilization Policy in a Developing Economy', *Journal of Development Economics*, Vol. 7, No. 3: 359–95.

National Bank of Hungary (NBH) (1991) *Monthly Report*, September (Budapest).

National Bank of Hungary (NBH) (1999a) *Annual Report*, various issues (Budapest).

National Bank of Hungary (NBH) (1999b) *The Hungarian Banking Sector*, various issues (Budapest).

National Bank of Poland (NBP) (1999) *Summary Evaluation of the Financial Situation of Polish Banks*, General Inspectorate of Banking Supervision, various issues (Warsaw).

Pawlowicz, L. (ed.) (1995) *Restrukturyzacja Finansowa Przedsiebiorstw i Banków – II Raport z Badan*, Gdansk Academy of Banking (Gdansk), mimeo.

PlanEcon (1995) *Commercial Banks in Poland: Who's Best?*, Vol. 10, No. 46–47, 31 January (Washington DC).

Polanski, Z. (1994) 'Building a Monetary Economy in Poland in the 1990s', National Bank of Poland, Research Department, Working Paper No. 9 (Warsaw: May).

Reisen, H. and Fischer, B. (1993) *Financial Opening – Policy Issues and Experiences of Developing Countries*, OECD (Paris).

Sagari, S. B. (1992) 'United States Foreign Direct Investment in the Banking Industry', *Transnational Corporations*, Vol. 1, No. 3: 93–123.

Seth, R., Nolle, D. E. and Mohanty, S. K. (1998) 'Do Banks Follow Their Customers Abroad?', *Financial Markets, Institutions, and Instruments* 7: 1–25.

State Banking Supervision (SBS) (1993) *Annual Report* 1992 (Budapest).

State Banking Supervision (SBS) (1994a) *Annual Report* 1993 (Budapest).

State Banking Supervision (SBS) (1994b) Amended Banking Act in Hungary (Budapest).

State Banking Supervision (SBS) (1995) *Annual Report* 1994–95 (Budapest).

Stiglitz, J. E. and Weiss, A. (1981) 'Credit Rationing in Markets with Imperfect Information', *American Economic Review*, Vol. 77, No. 1: 393–410.

Storf, O. (1999) 'Auslandsbanken im Transformationsprozess – Polen und Ungarn', *Deutsche Bank Research*, Sonderbericht, 16 December (Frankfurt am Main).

Tirole, J. (1994) 'Western Prudential Regulation: Assessment, and Reflection on its Application to Central and Eastern Europe', *Economics of Transition*, Vol. 2, No. 2: 129–50.

Vittas, D. and Neal, C. (1992) 'Competition and Efficiency in Hungarian Banking', World Bank, Policy Research Working Paper 1010 (Washington DC: October).

Wachtel, P. (1995) 'Foreign Banking in the Central European Economics in Transition', Issue Paper for the Institute for EastWest Studies (New York).

Walter, I. (1985) 'Barriers to Trade in Banking and Financial Services', Trade Policy Research Centre, Thames Essay No. 41 (London).

Weller, C. E. (1999) 'Financial Liberalization, Multinational Banks and Credit Supply: The Case of Poland', Working Paper B 10, Centre for European Integration Studies (Bonn).

Weller, C. E. and Scher, M. J. (1999) 'Multinational Banks and Development Finance', Centre for European Integration Studies, Working Paper B 16 (Bonn).

3
Refinancing Banks in an Unstable Financial Environment

Werner Neuhauss[1]

Introduction

Kreditanstalt für Wiederaufbau (KfW), the German 'Reconstruction Loan Corporation' as the original name read, primarily conducts credit activities aimed at promoting the German economy: infrastructure financing, export and project finance, small and medium-sized enterprise financing as a second-tier institution, refinancing of venture capital companies, and many other operations.[2] Another section works for the promotion of developing and transforming economies, mostly as an implementing agency for the German Federal Government within the framework of official German Financial Cooperation, but also as an agent of the European Commission or of other individual countries. Here KfW finances projects in various economic sectors, such as energy, water supply, health, infrastructure and others. Another important field of activity is the promotion of efficient and stable financial sectors. At present, financial sector support accounts on average for roughly 10 per cent of KfW's annual commitments.

In the transition countries KfW's financial sector projects are designed to pursue the following objectives:

- Promotion of economic development by improving access to credit (and other financial services) for micro, small and medium-sized enterprises

- Supporting transition by designing the programmes in such a way that they contribute to the development of a market-based financial system.

This chapter is structured as follows. After this introduction a short description of KfW's activities to promote financial system development in the transition countries is presented, followed by an analysis of the implementation of the downscaling approach to financial institution-building in the transition countries. After presenting the project design associated with this approach, a detailed description of the instruments used to deal with the instability of the local financial systems and the financial institutions operating within them is offered. There is then a brief overview of the results achieved in five transition countries. Since Ukraine was heavily affected by the spillovers from the Russian financial crisis, the German–Ukrainian Fund is used as an example to elaborate in detail the issues taken up. The chapter ends with a summary and conclusions.

The promotion of financial sector development in Central and Eastern Europe: a short description of KfW's activities

The general goals outlined above have led to three different strategies, each based on a different project design, which KfW is pursuing to promote financial sector development and to expand the 'financial frontier' (Von Pischke 1991) in the countries of transition. All three approaches are based on the same premises:

1. The development of private micro, small and medium-sized enterprises (SMEs) plays a key role in the transition from plan to market. SMEs are mostly young, dynamic and better managed than the enterprises run by directors from former state companies. It is therefore not surprising that they are the engine of economic growth in many transition countries.[3]
2. A major constraint to the development of the SMEs is their limited access to financial services, especially working and investment capital finance.
3. An appropriate supply of finance for SMEs must be provided by banks, as SMEs usually have no access to the capital markets (bonds, shares), even in countries where such markets exist.[4] In other words, they have practically no alternative but to turn to banks for financing – unless, that is, they are willing to risk the extremely expensive, unreliable and sometimes dangerous option of turning to informal lenders.[5]

Very briefly, the three approaches can be summed up as follows:

1. The 'downscaling' approach to financial institution-building[6] relies on the assumption that selected commercial banks are, at least in principle, interested in serving the new private sector, i.e. micro, small and medium-sized enterprises, but refrain from doing so due to a lack of funding resources, a shortage of qualified staff and the perception that SME lending is too risky and – given the small loan amounts involved – too costly. The downscaling approach is currently being implemented in Ukraine, Bulgaria, Bosnia, Armenia, Azerbaijan, Romania and Macedonia.[7]

2. Preconditions for the implementation of the downscaling approach are a certain degree of monetary stability and an organized banking sector with viable institutions which show some interest in embarking on SME lending. If these conditions are not met, a different approach is followed: building up a new financial institution from scratch. Together with international partners like the European Bank for Reconstruction and Development (EBRD) and the International Finance Corporation (IFC), KfW is not only refinancing the activities of these institutions, but also acts as an owner, holding shares and seats on the board of directors, i.e. KfW exercises corporate governance. New financial intermediaries have been set up in Albania, Georgia, Bosnia and Herzegovina and, most recently, Kosovo, to provide the target group not only with credit but also with account, payment and other services.[8]

3. Finally, in a number of countries KfW is also supporting state-owned promotional or development banks fulfilling first- and second-tier functions. The basic idea behind this approach is to enable commercial banks in particular, which receive loans for on-lending to the target group, to start providing long-term investment finance, for which there is particularly strong demand among the target group.[9]

The following remarks are confined to an analysis of KfW's experience with the downscaling approach.

Implementing downscaling projects in Eastern Europe

Project design

KfW is implementing the downscaling approach in the transition countries using the following project design (see also Figure 3.1).

In the framework of financial cooperation with the respective country,[10] the Financial Cooperation Funds are disbursed into an on-lending fund. This fund is administered by a so-called apex unit, which might be the central bank, a firm of auditors or sometimes a promotional bank. The apex unit concludes credit agreements with selected commercial banks, referred to as 'partner banks' (PBs), and ensures that the funds are channelled to them in accordance with the terms stipulated in the credit agreement. Partner banks are selected by two criteria: financial stability and target group orientation.[11] In practice, mainly private retail (first tier) banks are selected. However, public-sector banks are not excluded; this applies in particular to state-owned savings banks, provided that they are in the process of being transformed into savings and loan banks.

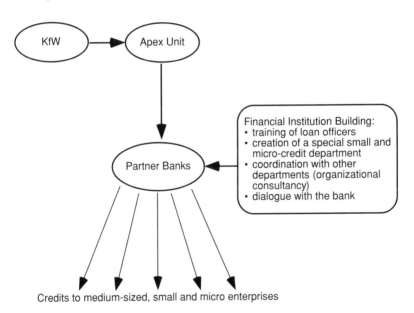

Figure 3.1   Project design of KfW-sponsored downscaling projects

Each of the PBs participating in the programme concludes a Framework Credit Agreement with the apex unit appointed to administer the Fund. The PBs pay an interest rate to the apex unit which is usually in line with the rates prevailing in the German interbank market. This means that the rate of interest charged to the banks is sufficiently low to keep the interest rates paid by sub-borrowers at a level which will attract customers from the service and production sectors and also avoid adverse selection, which can occur if interest charges are too high.[12] However, the banks are given scope to earn comparatively wide interest margins on their lending to the target group.[13] The rationale for this is to give the banks an incentive to assume the full credit risk, and to allow them to capture returns that will motivate them to supply the new product on a lasting basis.[14]

The PBs are fully liable for the funds they on-lend to the target group. Thus, they are not merely 'channelling organizations' through which funds flow, but rather institutions that bear full responsibility for all of their credit decisions. This is the only way of ensuring that the banks have an incentive to institute effective credit technologies and to use them as the basis for making well-founded credit decisions.[15] At the same time, the sustainability of the project is ensured, because the banks' positive learning experiences will motivate and enable them to continue serving the target group.

Particularly in the lowest market segments, there must be a maximum of flexibility in the types of economic activity that may be financed. In principle, all legal, ecologically sound activities can be financed.[16] However, loans to SMEs may not be used to finance pure trading operations, since the short-term trade activities of wholesale and import–export businesses are already being financed to an increasing extent by commercial banks. Accordingly, credit extension in the SME segment focuses on services and the producing sector.

Along with the financial cooperation funds the banks receive a technical assistance package which finances institution-building measures, in particular start-up costs related to SME lending. The main such measure is the training of newly hired loan officers, the purpose of which is to enable them to perform their assigned tasks without supervision in the future. The training focuses on teaching loan officers to use an appropriate credit technology, i.e. one which reflects the fact that in most countries the legal framework, including accounting and auditing standards, is still deficient and the enforcement of laws still weak. In addition, some countries have not yet developed a 'credit culture' in the sense that neither banks nor enterprises necessarily expect the borrowed funds to be paid back. In this environment, cash flow-based lending (including elements of character assessment) can succeed where traditional asset- and document-based lending fails. Every credit applicant has to be treated with respect, while administrative procedures must be reduced to a minimum. To avoid fraud and foster efficiency, there must be an appropriate incentive structure for loan officers which rewards efficiency and quality work.

The training measures and the know-how transfer are conducted by international experts who also assume the role of organizational consultants, assisting in the establishment of SME departments within the PBs, and initiating all measures required to set them up. In addition, they represent KfW's interests on the credit committees of the PBs. As a further measure, project-specific software is installed at the apex unit, allowing efficient processing and monitoring of all transactions between the apex unit and the partner banks.

Mechanisms used to deal with financial instability

During the first ten years of financial development most transition countries faced at least one financial or banking crisis.[17] This is a major challenge for the downscaling approach. Clearly, if partner banks collapse due to systemic failures or to their other business activities not related to their KfW-funded SME lending operation, the funds lent and the investments associated with institution building, which may be very substantial, could be lost. The appropriate response to this challenge varies with the different phases of downscaling project implementation.

In the first phase, the selection of the partner banks, the financial stability of the potential partner banks is checked on the basis of annual reports prepared by external auditors, together with information from the banking supervisory authority if available.[18] In cases where this information is insufficient, but the bank in question – due to its credible manifestation of willingness to serve the target group – is regarded as an attractive potential partner, a special due diligence review may even be conducted to ascertain whether the bank is in fact financially stable enough.[19] In addition, the partner banks are increasingly being required to provide collateral which, should they fail, the apex unit can seize and liquidate. Last but not least, cooperating with several partner banks in a given country, rather than just one, is another way of diversifying the risk of failure.

During the implementation of the programmes, the following measures have proved effective in limiting the risks associated with the refinancing of banks in an unstable financial environment:

- Ongoing monitoring of the financial stability of the PBs on the basis of audit and banking supervisory reports
- Limiting the loan volume granted by the apex unit to the PB based on an assessment of the financial soundness of the PB

- Imposition of certain limits to exposure, e.g. the value of the credit agreements concluded with the apex unit may not exceed, say, 15 per cent of a PB's equity and 50 per cent of its loan portfolio
- Limiting the volume of funds released at any one time: in order to ensure that the PBs do indeed use the funds provided to them for the purpose of financing loans to the target group, the loan amounts specified in the credit agreements are disbursed in tranches. The stipulation is that 85 per cent of the amount advanced by the apex unit to the bank has to be converted into loans to the target group before a new tranche can be disbursed. As an incentive to accelerate this process, the PBs have to pay a commitment fee on the contractually agreed total. Both measures reflect the experience that the portfolios built up under downscaling programmes are on average of a much higher quality than the loans the banks grant outside of our programmes.

Results

Since 1997 the downscaling approach has been implemented in five transition countries. The pioneer was the German–Ukrainian Fund, which was established in September 1996 and received the first disbursement from KfW in March 1997. Bosnia-Herzegovina was second, though here the funds which were provided by the European Union were specially earmarked to finance housing construction and improvement. Only later did KfW also start a credit programme for SMEs, with the initial funding being provided by the governments of Germany, Austria and Switzerland. Finally, in late 1998 and the early summer of 1999, programmes were launched in Bulgaria, Romania and Armenia.

As Table 3.1 shows, the total volume of on-lending funds provided by KfW comes to DM82.7 million, of which DM70.1 million has so far been on-lent to the target group. Ukraine and Bosnia are not only the oldest but also the largest programmes. The large size of the outstanding portfolio in Bosnia partly reflects the fact that housing loans have a comparatively long maturity.[20] The numbers of loans and average loan amounts show that the target group is indeed being reached in the respective countries. Finally, the low arrears rate proves that the credit technology is successful in keeping the quality of the portfolios high.

The overview indicates, however, that macroeconomic and financial instability as well as institutional deficiencies are indeed major problems confronting the downscaling approach. By way of illustration, in the following I examine the German–Ukrainian Fund.

Table 3.1 Key indicators of KfW's downscaling programmes as of 31 December 1999

	Start[1]	Financial Cooperation funds*	Number of loans granted	Total volume of loans granted*	Average loan amount**	No. of loans outstanding	Outstanding portfolio*	Arrears rate (PAR[3])	Main problems encountered
Ukraine	03/97	12.0	1,150	33.5	29,000	375	5.1	5.0%	Macroeconomic and financial sector instability; lack of commitment by partner banks, bureaucratic procedures
Bosnia[2] (SME + HCLP)	01/98	47.7	1,565	30.5	19,000	1,560	27.6	1.0%	Small size and financial instability of banks, governance problems, political pressures
Bulgaria	12/98	8.5	140	2.8	20,000	121	2.1	0.0%	Banks show varying levels of commitment; entrepreneurs distrust banks
Romania	12/98	8.5	55	1.2	22,000	51	0.9	2.3%	Macroeconomic and financial sector instability; bureaucratic procedures
Armenia	05/99	6.0	130	2.6	20,000	130	2.0	0.0%	Banks show varying levels of commitment

Notes:
* In DM millions.
** In DM.
[1] First disbursement by KfW.
[2] SME = Small and Medium Sized Enterprises Credit Programme; HCLP = Housing Construction Loan Programme.
[3] PAR = Portfolio at risk.

Source: author's compilation.

Downscaling in detail: the case of Ukraine

The German–Ukrainian Fund (GUF) was set up in September 1996 with an initial endowment of DM10 million, accompanied by a substantial institution-building component.[21] The agencies responsible for implementing the programme are Germany's Kreditanstalt für Wiederaufbau (KfW) and the National Bank of Ukraine. In July 1999, the National Bank of Ukraine and the Ministry of Finance of Ukraine together with KfW became co-sponsors of an expanded German–Ukrainian Fund with its statutory capital increased to DM32 million.[22] In line with the general features of the downscaling approach outlined above, the GUF has several complementary objectives:

- to provide credit to micro and small enterprises
- to give technical support to Ukrainian banks with a view to promoting the designated target groups
- to establish a long-term funding mechanism, the GUF, which is to function as a 'perpetual' revolving fund
- to acquire an equity stake in a new microfinance bank which is to be established

Accordingly, the programme's target groups are, on the one hand, Ukrainian micro and small enterprises and, on the other, Ukrainian commercial banks which are to receive systematic technical assistance to prepare and train them for the task of SME lending.

The financial sector environment prevailing in Ukraine is a very difficult one. As in other countries in Central and Eastern Europe, the financial system in Ukraine is dominated by former state-owned banks and a huge number of private-sector intermediaries founded at the beginning of the transition process (see Table 3.2), when the licensing policy of the National Bank was of the *laissez-faire* type.[23] Despite this surge in the number of banks, in the hyperinflationary environment of the first half of the 1990s the level of monetization dropped from 33.7 per cent to 15 per cent.

In 1997, when the GUF started its activities, progress was being made towards macroeconomic stabilization but the instabilities and deficiencies in the banking system were still very apparent. The banks' loan portfolios consisted of a few large loans, which were often non-performing. Lending was constrained in particular by bureaucratic requirements stemming from the days of central planning and by continual changes in relevant legislation which created great uncertainty as to precisely what the law was in a given case. As Table 3.2 shows, credit to the private sector, expressed as a percentage of GDP, is extremely small, even though the private sector accounts for 55 per cent of GDP. Evidently, the banks that were established in Ukraine after 1992 did not engage in financial intermediation, and were even less involved in providing financial services to the SME sector.[24]

Table 3.2   Key indicators of private-sector and financial-system development in Ukraine, 1993–8

	1993	1994	1995	1996	1997	1998
Inflation rate	4,735	891	377	80	16	11
Number of banks	133	211	228	230	229	227
(of which foreign owned)	(n.a.)	(n.a.)	(1)	(1)	(6)	(12)
Broad money/GDP	33.7	26.7	12.5	11.3	13.4	15.1
Private sector share in GDP	15.0	40.0	45.0	50.0	55.0	55.0
Credit to private sector (% of GDP)	1.4	4.6	1.5	1.4	2.5	7.6

Source: EBRD (1999, pp. 280ff.).

In accordance with the general principles explained above, the GUF selected as its partner banks two of the country's larger institutions, which had an extensive nationwide branch network and a combined volume of total assets that accounted for about 25 per cent of the Ukrainian banking system, and three small, rather dynamic private banks with one to five branches and a combined volume of total assets accounting for roughly 3 per cent of the Ukrainian banking system. Substantial institution-building measures have been carried out at these banks. The most important has been the training of around 100 loan officers, mainly 'on the job' by expatriate long-term experts. In addition, several courses and seminars in Ukraine and abroad have been organized.

Micro and small lending departments have been established at 20 of the branches run by the partner banks. The lending procedures have undergone a process of adaptation to the requirements of micro and small lending, and the new product has been accepted by the partner banks and integrated into their operations.

The new credit product met with strong demand: the funds originally provided by KfW were completely disbursed in a single year, with all loan repayments being 'recycled' in the form of new lending. However, in September 1998 the Russian financial crisis spilled over into Ukraine, cutting into both the demand for and the supply of credit. Financial crises are periods of uncertainty, output decline, rising interest rates and turmoil in the exchange markets. Each of these aspects alone reduces the demand for credit, but together they can lead to an almost complete standstill in credit applications. On the supply side the banks rushed into safe and liquid assets, supported by the National Bank (IMF 1999, p. 161). For lending operations under the GUF this meant that the analysis of borrowers' creditworthiness had to be conducted in an even more stringent way. If loans were granted at all, they became increasingly short-term and higher collateral requirements were introduced. To sum up, the partner banks became even more risk averse than they already were.

Their stance was reinforced by the fact that some of the micro and small enterprises could not service their loans on time due to problems related to a lack of foreign exchange in the market.[25] In general, however, even during the crisis the advantages of the credit technology described above remained apparent. Because the borrowers' revenues had been estimated conservatively, their monthly payment capacity was generally well in excess of the instalments they actually had to pay. Accordingly, when the crisis hit, most of them were soon able – after initial difficulties – to continue servicing their debts on time. To this day, not a single loan has had to be written off, late payments amount to only 0.4 per cent of credits disbursed, and merely 2.7 per cent of the portfolio is at risk.

In contrast to Russia, most of the banks survived the crisis.[26] At the start of 1999 the number of loans disbursed per month by the partner banks of the GUF rose steadily. As a consequence of the depreciation of the local currency, the Hryvnia, and the retention of the policy of granting short maturities, the outstanding portfolio in DEM terms grew only very slowly during 1999, however, and it was not until the start of 2000 that business began to regain its pre-crisis momentum.

The range of industries financed includes nearly every kind of business that small firms are engaged in. Enterprises in the service and production sectors each account for around 40 per cent of the total outstanding loan portfolio, while the remaining 20 per cent has been issued to trade businesses. On average the enterprises employ 25 people; however, 40 per cent of them have fewer than 10 employees, which is a clear indication that the target group of micro, small and medium-sized enterprises is being reached.

From the viewpoint of the partner banks too, the GUF's significance has become unmistakable. Despite the small loan amounts involved, the share of the GUF portfolio in the partner banks' overall portfolio is already quite significant: at some branches it is as high as 40 per cent, while the average is around 10 per cent. In terms of the number of loans issued, the outreach is even greater: in half of the branches implementing the GUF, 30 per cent of all loans are financed with GUF funds. Finally, it is interesting to note that around 20 per cent of the loans outstanding have been disbursed to clients that have already received and paid back at least one previous loan. This shows that the GUF is on its way to establishing lasting bank–enterprise relationships, i.e. relationships based on the 'Hausbank' principle.

Summary and conclusions

The downscaling approach has proven itself to be a successful way to support the development of the financial systems of countries in transition by expanding the frontier of finance to include micro, small and medium-sized enterprises. However, it has also become clear that not only on-lending funds, but also a substantial amount of technical assistance funding for training and monitoring is needed to overcome the institutional deficiencies and the lack of know-how at the partner banks.[27] In addition, reacting quickly and flexibly is crucial to protect the value of financial cooperation funds disbursed under conditions of systemic and institution-specific instability.

Notes

1. I thank my colleague Wolfgang Beck, and Carol Reichelt and Volker Renner, both of IPC, for preparing detailed information on the results of the German–Ukrainian Fund. The views expressed are those of the author and do not necessarily represent those of Kreditanstalt für Wiederaufbau.
2. A thorough review of KfW's activities, its rationale and its history, is provided by Harries (1998).
3. See also EBRD (1999, p. 92).
4. Capital markets play a virtually negligible role in the financing of enterprises in transition countries, as is also concluded in EBRD (1998, p. 95).
5. In developing countries, the importance of the informal financial sector as a source of financing for micro and small enterprises has long been recognized. A brief, incisive overview of the literature on informal financing in developing countries can be found in Robinson (1998) and Rutherford (2000, pp. 60 ff.).
6. A detailed description of this approach can be found in Schmidt and Winkler (2000).
7. Other international financial institutions are also applying the downscaling approach. One example is the EBRD's Russia Small Business Fund (for a short description see EBRD (1995, p. 145) and Wallace (1996)). In some countries, such as Ukraine and Bulgaria, the EBRD and KfW programmes complement each other.

8. See also the chapter by Zeitinger, this volume.
9. For an in-depth account of this approach, see KfW (1997).
10. The funds are made available under an intergovernmental agreement concluded between the Federal Republic of Germany and the respective transition country. In addition, KfW concludes a loan agreement with the respective government, usually represented by its Ministry of Finance.
11. See also Schmidt (1999).
12. See Stiglitz and Weiss (1981).
13. It should be remembered that often the target group's only alternative to bank loans is to borrow from the informal sector. There, however, it is not unusual to find that real interest rates of 5 per cent per month and more are charged – and paid; see also Orszag-Land (1998).
14. This implies that there is usually no pre-set interest margin on loans to micro enterprises.
15. On this point see also Webster et al. (1996, p. 36).
16. This is a result of the experience gained in many credit programmes, some of them in transition economies (for a general discussion see Adams (1998) and Von Pischke (1999)). It was found that credit lines where the funds were not to be used to finance working capital unless fixed assets were also acquired at the same time ran into severe problems. The funds were not reaching the target group, because this stipulation was at odds with the target group's actual financing needs. This conflict was and is particularly likely to occur in cases where the ratio of fixed assets to working capital is predefined.
17. On this point, see also Bokros, this volume, as well as Talley et al. (1998).
18. The importance of selecting stable partner banks for the success of any SME project is also stressed by Webster et al. (1996).
19. Unfortunately, experience has shown that the more stable and successful a partner bank's other business operations are, the less developed is the bank's eagerness to engage in micro and small business lending. Therefore, a trade-off between stability and target group orientation is often inevitable.
20. For more details on the housing loan programme in Bosnia, see Erhard (1999).
21. See also Bundesministerium für Wirtschaft/Kreditanstalt für Wiederaufbau (1998).
22. In November 1998, the European Bank for Reconstruction and Development joined the German efforts by starting its Micro Lending Programme as an extension of an SME credit line for small and medium enterprises. Special attention is paid to a usually neglected and even maligned group: micro entrepreneurs engaged in small trade activities on local markets, which are mainly women. Programme implementation is supported by TACIS (the European Union Tacis Programme) and USAID (United States Agency for International Development).
23. For a short but comprehensive overview of the development of the Ukrainian banking system, see IMF (1999).
24. Indeed, for two of the five partner banks, participation in the GUF was their first experience of lending activities.
25. The GUF sub-loans are disbursed in DM or DM equivalents.

26. This is mainly due to the fact that in Ukraine the government was able to avoid defaulting on its bills and the exposure to foreign claims was much smaller than in Russia; see Aslund (1999).
27. A similar conclusion – with reference to the Ukrainian banking system – is drawn by IMF (1999, p. 162).

References

Adams, D.W. (1998) 'The Decline in Debt Directing: An Unfinished Agenda', Paper presented at the Second Annual Seminar on New Development Finance, Frankfurt am Main.

Aslund, A. (1999) Statement at the Panel Discussion 'Getting it Right: Sequencing Financial Sector Reforms', http://www.imf.org/external/np/tr/1999/tr990715.htm

Bundesministerium für Wirtschaft/Kreditanstalt für Wiederaufbau (1998) *5 Jahre Transform – Beratung für Mittel- und Osteuropa, Bilanz und Ausblick*, Bonn/Frankfurt.

EBRD (1995) *Transition Report* 1995, London.

EBRD (1998) *Transition Report* 1998, London.

EBRD (1999) *Transition Report* 1999, London.

Erhard, M. (1999) 'Long Term Housing Loans to Low and Medium Income Households in Bosnia and Herzegovina – The Experience of Developing an Appropriate Credit Technology', Paper presented at the Third Annual Seminar on New Development Finance, September 1999, Frankfurt am Main.

Harries, H. (1998) *Financing the Future, KfW – The German Bank with a Public Mission*, Frankfurt.

IMF (1999) 'Ukraine: The Banking System in Transition', in *Ukraine: Recent Economic Developments*, IMF Staff Country Report No. 99/42, Washington DC.

KfW (1997) *KfW-Förderbankenberatung*, Frankfurt.

Orszag-Land, T. (1998) 'Underworld Bankers Lend to Small Businesses in Transition Economies', *Transition, The Newsletter about Reforming Economies*, Vol. 9, No. 4: 15–16.

Robinson, M. S. (1998), 'Microfinance: The Paradigm Shift from Credit Delivery to Sustainable Financial Intermediation', in M.S. Kimenyi, R.C. Wieland and J.D. Von Pischke (eds), *Strategic Issues in Microfinance*, Ashgate, Aldershot et al., pp. 55 – 85.

Rutherford, S. (2000) *The Poor and Their Money*, Oxford University Press, Oxford, New York.

Schmidt, R.H. (1999) 'Selecting Partner Institutions', in J. Ledgerwood (ed.), *Microfinance Handbook: An Institutional and Financial Perspective*, Washington DC, pp. 93–106.

Schmidt, R.H. and Winkler, A. (2000) 'Financial Institution Building in Developing Countries', in *Journal für Entwicklungspolitik*, Vol. XVI, No. 3.

Stiglitz, J.E. and Weiss, A. (1981) 'Credit Rationing in Markets with Imperfect Information', *American Economic Review*, Vol. 81: 393–410.

Talley, S., Giugale, M. and Polastri, R. (1998) 'Capital Inflow Reversals, Banking Stability, and Prudential Regulation in Eastern Europe', World Bank Policy Research Paper No. 2023, Washington DC.

Von Pischke, J. D. (1991) *Finance at the Frontier*, Washington DC.
Von Pischke, J. D. (1999) 'Overcoming Access Barriers', in S. A. Breth (ed.), *Microfinance in Africa*, Sasakawa Africa Association, Mexico, pp. 1–11.
Wallace, E. (1996) 'Financial Institutional Development – The Case of the Russia Small Business Fund', in J. Levitsky (ed.), *Small Business in Transition Economies*, London, pp. 76–84.
Webster, L. M., Riopelle, R. and Chidzero, A.-M. (1996) 'World Bank Lending for Small Enterprises 1989–1993', World Bank Technical Paper Number 311, Washington DC.

Part III
Financial Crises in Retrospect

4
Models of Financial Crises and the 'Boom' of Financial Crises in Transition Countries

Zsófia Árvai and János Vincze[1]

Introduction

Financial vulnerability became a much-studied topic in recent years. The Mexican crisis of 1994–5 reinvigorated interest in developing country capital market crises, and the 1997 events in East Asia widened the range of possible causes and mechanisms. The Russian crisis of 1998 brought the issue especially close to the transition countries in Central and Eastern Europe, where exchange rate, banking and stock market upheavals have been quite frequent. Countries with a view towards joining the Economic and Monetary Union (EMU) must regard vulnerability to crises as one of their most important concerns, since preconditions of candidature explicitly require that violent movements in certain financial variables, such as exchange and interest rates, do not occur.

In this chapter we first ask whether there has been a veritable boom of financial crises in transition economies. We then briefly list some facts about the incidence of financial crises in 11 transition economies, restricting our attention to the period 1995–9, in order to avoid issues pertaining to the beginning of transition. Thereafter we focus on currency crises and ask what the theoretical models tell us about these. We then recapitulate the theoretical literature, and assess in what sense it explains currency crises. Following this, we draw on 11 case studies presented in a companion paper (Árvai and Vincze 2000), and summarize their lessons in the light of the literature. We then suggest the existence of missing links, and speculate on features models should exhibit to better explain the transition experience. Finally, we offer brief comments related to policy.

The boom of crises?

A crisis is something that develops abruptly, though not necessarily unexpectedly. A financial crisis is one that occurs in one of the financial markets. The principal types include currency, debt, stock market and banking crises. There is no generally accepted definition of any of these, but there are phenomena that have the distinctive flavour of crises. In the case of a large quantitative study it would be necessary to give precise definitions; here we can list a few features in an informal way.

A *currency crisis* can happen when a precommitted peg is abandoned resulting in a devaluation and either in a new fixing or in letting the currency float. In the latter case the ensuing depreciation often overshoots the new equilibrium level. Alternatively, a large depreciation of a floating (or managed floating) currency might occur. In this case the change in the exchange rate is not a discrete jump, but is large and abrupt. The currency crisis definition may include unsuccessful attacks that do not end in a devaluation, as attacks may cause suffering since they are frequently associated with high interest rates or significant loss of official reserves.

We talk of a *debt crisis* when a country is unable to meet its obligations to repay its official foreign debt, and asks for a rescheduling or a writing-off of the debt. Also, there may be an official ban on honouring foreign debt by private entities, or a significant number of corporations may be in default towards foreign lenders.

By a *stock market crisis* we mean a sufficiently high drop in share prices, where many agents in the market (securities firms, brokers, investors, etc.) go bankrupt. During such a crisis turnover usually reaches extremely low levels.

Finally, in a *banking crisis* the illiquidity or insolvency of some of the banks disrupts the normal functioning of the banking system. A crisis can start from one bank and spread to other banks through the payments system; or several banks may face difficulties for similar reasons. A banking crisis is characterized by bank runs and/or a breaking down of the payments system. In a broader sense one may include in the definition of a banking crisis bank consolidation schemes without the symptoms of runs or payments system problems, as these can involve substantial fiscal costs, and a disruption in the form of a sharp reduction in the volume of credit.

Usually, these types of financial market crises are related to each other, though one type of crisis does not necessarily bring about another. A currency crisis may put pressure on the stock market, as foreign investors try to flee the country. A large devaluation may also lead to a banking crisis, for example, if the currency mismatch is high in the banking sector's balance sheet. A banking crisis may induce a currency crisis if the confidence of residents in the domestic banking system is shaken and they reallocate their savings in foreign currency. Debt crises and currency crises usually go together, as confidence in the local currency is shattered.

We examined the crisis history of 11 transition countries. These included the five first-round EU accession countries (the Czech Republic, Estonia, Hungary, Poland and Slovenia), the five second-round accession countries (Bulgaria, Latvia, Lithuania, Romania and the Slovak Republic) and finally Russia, because of its obvious importance. As the early 1990s were characterized by the elementary structural reforms (some of the countries are still struggling with that), and the economies were not functioning as market economies, we focused on the period since 1995. By the above definitions most of the transition countries have experienced some type of financial crisis since 1995.

The clearest case is probably *Russia*. Here, virtually every type of crisis appeared in 1998: first, a stock market crisis with significant real repercussions, then a sharp devaluation with foreign (including private) debt moratoria, and then bank runs resulting in a collapse of the payments system.

In 1997, *Bulgaria* saw after years of currency instability and banking sector problems, a veritable (successful) currency attack, and a full-blown banking crisis with runs developed. Default was avoided, and there was no stock market crisis because there was no stock market to speak of.

In *Romania* a continuous state of banking and currency problems has prevailed. In 1997–8 the foreign exchange situation exhibited the features of a crisis with large depreciation, though no bank runs or financial intermediation collapse ensued. Financial markets and the stock market have not been developed enough to cause much trouble in themselves.

The *Russian* crisis had quite a severe impact on *Latvia* due to the economy's high exposure to Russian markets, but the currency board system did not have to be abandoned. Even though we cannot speak of a full-blown banking crisis, several banks experienced bank runs and liquidity crises following the Russian crisis. There was a modest rise in

interest rates, though capital flight was not substantial as foreign participation in Latvia's capital markets is insignificant. Stock prices had
been declining for several months already by the time of the crisis; thus,
there was no significant immediate effect on the stock market.

Although *Lithuania* was also quite vulnerable to contagion from
Russia, the currency board arrangement survived the storm and the
consequences of the Russian crisis were more substantial in the real
economy than in the financial markets. Financial markets basically
reacted the same way as in Latvia.

Estonia is a similar case to the other two Baltic economies, though with
less damaging consequences to the real economy due to its lower
exposure to Russia. The stock market, however, was hit hard by the loss
of confidence of foreign investors in emerging markets. As an automatic
response to the liquidity shortage in a currency board system, there was
an immediate rise in interest rates, but capital flight was not substantial.

The *Slovak Republic* was able to defend its fixed exchange rate system
despite an attack during the Czech crisis of 1997. The Russian crisis of
1998, however, triggered the collapse of the fixed exchange rate system
and led to a large depreciation of the crown. The banking system has been
struggling with serious problems for years, but Slovakia's case is the type
of banking crisis which takes the form of bank consolidation schemes.

The *Czech Republic* was hit by speculative attacks on the Czech crown
in May 1997 which the monetary authorities were not able to withstand
and which meant that the fixed exchange rate system had to be
abandoned. The repercussions of the currency crisis in the capital market
were less severe than expected. Though the currency crisis did not lead
to a liquidity crisis in the banking system, the serious problems of the
Czech banking sector – which had been accumulating for years – became
more visible.

Poland's monetary authorities widened the fluctuation band in several
steps, which finally let to the zloty being floated in April 2000. This may
have been influenced by the consideration of having an 'independent'
monetary policy, and may also have been taken with a view towards pre-
empting potential speculative attacks.

In *Hungary* banking problems were solved via consolidation before
1995, though the cost of this may have contributed to the recurrent
small attacks on the currency throughout 1994–5. The currency problem
was managed via a larger devaluation and the implementation of a stabilization programme. In 1998, after the Russian crisis, stock prices
dropped sharply, but without important real effects. The exchange rate
came under some pressure, but was defended at almost no cost.

Slovenia is a case of avoiding all sorts of crises at the cost of maintaining relatively strong capital controls, and pursuing extremely cautious macroeconomic policies.

Theories of currency crises

Here, the main models of currency crises and speculative attacks will be reviewed. The theory of currency crises has a rather rich literature, of which we do not aim to give a full review. A few years ago there seemed to be a consensus in the literature about the existence of two major families of models, namely first- and second-generation models. However, here we follow Jeanne (1999) and distinguish between *currency attack* and *escape clause* models.

Currency attack models

The main features of the currency attack model include the following:

1. There exists a prespecified level below which central bank reserves cannot fall.
2. There exists a monetary policy rule.
3. The shadow exchange rate is defined as the floating exchange rate that would prevail if the level of reserves were at the lower bound from period *t* indefinitely.
4. The model starts with a fixed rate, which remains the actual exchange rate until the shadow rate becomes larger than the fixed rate.
5. In that period speculators attack the currency, reserves fall to their lower limit and the exchange rate becomes equal to the shadow exchange rate.

The crucial point in this type of model is that reserves cannot be acquired instantaneously to replete the stock at the time of an attack. Thus, when the shadow rate exceeds the fixed rate the attack leaves the monetary authorities helpless, and there is nothing to do but float. A subcategory in this class are the so-called first generation models (see Krugman 1979, Flood-Garber 1984) where the floating rate is unique (or, to be more precise, a unique floating rate solution is considered as non-stationary exchange rate bubbles are disregarded), and the policy rule is invariant to the occurrence of an attack. Here one can rightfully say that attacks come for fundamental reasons, and are caused by monetary–fiscal policy mixes that are inconsistent with the peg. The models are silent, however, on why this is the case.

Other currency attack models, such as that of Obstfeld (1986), were described as second-generation models. These assumed that policy is altered after an attack occurs; indeed, becomes looser. The explanation of this assumption is not part of the formal framework, though informal justifications are offered in the literature. In concrete examples it can be proven that within certain parameters this small change in the framework can result in multiple equilibria and an independent role for expectations even if we still disown the possibility of non-stationary bubbles. It has been shown, however, that self-fulfilling equilibria can be obtained in other ways, too. The trick is to devise a model where the stationary shadow rate solution is not unique, and this multiplicity once more results in an independent role for expectations (see Flood and Marion 2000).

The second-generation models were developed to explain speculative attacks in cases where the exchange rate seemed sustainable for a long period of time, but was still attacked. The switch in beliefs concerning the future paths of fundamentals can be attributed to numerous factors, i.e. political reasons, contagion, etc. Second-generation models focus on the panicky nature of speculative attacks; the main idea here is very similar to the famous (Diamond and Dybvig 1983) bank-run model with a 'good' (no attack) and 'bad' (attack) equilibrium. The attack is self-fulfilling: if everybody believes that everybody else is going to panic, then the flight is rational – independently of what one thinks about the fundamental reasons behind it.

Escape clause models

In contrast to currency attack models, escape clause models can be characterized by the following features:

1. There exists an initial peg.
2. It is supposed that there exists a loss function defined on the state of the economy.
3. There is a fixed opting-out cost that must be incurred if the fixed arrangement is given up.
4. Monetary policymakers want to minimize expected loss plus the opting-out cost by setting their instruments in an appropriate way, including the decision on whether the initial peg is maintained.
5. A crisis occurs when the peg is 'deliberately' abandoned.

In escape clause models expectations are important because they can result in policies that keep the fixed arrangement costly. The authorities' decision on the fate of the peg is based on a cost-benefit analysis.[2] There is a built-in discontinuity via the fixed opting-out cost that leads to a regime change in policy after the peg is abandoned. Here one can also define a shadow exchange rate as the one that prevails in period *t* if the authorities decide to abandon the peg in that period. However, because of the fixed opting-out costs, this shadow rate must exceed the peg with a finite amount to make the abandonment of the peg worthwhile to the monetary authorities. Because of the policy regime change one can construct examples where multiple equilibria and expectations can be self-fulfilling (see for instance Bensaid and Jeanne 1997). Because of this feature the traditional classification put these models into the second-generation class. However, we think that this similarity is more superficial, whereas the differences between currency attack and escape clause models as described above are essential.

There exist a wide variety of formulations leading to a specific loss function, and to a mechanism that may result in the eventual abandoning of a peg. In theory, there is always an interest rate level at which it is more profitable to invest in domestic assets rather than foreign assets. It is obvious, however, that high interest rates cannot be maintained forever, since their maintenance is costly. This cost can take the form of increasing interest expenditures on existing debt by the budget (countries with high public debt are particularly sensitive to this), or it can contribute to a slowdown in economic growth (which is particularly important in cases where the economy is in a recession anyway or there is political interest in high growth). The Central Bank may also be hesitant to maintain high interest rates in those cases where private-sector indebtedness is significant, and this debt bears floating interest rates (for example mortgage). It is obvious that the outcome of the crisis depends on who is able and willing to bear the costs of high interest rates longer: the monetary authorities or speculators. Usually there are three possibilities within the parameters:

1. No change in regime.
2. The regime necessarily changes.
3. Self-fulfilling (multiple) equilibria.

The 1997 Asian crisis gave incentives again to reconsider the theory of currency crises, since it could not be explained by either of the existing models (see Corsetti et al. 1998). Was the Asian crisis new in the sense that models aiming at its explanation need to be called third generational? We think that this is not necessary and regard these as either currency attack or escape clause models where the set of fundamentals determining the shadow exchange rate is widened, including financial fragility, banking collapse, balance sheet quality, (implicit) government guarantees, etc. In fact, this tendency to extend the set of fundamentals was present in the former escape clause models that were called second generational.

Explanation with the help of the models

Most models have focused on specific crises or on a certain type of crisis. The comparison of speculative attacks and currency crises in the 1990s shows that the reasons behind and the dynamics of the attacks may vary substantially, and different model types explain different crises. Although the literature on currency crises is becoming more and more extensive, the new models are usually lagging behind events. Models emphasizing self-fulfilling prophecies were developed and became popular after the 1992–3 ERM crisis when some of the currencies attacked (e.g. the French franc) apparently had no problems with fundamentals. The theoretical aftermath of the 1997–8 Asian events also indicates that speculative attack models are mostly *ex post* justifications rather than predictions (see Krugman 1998).

One can claim that currency attack models do not explain crises; rather they focus on certain features, such as sudden reserve loss, timing of attack, existence of multiple equilibria, the 'fundamental' or 'sunspot' nature of crises, the path of interest rates, role of guarantees, role of financial intermediation, the effect of bond financing, etc. Policy inconsistency is a built-in feature of these models; thus we cannot really say that they offer an explanation. On the other hand, escape clause models are so general that they can virtually explain anything by a judicious choice of fundamentals and government preferences.

Below, we try to categorize the crises observed in transition countries as falling in the domain of a currency attack or an escape clause model. However, crisis models should also shed light on periods or cases where no attack occurs. Of course, it is a much more complicated issue to decide whether a period is essentially tranquil, or is one leading up to an attack despite the calm surface. We will attempt to make such categorizations, and ask whether the models inform us about such episodes. Crisis models must also have something to say about the exchange rate arrangements itself, as it is obvious that the sustainability of a peg, or a quasi-peg, has been a very important consideration when exchange rate regimes are devised or operated. Thus we can try to explain the choices of exchange rate regimes with the help of crisis models whenever the regimes are created with a view towards pre-empting currency attacks.

We believe that in our non-experimental investigation there is no reliable way to distinguish between a fundamental and a sunspot equilibrium. The old rationale for self-fulfilling equilibria, namely the observation of fast switches in behaviour, has been criticized on the grounds that one can set up models with rational learning, informational cascades or convex adjustment costs producing such abrupt behaviour changes for no 'visible' reason. Indeed, there is an easy way to find sunspot equilibria: build a poor empirical model and conclude that fundamentals cannot explain the crisis. On the other hand, models featuring multiple equilibria are not without fundamental reasons. As we mentioned, the parameters usually contain a region where fundamentals are bad enough to make an attack possible, but not as bad as to make one inevitable.

The models and the facts

The following is based on the case studies of 11 transition economies in Central and Eastern Europe (see Árvai and Vincze 2000). We try to identify the causes why certain countries experienced a currency crisis, while others did not. In the time period under investigation, six countries were hit by speculative attacks and finally had to abandon the former exchange rate system (Russia, Bulgaria, Romania, the Czech Republic, the Slovak Republic and Hungary). It was a common feature in all the six cases that these economies had major macro- and/or microeconomic problems, which finally led to the collapse of the exchange rate, so none of them can be considered for sure as a second-generation currency attack-type crisis, e.g. a self-fulfilling prophesy. There were, however, significant differences in the causes of and reactions to the speculative attacks as these countries were at different stages of transition, and the degree of capital account liberalization was also different.

Patently weak microeconomic foundations and inconsistent policies characterized Russia, Bulgaria, and Romania. These three countries had several elements in common in the years preceding the crisis: soft budget constraints, asset stripping, weak supervision of financial markets, lack of efficient privatization, severe fiscal imbalances, high inflation, real appreciation of the exchange rate, increasing foreign debt. The Russian currency crisis can be clearly classified as a currency attack crisis. Romania and Bulgaria had floating exchange rate systems, so currency crises occurred in the form of sharp depreciations, so this type can best be described as a 'would-have-been a currency attack crisis'.

Of the remaining three countries attacked, the Czech Republic and Slovakia have much in common. In these two countries macroeconomic indicators painted a rather favourable picture of the economy, but they concealed very serious microeconomic problems. The slow pace of restructuring and privatization together with the overvalued exchange rate led to a deterioration in external competitiveness, and the resulting high current account deficit made the two countries vulnerable to speculative attacks. The Czech and Slovak crises were closer to the escape clause model type, as the decision about the fate of the exchange rate resulted from a cost-benefit analysis. The comparison of the first and second speculative attacks on the Slovak crown is an especially good example for illustrating the escape clause model, as the costs of maintaining the peg were valued differently in the May 1997 and September 1998 attacks. In the first case Slovak monetary authorities were determined to defend the exchange rate as they regarded the political and real economic costs as being higher than the benefits resulting from the devaluation, whereas in 1998 the currency was not defended for too long, especially because political considerations did not play a large part in the decision. Hungary's 1995 devaluation also belongs to the escape clause model in our view, as prevailing macroeconomic policies would have been sustainable for some time but the costs of having a strong real exchange rate were considered too high.

The remaining five countries which did not go through a currency crisis in the second half of the 1990s can be divided into two distinct groups. One group introduced a currency board system (Estonia, Latvia and Lithuania) in order to facilitate macroeconomic stabilization and to increase the credibility of the exchange rate system. The implementation of the reform measures was fast and successful enough to avoid abandoning the peg, even at the time of the Russian crisis which had a significant impact on these economies. The key in this group's case was that they did not experiment too much with other exchange rate regimes but introduced the currency board at an early stage of the transition process, which in turn served as a crucial support in macroeconomic stabilization.

Slovenia and Poland in different ways tried to retain some flexibility in influencing the exchange rate in order to respond to macroeconomic developments. Slovenia did not make exchange rate announcements, but the Central Bank has always heavily managed the exchange rate and the interest rate together, which was made feasible by significant controls on capital flows. In contrast, Poland adopted increasingly flexible exchange rate regimes to pre-empt currency attacks and to target inflation via managing the domestic interest rate. The intervention band was widened gradually and the exchange rate was finally allowed to float in April 2000. On the other hand, Hungary's successful sticking to a crawling system with a rather narrow band, puts its more recent experience closer to the Baltic countries, demonstrating that increased exchange rate flexibility is not necessary for avoiding delicate situations.

It is important to note that the incidence of currency crises was independent of the degree of exchange rate rigidity – both floating rate countries and fixed rate countries suffered from it. The analysis of the achievements of the 11 countries suggests that transition has been a painful process in every country and the choice of the exchange rate regime was not a determining factor in the pace of their development. The incidence of currency crises was more of a sign that there was a lack of political will to bring the exchange rate regime and economic policies in line.

What is missing from the literature?

It is a general feature of the models surveyed above that they consider a period of pegging the exchange rate, whether a constant or a crawling peg, and ask when this arrangement will be abandoned. In practice very few actual exchange rate regimes belong to this category in the strict sense. In the continuous scale from strict pegs to pure floating one can observe regimes that switch between these extremes: monetary authorities sometimes intervene and virtually peg the exchange rate in certain periods, and at other times they let it float. Wide bands and managed floats can describe the announced regimes but within either of these classes the operations of central banks can exhibit large differences. The literature has focused exclusively on pegs or target bands. Both general experience and our transition examples reveal that most developing countries manage their exchange rates to some extent, but fewer and fewer apply pegs in the strict sense. In our sample Estonia, Lithuania and, more recently, Bulgaria have adopted very rigid exchange rate arrangements (currency boards), whereas none of the others have exhibited a policy of absolutely no intervention. However, attacks can occur on currencies that are flexible to a significant degree. Of course, modelling a managed float is difficult because there exists a very wide range of policy rules that monetary authorities may follow, lying between a peg and a pure float. Still, it is possible that certain types of exchange rate management strategies can be distinguished. With such intermediate types of monetary policies the definition of a crisis or an attack becomes a non-trivial issue. Clearly a possibility is to define a successful attack as a change in the policy rule from a partially managed float to a strict float. Or more generally the abandonment of a certain exchange rate rule for the sake of another with an enhanced degree of flexibility can be an appropriate definition.

The two models can in principle be merged, that is one can set up a model where reaching some domain in the state space results in a currency attack, whereas in some other domain an escape clause attack materializes. Here, two shadow exchange rates would exist: one defined by reserves falling to their minimum level, the other via policy preferences. Indeed, in such a model the type of crisis would itself be an endogenous (stochastic) event. Several of the transition country cases suggest that for many countries both crisis regimes may have been relevant, and contingencies pushed these economies into one or other compartment. Indeed, it seems plausible that an escape clause scenario occurs earlier than a currency attack-type one, and the danger of the latter can be a powerful reason why central banks act pre-emptively, by abandoning a commitment they may keep today but are afraid that they might be forced to give up in the future. The assumption of a minimum feasible level of reserves is an expression of this idea, but in a rather specific manner.

Existing models treat the political dimension rather simplistically. In currency attack models the reserve bound can be interpreted as an expression of some political constraint, whereas in escape clause models the government's preferences may have this role. However, as several examples (Russia, Bulgaria, the Slovak Republic) have proved, the development of crises has had a more intimate, even endogenous, relationship with political events. Political changes could effectively alter social preferences, and these are partly the outcome of the economic situation. While it is true that making politics and financial crises endogenous would be very difficult, neglecting it is a disadvantage when one wishes to match models with the facts. In particular the Russian example has taught us that politics can have a truly international dimension, at least as much as a run on foreign exchange reserves does.

It has been noticed for many years that in currency attack models reverse attacks can be studied in essentially the same framework as normal ones. The simple trick is to assume an upper, rather than a lower, bound for reserves. Though formally correct this solution has much less of an appeal as a plausible hypothesis. On the other hand, escape clause models can also be rephrased in a way in which the monetary authorities may be willing to give up a peg, because its defence requires too low rather than too high interest rates. Indeed, in several transition country cases policymakers were intent on fighting inflation with high interest rates, and this, together with good fundamentals, led to capital inflows and to a reverse attack (Poland, Slovenia, Hungary and the Czech Republic). Policymakers either had to give in and decrease interest rates (Hungary), or had to apply capital controls (Slovenia), or make the exchange rate regime more flexible (Poland). The analysis of these policy options is completely missing from the theoretical literature. This issue can be particularly interesting since attacks have in many cases been preceded by reverse attacks, where the bulk of the problem consisted in a sudden reversal of capital flows, and not just a flight.

Today it is almost commonplace that micro behaviour on stock and foreign exchange markets should be invoked to explain the development of financial prices, and a purely macroeconomic approach toward the exchange rate is insufficient. Therefore, it is somewhat surprising that this aspect is largely absent from crisis models. Of course, the difficulty in approaching this is obvious, and there does not seem to be any fully general approach. However, from an empirical point of view, our case studies indicated that the market microstructure facet can clarify why certain countries suffered and others did not (or not so much). At least the timing of collapses must have been directly influenced by market microstructure (see Darvas and Szapáry 2000).

Finally there is an issue pertaining to financial crises (emphasized by Allen and Gale 1998) that has apparently not been raised by scholars of currency upheavals. This is the possible 'optimality', or at least Pareto improving feature, of a crisis scenario. The Allen and Gale idea is based on the observation that a traditional loan contract does not have good risk-sharing characteristics. In this view bank runs that are implied by real causes, e.g. a true collapse of asset values, may improve risk-sharing with respect to a contract where depositors never suffer. Indeed, if crisis-prone developing countries issue domestic currency denominated debt to foreigners, and a currency crisis ensues when things turn bad for a perfectly good extraneous reason, then a crisis would reduce the yield of foreign investors in order to make them share the losses with the developing country. This might be a less costly way of implement risk-sharing than outright default. Of course, the incentive compatibility of this implicit contract may raise interesting questions, but it is not too far-fetched to interpret some of the crises in our sample in such a manner (Hungary, the Czech Republic, Russia).

Concluding remarks

We have described the multicoloured financial crisis experience of 11 transition countries and arrived at the conclusion that there is no unique explanation for their behaviour, and several existing models should be invoked to clarify it. As we pointed out, the story is complex enough to request theoretical progress in the field.

Moving from the vantagepoint of contemplation to that of action, we can now ask what message our investigation bears on policy. As we have not focused on this aspect we can offer only a few tentative remarks on this topic.

First, it seems that crises were not a really devastating experience for most transition countries. Where they were, Russia being probably the most obvious example, they were associated with inconsistent macroeconomic policies and the weakness of structural (micro) reforms.

Second, the Czech and Slovak examples can show that macroeconomic stabilization can be an illusion without accomplishing the *de facto* market economy transformation.

Third, though capital controls may be useful for avoiding crises, one can argue on quite traditional grounds that they have clear disadvantages. In the case of Slovenia they may have inhibited growth, whereas the lack of capital market discipline may have been instrumental to the developments in Hungary before 1995, in Bulgaria before 1997, in the Slovak Republic more recently, or in Romania during the whole period.

Fourth, having said that we cannot deny that financial market liberalization may add to the vulnerability of these countries in the foreseeable future, and especially before they join the European Union, we believe that admitting this necessity and accepting some concomitant pains would be wiser than insisting on avoiding financial market turbulence at all costs.

Notes

1. The authors would like to thank the participants of the conference 'Financial Development in Eastern Europe: The First Ten Years' (Klaffenbach Castle, Chemnitz) for their comments. The views expressed are those of the authors and do not necessarily reflect the official view of the National Bank of Hungary.
2. Note that reserves are not necessarily part of the model.

References

Allen, F. and Gale, D. (1998) 'Optimal Financial Crises', *Journal of Finance*, LIII: 1245–84.

Árvai, Z. and Vincze, J. (2000) 'Financial Crises in Transition Countries: Models and Facts', National Bank of Hungary, Working Paper Series.

Bensaid, B. and Jeanne, O. (1997) 'The Instability of Fixed Exchange Rate Regimes when Raising the Nominal Interest Rate is Costly', *European Economic Review*, 41: 1461–78.

Corsetti, G., Pesenti, P. and Roubini, N. (1998) 'What Caused the Asian Currency and Financial Crisis?' NBER Working Paper, 6833–4.

Darvas, Z. and Szapáry, G. (1983) 'Financial Contagion in Five Small Open Economies: Does the Exchange Rate Regime Really Matter?', *International Finance*, 3 (1).

Diamond, D. and Dybvig, P. (1983) 'Bank Runs, Deposit Insurance, and Liquidity', *Journal of Political Economy*, 91 (3): 401–19.

Flood, R. and Garber, P. M. (1984) 'Collapsing Exchange-Rate Regimes: Some Linear Examples', *Journal of International Economics*, 17: 1–17.

Flood, R. and Marion, M. P. (2000), 'Self-fulfilling Risk Predictions: An Application to Speculative Attacks', *Journal of International Economics* 50 (1): 245–68.

Jeanne, O. (1999) 'Currency Crises: A Perspective on Recent Theoretical Developments', CEPR Discussion Paper No. 2170.

Krugman, P. (1979) 'A Model of Balance-of-Payments Crisis', *Journal of Money, Credit, and Banking*, 11: 311–25.

Krugman, P. (1998) 'What Happened to Asia?' mimeo, MIT.

Obstfeld, M. (1986) 'Rational and Self-fulfilling Balance-of-Payments Crises', *American Economic Review*, 76(1): 72–81.

5
Promoting Financial Development: Lessons from Poland

Zbigniew Polanski[1]

Introduction

The first decade of post-socialist transformation in Poland, i.e. the 1990s, proved to be a remarkable success. In ten years Poland switched from the chaos of the late 1980s to an economic system rapidly converging towards European Union standards. Political and institutional changes not only allowed for a quick economic recovery and enduring growth, but also led to the opening of accession negotiations with the EU in the spring of 1998.

One of the outstanding features of Poland's development in the past decade is that, contrary to most other post-communist countries, it managed to avoid any major type of economic disturbance. Of course, at the beginning of the decade Poland passed through a typical transformational recession. However, since mid-1992 it followed a relatively balanced growth supported by a smoothly developing financial system. Only at the end of the decade did both external and internal developments result in an economic slowdown accompanied by a quickly growing balance of payments' current account gap, demonstrating that important threats to Poland's economic and financial stability still remain.

By and large, however, there is no doubt that for Poland the 1990s was the most successful decade within living memory. In what follows we attempt to explain these developments, asking for possible lessons to be learnt.

Below we present a short bird's-eye view of Polish economic development since the late 1980s, followed by a sketch of the evolution of the financial system. We then move on to link financial issues with economic development, stressing both the methods adopted to solve problems inherited from the socialist economy in the first half of the 1990s and the currency crisis prevention measures of the second half of the decade. We conclude with an attempt to generalize Polish experience.

Poland's economic development in the 1990s: A bird's-eye view

The late 1980s social and political developments led to a peaceful collapse of the Polish communist regime and the establishment of a new, democratically elected government in August 1989.[2] Consequently, from the beginning of 1990 new economic policies were launched, well-known as the Balcerowicz Plan (named after Leszek Balcerowicz, the deputy Prime Minister responsible for economic policy at that time).

The initial phase of these policies is also known as the big bang. This latter expression stresses the essential feature of new policies, i.e. the fact that they were a drastic break from the previous approach to economic policy. At the macroeconomic level a restrictive stance was coupled with limited convertibility of the local currency (the zloty). At the microeconomic level far-reaching liberalization of prices and contractual relations was implemented. In the institutional dimension these moves were accompanied by regulations promoting market structures and ownership changes (i.e. privatization).

The policies started at the threshold of the decade evolved over time. However, the basic logic of the new system was not distorted by subsequent decisions. Poland followed a cautious, pragmatic, and relatively consistent approach to economic reforms. By the end of the decade a new generation of reforms was launched (once again linked mainly with Balcerowicz), this time dealing mostly with the public sector.

After a short transformational recession[3] strong economic growth appeared, acutely contrasting with the sluggishness of the previous decade. The 1990–1 collapse was the mildest among post-socialist economies. As a result Poland was the first post-communist country in which GDP exceeded its pre-transformation level; that was in 1995. By 1999 Poland's GDP was larger by approximately 27.5 per cent than in 1989.

A steady inflation reduction and an increasing openness of the economy accompanied these developments. Obviously Poland has not suffered from any major reversals. Nonetheless, it cannot be denied that an economic slowdown and rising unemployment marked the end of the decade. Other important imbalances appeared as well, especially in the area of the balance of payments.

Table 5.1 Poland's economic development, 1989–99 (selected indicators)

Year	GDP[a]	Inflation[b]	Unemployment rate[c]	Openness[d]
1989	0.2	251.1	–	–
1990	–7.5	585.8	6.5	–
1991	–7.0	70.3	12.2	–
1992	2.6	43.0	14.3	30.7
1993	3.8	35.3	16.4	32.2
1994	5.2	32.2	16.0	35.3
1995	7.0	27.8	14.9	37.7
1996	6.0	19.9	13.2	39.9
1997	6.8	14.9	10.3	46.0
1998	4.8	11.8	10.4	47.0
1999	4.1	7.3	13.0	43.5

Notes:
[a] Percentage change.
[b] Consumer Price Index yearly average change.
[c] End of year.
[d] Exports and imports (as registered in the balance of payments on a cash basis) to GDP.
Sources: Central Statistical Office and National Bank of Poland.

Poland's financial development in the 1990s: An overview

The socialist economy legacy

The first important reason explaining Poland's success, however surprisingly it may sound, lies in the socialist economy period, although – at the same time – the socialist system's legacies resulted in important problems (touched on later in this chapter).

The Polish experience pre-1990s was not encouraging. In the 1980s (and earlier decades) Poland conducted unsuccessful reforms which led to deep macroeconomic imbalances (as evidenced by increasing inflation and state budget deficits) coupled with economic stagnation.[4] Nonetheless, the important point to note is that these attempts to reform the socialist system had several beneficial aspects.

First, they led to practical conclusions that became accepted by most of the society and a majority of influential policymakers. Among these practical conclusions two should be mentioned in particular: the conviction that consistency, credibility and transparency are crucial for the efficacy of economic policy, and that ownership changes (privatization) are indispensable for market mechanisms to work properly.

Second, by the end of the 1980s such intellectual developments led to some institutional and behavioural changes, which allowed for Poland's quick revival in the next decade. Above all one should recall that a radical liberalization of business activity took place as early as 1988. In the finance area it must be noted that banking reform started in 1988–9, leading to the breakdown of the socialist banking system.[5] Consequently, it was prior to the summer 1989 political changes that Polish banks became true intermediaries. In 1989 the legal basis for a relatively independent Central Bank (the National Bank of Poland – NBP) was adopted. These activities were accompanied by the creation of a banking supervision unit housed by the Central Bank.

New legal solutions would not lead to institutional and behavioural changes so smoothly if some pre-war regulations were non-existent. Of particular importance among them was the 1934 Commercial Code which was able to be reintroduced easily; other inherited regulations important for financial development were the Check Law and the Bill-of-Exchange Law (both from 1936).

Financial development in the 1990s

Broadly speaking, both the legal and the quantitative development of Poland's financial system in the 1990s can be described as following a pattern of two major 'waves'. The first wave of changes started actually prior to 1990 (as mentioned above, its beginning can be traced back to 1988) and lasted until 1993. The second wave began in 1997 and finished in 1999. These dates clearly suggest that financial development was closely linked to efforts aiming at the reform and modernization of the economy.

The first wave coincides in its most intensive part with the introduction of the Balcerowicz Plan. From the end of 1989 many laws were amended (e.g. the Banking Law and the NBP Act) and completely new regulations were introduced (e.g. the regulations pertaining to capital markets). It should be noted that in December 1991 Poland signed an Association Agreement with the EU, which provided for the harmonization of all new legal regulations with the EU standards. Although this Agreement came into force in February 1994, it has been an important reference point for the legislators since 1991.

On the quantitative side these changes were associated with a far-reaching liberalization of financial institutions creation and a gradual development of the securities market.

Table 5.2   Quantitative development of the main financial institutions in Poland, 1986–99 (selected years; end of year)

Financial institutions	1986	1993	1995	1998	1999
Banking institutions					
Central bank	1	1	1	1	1
Commercial banks	3	87	81	83	77
Cooperative banks	1662	1653	1510	1189	781
Credit unions	–	36	126	290	417
Non-bank institutions					
Insurance companies	2	28	40	55	63
Mutual funds					
Open-end	–	1	4	41	62
Closed-end	–	–	15	15	16
Private pension funds	–	–	–	–	21

Sources: National Bank of Poland and Central Statistical Office.

The first stage of financial development can be considered at an end with the adoption of two important acts: the Law on Financial Restructuring of State Enterprises and Banks, which will be discussed below, and the Law on National Investment Funds, a regulation related to the Polish Mass Privatization Programme.[6]

Institutional reforms slowed down during 1994–6. Nonetheless, it should be mentioned that in 1995 legislation on deposit insurance became effective and the Bank Guarantee Fund came into existence.

The beginning of the second wave of legal and quantitative changes can be linked to the new Constitution of the Republic of Poland, adopted in 1997. The Constitution has created a new framework for macro-economic policy, that is, it has forbidden budget deficit financing by the Central Bank as well as introducing the Maastricht Treaty provision on public debt, which places its limit at 60 per cent of GDP. It has also guaranteed a large degree of autonomy to the NBP, similar to that enjoyed by institutions belonging to the European System of Central Banks.

On the micro side a new Banking Law, a much more restrictive act than the previous regulation,[7] complemented these changes. In the capital market, insurance and foreign exchange areas, various regulations were amended and new laws were implemented. In 1997–8 a set of laws laying grounds for the pension system reform (started in 1999) was passed. Finally, in 1999 a new Public Finance Law became effective, leading to the decentralization of the state (administrative reform) and stimulating the development of a market for local government debt.

As Table 5.2 shows, the 1997–9 legal changes were accompanied by important developments in the number of financial institutions, resulting from, among others, the consolidation of the banking sector. These data, however, do not capture the process of privatization. As in the corporate sector, privatization of financial institutions proceeded gradually but consistently. In 1993, 58 institutions out of the operating 87 commercial banks were controlled by private owners, while 10 were controlled by foreigners. By the end of the decade private owners controlled 70 commercial banks (out of 77) and 39 were in the hands of foreign investors. While foreign ownership accounted for 56 per cent of total capital of Polish banks, it is estimated that, when all types of property links are considered, foreign investors controlled over 70 per cent of total assets of commercial banks by the end of 1999.[8]

In the second half of the 1990s processes of the same kind were taking place in other segments of the financial system. For example, the insurance sector quickly expanded with the growing participation of foreign ownership. By the end of the decade approximately half of the equity capital of insurance companies operating in Poland belonged to foreign investors.

The financial system's depth and soundness by the end of the 1990s

There is no doubt that despite the last decade's accelerated expansion, the Polish financial system cannot be considered as particularly well-developed. The typical financial deepening indicators for Poland are much lower than those for industrialized countries; for most of the decade they were also usually lower than those for the most advanced post-communist countries (i.e. Hungary and the Czech Republic).

Table 5.3   Selected financial deepening indicators for Poland, 1994–9 (selected years; % of GDP)

Indicator	1994	1998	1999
Commercial banks' assets	55.8	60.5	62.3
'Monetization'[a]			
For M2	34.5	40.2	43.1
For M1	16.3	14.8	16.3
Credit market	18.6	25.2	28.8
Corporate credit	17.1	20.9	22.8
Consumer credit	1.5	4.4	6.0
Warsaw Stock Exchange capitalization	3.3	13.2	20.2

[a]   Ratio of a monetary aggregate to GDP.

Sources: National Bank of Poland and Central Statistical Office.

Despite its modest size, the Polish financial system seems to be relatively sound. As a result of the 1980s chaotic experience and the problems of the first half of the 1990s (described below), tough regulatory frameworks and efficient supervisory institutions were implemented. In the second half of the decade, the stability of the financial system was assured. However, detailed research shows, for example, that the efficiency of Polish banks is still lower than that of banks in Hungary and the Czech Republic and, obviously, lower on average than that of banks in the EU.[9]

Poland's financial development in the 1990s: legacies, imbalances and crisis prevention

Here we look at Polish financial development from the point of view of the problems which had to be tackled. We start by looking at the first half of the decade, then move on to current issues.

Dealing with the legacies of the socialist economy

We briefly touch upon three issues. All of them are essentially property rights problems. The first two deal with internal developments, the last one involves international considerations.

The 'payment jams' problem

In the socialist economy 'payment jams', i.e. inter-enterprise arrears or overdue trade debts of enterprises, developed when monetary authorities attempted to conduct stringent credit policies.[10] The beginning of the 1990s was not different in this respect as the state-owned enterprises initially neutralized the new macroeconomic policy by accumulating overdue payables and receivables.[11]

The 1990s experience, however, differed essentially from previous attempts at tightening economic policies as the new macroeconomic management was coupled with privatization and the enforcement of bankruptcy procedures. Thus, enterprises were forced to control 'payment jams', so that the resulting barter trade never reached unmanageable proportions, losing importance by 1993.[12] Polish experience showed not only that *effective economic policies must be internally consistent but also that macroeconomic actions need to be accompanied by appropriate microeconomic and institutional reforms.*

It would be unfair to suggest that Poland solved these types of problems entirely in the first years of transition to the market economy. During the whole decade large state-owned enterprises created tax and customs arrears. In 1999 important delays in social contribution payments took place, fuelling public sector deficit. Such developments confirm that microeconomic restructuring is not yet complete. However, these property rights problems were reduced to an extent that they no longer threaten the stability of the financial system.

The 'bad loans' problem

The corporate sector's payment problems not only took the form of temporary growing inter-enterprise arrears, but also resulted in the expansion of so-called 'bad loans'.

The relative volume of bad bank loans, more formally known as non-performing loans (or assets), grew quickly from the start of the decade, reaching its peak in 1993 (see Figure 5.1).[13] Broadly speaking, the origins of the problem can be linked to the transformational recession. Looking in more detail, two groups of factors responsible for their development can be established. First, bad loans were due to factors external to the financial system, that is to loans inherited from the socialist economy period, to the collapse of the Council for Mutual Economic Assistance (Comecon) and to new stringent macroeconomic policies. Second, bad loans resulted from the financial system's internal factors, most notably from the lack of expertise by newly created – both state-owned and private – commercial banks which often extended credit to unreformed state-owned enterprises or newly created private businesses without proper evaluation of the risks involved. In other words, non-performing

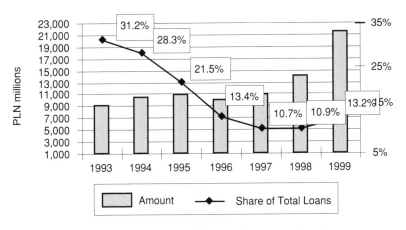

Figure 5.1   Non-performing loans, 1993–9 (% of total bank loans)

Source: National Bank of Poland.

loans to a large extent originated from bankers' lack of knowledge of credit management.

The Polish approach to resolve the problem of quickly growing non-performing loans focused on these latter factors. A *decentralized approach* was followed, meaning that commercial banks were burdened with solving the problem. Of course, a general framework was prepared for the banks to act.

The focal point of this framework was the Law on Financial Restructuring of State Enterprises and Banks, which became effective in March 1993. This act, however, should be seen in a broader context of steps aimed at creating incentives for a more efficient and stable financial system. In particular, it should be mentioned that in late 1991 a programme of state bank privatization was made public and the quality of banking supervision gradually improved.[14]

The Law on Financial Restructuring assumed some governmental recapitalization of banks (based on their end of 1991 balances). However, as mentioned, it promoted a decentralized approach. Banks were obliged to create special departments to deal with the restructuring process. To facilitate this, new, additional legal procedures were established, such as the bank-led conciliation, public sell-out of enterprise debt and debt-to-equity swaps. These procedures gave a lot of power to banks *vis-à-vis* their corporate clients, while at the same time they forced banks to work out their problems individually.[15] Further developments showed that this latter characteristic of the Polish approach to solving the bad loans issue proved to be of crucial importance. *Banks became motivated to tackle the problem, and in the process learned how to deal with financial risks and how to avoid the emergence of new non-performing assets.*

Bad loans increased again in 1999. This was partly due to the economic slowdown resulting from the August 1998 Russian crisis, and partly due to policies aiming at inflation and current account imbalance reduction. (More details on these issues are presented below.) Here we should stress that the end of the decade proved that Polish banks were able to accommodate flexible monetary and exchange rate policies. This would not be possible if banks had not learned how to evaluate financial risks properly.

Summing up the Polish experience with bad loans, the following points should be emphasized. First, problems resulting from non-performing loans *did not turn into bank runs and systemic difficulties.* Thus, non-performing assets did not lead to a fully-fledged banking crisis. Second, the adopted decentralized approach *had a positive long-term impact on banking behaviour* as it helped banks to build up better information about their customers and avoid excessive risk. In subsequent years this fact enabled Polish authorities to privatize the banking sector in such a way that it generated substantial revenues to the state budget. Furthermore, the decentralized approach allowed for the creation of a relatively sound banking system able to accommodate changing macroeconomic conditions. Third, the adopted approach stressed banking questions, placing, however, *less emphasis on enterprise restructuring*. Consequently, as suggested, the latter proved insufficient.

Solving the foreign indebtedness problem

Poland entered the 1990s with another property rights issue: by the end of 1989 its foreign public debt *vis-à-vis* Western countries reached US$40.8 billion, i.e. it exceeded the value of its exports fourfold. Polish authorities had not serviced this debt, originated in the 1970s, since 1981.

At the threshold of the new decade it was obvious that without forgiveness Poland would face an important obstacle in its development. Consequently, negotiations on foreign debt rescheduling started. In 1991 an agreement with the Paris Club creditors (i.e. creditors whose claims were guaranteed by governments) was signed. As a result Polish debt was cut by approximately 50 per cent while the rest is to be repaid over a period ending in 2009. Three years later, in 1994, an agreement with the London Club creditors (i.e. creditors whose claims were not guaranteed by respective governments) was reached. This time Polish debt was cut by approximately 45 per cent while the rest is to be repaid over a period ending in 2024.

What is important to note is that these changes in Poland's external debt position coincided with a gradual relaxation of foreign exchange administrative controls. In the first half of the 1990s the zloty's convertibility in the area of balance of payments current account transactions expanded substantially. By mid-1995 Poland accepted the IMF's Article VIII obligations confirming the convertibility of its currency in this matter.

In the first half of the decade capital controls were gradually relaxed as well. This process is not yet complete as a major part of short-term capital flows continues to be subject to administrative controls. Nonetheless, by mid-decade most long-term and part of the short-term flows (e.g. resulting from T-Bill transactions) were liberalized. Thus, legal conditions were created allowing foreign investors to participate actively in the Polish capital market.

Currency crisis prevention in the second half of the 1990s

Having signed the agreement on foreign debt rescheduling with the London Club, Poland faced a new situation: it became a credible debtor, as confirmed by the first credit ratings published by mid-1995. Consequently, given the gradual relaxation of capital controls, a major inflow of foreign capital followed.

Balance of payments developments

Poland's decisive opening to international capital movements coincided with important changes in its balance of payments. In the second half of the decade the current account gap grew quickly, reaching 7.5 per cent of GDP by the end of the 1990s. In the beginning of 2000 it continued to expand, increasing to over 8 per cent of GDP in the first quarter of the year.

Table 5.4   Polish balance of payments, selected items, 1995–9 (US$ billions)

Item	1995	1996	1997	1998	1999
Current account (C/A)					
Relative to GDP (%)	4.6	−1.0	−3.0	−4.4	−7.6
Total C/A	5.5	−1.3	−4.3	−6.9	−11.6
Merchandise trade balance	−1.8	−8.1	−11.3	−13.7	−14.4
Unclassified C/A transactions	7.7	7.1	6.0	6.0	3.6
Capital account	2.8	4.8	5.4	10.8	9.2
Foreign direct investments	1.1	2.7	3.0	5.0	6.6
Portfolio investments	1.2	0.2	2.1	1.3	1.1
Credits	0.2	−0.16	0.8	1.5	2.4
Long-term credits	0.16	−0.2	0.3	1.6	2.0
Short-term credits	0.07	0.08	0.5	−0.06	0.4
Gross official reserves (stock)	15.0	18.0	20.7	27.4	25.5

Notes:
1. These balance of payments statistics are based on bank processed payments (i.e. it is a cash-based balance of payments, not a transactions-based balance).
2. Totals may differ from sums because of rounding errors.

Source: National Bank of Poland.

The direct factor responsible for the quickly expanding current account gap is to be found in the area of foreign trade. This is particularly true of the officially registered merchandise trade balance. It has been in permanent deficit since 1993, showing a tendency for fast expansion since 1996. In 1995 the deficit in officially recorded trade flows was, however, counterbalanced by a substantial surplus in cross-border, unregistered trade flows (Table 5.4, 'Unclassified C/A transactions'). Consequently, overall, Poland enjoyed a positive trade balance resulting in a surplus current account in 1995.

The positive trade developments of 1995 were accompanied by increasing capital inflows. After a very modest first half of the decade, capital inflows began picking up, most notably foreign direct investment (FDI). By the end of the decade Poland became a leading Central–East European country in this respect.[16] Portfolio investments and credit flows were substantially lower, although the role of the latter has gradually increased.

The 1995 surpluses in the current and capital accounts led to a sharp increase of foreign reserves: NBP gross official reserves increased 2.5 times (from US$6 billion to US$15 billion) in 1995 alone. This growth trend continued until 1998. In 1999 reserves declined as a result of two main factors. On the one hand, NBP stopped intervening on the foreign exchange market. Thus, Central Bank reserves did not increase despite continued capital inflows. On the other hand, Poland was servicing its foreign debt as stipulated by the agreements with Paris and London Clubs.

There are three basic reasons explaining the dramatic increase in Poland's balance of payments current account deficit.

The first is the *long-term weakness of the export sector*. Putting it simply, Polish products are not competitive enough on quality grounds. Obviously, despite the modernization efforts of the 1990s, Poland's real sector has not been sufficiently restructured to secure its international competitiveness. On the import side, the gradual reduction of tariffs and the abolition of the import tax led to the domestic cheapening of foreign products. With regard to the positive balance of cross-border trade in the mid-1990s, its size can be explained by substantial price differentials between Germany, Poland and post-USSR countries. As they have gradually diminished, there has been a long-term trend for cross-border trade to decline. These developments were, however, accelerated by the Russian crisis, which led to a decline of 40 per cent in the unclassified trade flow balance in 1999.

Trade balance developments, however, not only reflect the structural backwardness of the export sector and its lack of competitiveness. As suggested by economic theory, current account developments can be analysed from the perspective of the economy's saving and investment behaviour. Table 5.5 suggests that such an approach gives an additional insight into the Polish situation. On the one hand, it shows that while private savings relative to GDP were declining, the ratio of private investment to GDP was quickly increasing, leading to *a savings-*

investment imbalance since 1996. Such investment developments can be largely explained by the above-mentioned inflows of FDI. Since 1995 Poland has been attracting foreign long-term capital, which has resulted in the expansion of real investment-related imports. On the other hand, this savings–investment imbalance has been further aggravated by the *deficit of the fiscal sector*. Table 5.5 shows that in 1997–9 the fiscal sector gap was largely generated by extra-budgetary funds performance, which in turn mostly reflected the costs of some of the reforms of the public sector (especially the pension system reform).

Table 5.5   Savings–investment and fiscal balances, 1995–99 (% of GDP)

Items	1995	1996	1997	1998	1999
Savings–investment balance[a]	1.6	–1.1	–3.0	–3.9	–5.3
Savings	17.1	16.1	16.2	16.6	15.6
Investment	15.5	17.2	19.2	20.5	20.9
Total fiscal sector balance	–2.6	–3.1	–2.9	–2.6	–3.2
State budget balance	–3.3	–3.3	–2.6	–2.4	–2.0

Note: [a] Household and enterprise sectors.

Sources: Central Statistical Office and Ministry of Finance.

Polish 1999 reforms overlapped with the impact of the 1998 Russian crisis. Consequently, their costs were aggravated as the economy slowed down. In the last three months of 1998 Polish GDP growth declined to 2.9 per cent (on a year-on-year basis), further declining to 1.6 per cent in the first quarter of 1999. Economic growth, however, accelerated in the following period, so that by the last quarter of 1999 it reached 6.2 per cent and approximately 6 per cent in the first quarter of 2000. This *acceleration of economic growth* seems to be the third reason explaining the rise of the Polish current account deficit. As Polish GDP picked up, imports followed, but they were not matched by increasing exports.

Macroeconomic policies

The above analysis has shown that in order to control the current account gap, policies in several areas could, and probably should, be adopted. Polish authorities, however, concentrated essentially on macroeconomic policies. Microeconomic measures (e.g. in the form of an industrial policy focusing on the restructuring of the export sector) were not designed and, consequently, not implemented.

The Polish monetary authorities reacted quickly to the new macroeconomic environment resulting in the increasing inflow of foreign capital. When it became evident that Poland had evolved into a typical small-open economy, subject to interest rate parity conditions, a new exchange rate arrangement was introduced. In order to discourage unwanted inflows of short-term capital, the volatility of the exchange rate was increased: in mid-May 1995 the 'pre-announced crawling peg mechanism' was replaced by a 'pre-announced crawling band system'. Initially, as visible in Figure 5.2, the fluctuations of the exchange rate were not particularly large. However, in 1997 a new approach was adopted allowing for a major volatility of the market rate *vis-à-vis* the (subject to the crawling devaluation) central parity rate. In the subsequent period, a further increase of the volatility in the exchange rate was permitted: in March 1999 fluctuation bands were widened to ±15 per cent and in June that year the Central Bank finally stopped intervening in the forex market. Thus, despite its official form of a 'pre-announced crawling band system', the Polish exchange rate regime gradually evolved into a floating exchange rate mechanism. This evolution was finally confirmed by the official adoption of a floating exchange rate system on 12 April 2000.

Such developments in the area of the exchange rate were to a large extent stimulated by the 1997–9 international financial turbulence. Exchange rate flexibility proved to be very helpful in absorbing external shocks and discouraging short-term portfolio inflows.[17]

The rationale for the policy emphasis on exchange rate fluctuations should also be seen from the perspective of internal developments. As Table 5.5 shows, fiscal policy was not consistently focused on economic stability. Although major efforts were made in order to prevent further deterioration of fiscal imbalances,[18] the deficits of the fiscal sector increased throughout the second half of the decade. Consequently, only monetary policy (together with the exchange rate policy) could play a major active role in trying to prevent the expansion of the current account gap.

Polish monetary policy had been focusing on inflation control since the early 1990s.[19] Consequently, during the entire decade relatively restrictive policies were followed by the Central Bank. Nonetheless, when dangers stemming from current account deficits were detected, the NBP – relying on its extensive autonomy – started policies aiming at 'cooling down' the quickly expanding economy (see Table 5.1), so that from December 1996 it began raising the restrictiveness of its policies further. (See Figure 5.3.)

These policies not only allowed for a substantial inflation reduction (in autumn 1998, year-on-year inflation dropped to single-digit levels),

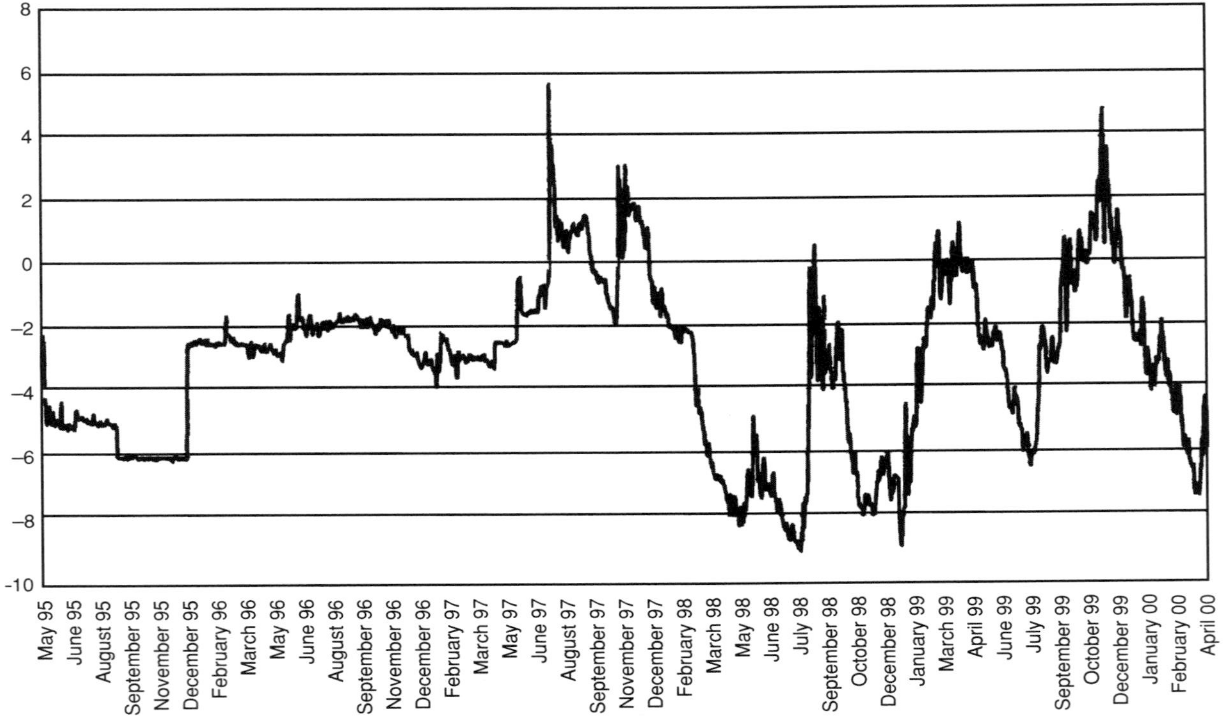

Figure 5.2 Deviations of the market rate of the zloty from the central parity rate against the currency basket, 1995–2000 (%)

Source: National Bank of Poland.

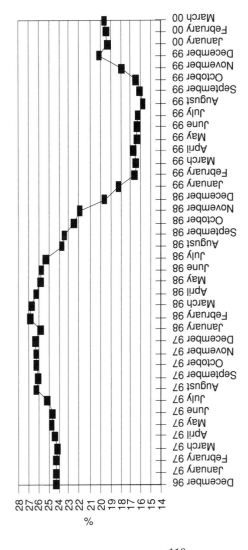

Figure 5.3   Average interest rate on one-year bank loans for business, 1996–2000 (%)

Source: National Bank of Poland.

119

but also put the current account developments under relative control until the Russian crisis hit the economy, i.e. until August 1998.[20]

As inflation rates were declining the Central Bank lowered interest rates several times. However, when inflation picked up at the end of 1999, monetary policy was tightened again.

At the time of writing, it is difficult to predict what the impact on the current account of this recent monetary policy tightening will be. However, let us end this short description of Polish macroeconomic policies with the following observation. Such exchange rate and monetary policies aiming at avoiding macroeconomic destabilization *would not have been possible without a relatively healthy financial system*. It is well-known that high interest rates strengthen the adverse selection and moral hazard risks in credit relations. This is probably the main explanation for the increase in classified loans at the end of 1998 and in 1999 (see Figure 5.1). Similarly, floating exchange rates induce additional risks in business activity, which can be successfully avoided only by a modern (i.e. providing hedging services) and sound financial system. Obviously, Poland in the first half of the 1990s managed to create a financial infrastructure permitting the conduct of flexible macroeconomic policies.

The sustainability of Polish external imbalance

The size of Poland's balance of payments current account gap raises the question of its sustainability, i.e. concerning its future financing. Many countries, sometimes with lower current account gaps than Poland's, suffered from abrupt capital inflow reversals, which led to a sharp exchange rate depreciation and the loss of foreign reserves, i.e. currency crises, often followed by financial crises and economic crises.

Before briefly commenting on Poland's situation, let us make two remarks. First, *there is no mechanical relationship between the size of the current account gap and the development of a currency crisis*. Some countries with deficits similar to Poland's (e.g. Australia and New Zealand in the 1990s) or larger (e.g. Norway in the second half of the 1970s) did not face currency crises; while others, with lower deficits (e.g. most East Asian countries prior to 1997), suffered from speculative behaviour. Second, *in Poland there is currently no institutional set-up for a traditional currency attack*. This is because the exchange rate system is a floating one and the Central Bank conducts no interventions in the forex market. Consequently, there is no place for a sharp decline in Poland's foreign reserves.[21]

Table 5.6   Poland's selected external financial safety indicators, 1996–9

Year	Foreign official reserves (in months of imports)	FDI to C/A deficit (%)	External debt to GDP (%)	Debt–service ratio[a] (%)	Short-term external debt to foreign official reserves (%)
1996	6.6	202.7	33.1	8.6	26.5
1997	6.4	70.5	34.2	6.7	21.2
1998	7.5	72.4	36.2	9.5	22.2
1999	7.5	57.0	39.3	14.4	28.8

Note: [a] Foreign debt service/exports.

Source: National Bank of Poland.

Table 5.6 presents some ratios traditionally interpreted as indicators of an economy's vulnerability to a currency crisis. As is usually the case with economic indicators, their predictive power can be easily questioned. Nonetheless, they can be treated (with caution) as a reference point for further discussion.

Similar to our earlier observations, these ratios seem to suggest that despite the existing imbalances, the situation is basically under control. Clearly, most of the indicators worsened, especially in 1999.[22] In this context two observations must be made. It is true that in recent years Polish external indebtedness increased mostly due to enterprise sector behaviour. Nonetheless, both total and enterprise foreign debt as well as the costs of their service are at a relatively low (although increasing) level. What is essential, however, is that *enterprise debt is mostly medium- and long-term* as capital controls on credits up to one year are still in place. Moreover, a major part (approximately 32 per cent at the end of 1999) of business sector foreign indebtedness comprises intercompany loans, i.e. credits granted by parent companies to their Polish affiliates and daughter companies.

The second remark refers to *the role of FDIs in current account gap financing*. Their role obviously declined in 1999. This, however, seems rather a temporary phenomenon as it resulted mostly from delays in the privatization process. The year 2000, however, is set to be a record one in terms of financial flows resulting from privatization. Large-scale privatization is expected to continue up to 2002.

In the last few years the quickly expanding current account deficit has been easily financed by capital inflows resulting from the privatization process. The crucial question for the future is *what will happen when privatization is completed*? Obviously, exports must resume if the current account gap is to start declining. This means that in a relatively short span of time the Polish export sector must be profoundly restructured, so that it starts providing internationally competitive goods and services. Time will tell, however, if Poland is able properly to utilise the remaining time left.

The lessons

Without aiming at easy generalizations, one can try to draw some conclusions from the experience described above.

First, *history matters*. It is not a coincidence that the countries most advanced in economic reform (as confirmed by the Hungarian and Polish cases) are countries that started their reforms first. In Poland, the unsuccessful reforms of the 1980s resulted in a general acceptance of the view that *clear vision of the goals to be achieved and persistence in maintaining the main lines of reforms are crucial.* In particular, the Polish experience confirms that the *efficacy of economic policy results from its consistency, credibility and transparency.* The 1980s reforms also showed that *privatization is indispensable for market mechanisms to work efficiently.*

Another important conclusion relates to the correct sequencing of reforms and their proper pace. This was most notably evidenced by the fact that problems inherited from the socialist system ('payment jams' and 'bad loans' problems) were worked out before the decisive opening to international capital flows. With regard to the pace of reform, the Polish experience suggests that gradual privatization is crucial for the promotion of a sound financial system and the sustainability of large current account deficits.

Poland's transformation also shows that *enduring financial stability can be achieved only when economic agents' incentive structures are correctly designed.* The way in which the legacies of the socialist economy were dealt with and new regulations were implemented confirms that appropriate incentive structures are crucial for the emergence of a sound financial system.

Obviously, Polish experience confirms the well-known truth that macroeconomic policies should react in a proper and timely fashion. However, it also suggests a less widely held view that exchange rate flexibility is crucial in absorbing external shocks and discouraging speculative capital inflows.

Finally, the Polish transition allows for the observation that it is extremely beneficial *to combine financial development with policies aiming at preventing financial and currency crises.* In the Polish case such an approach stimulated the development of a sound financial infrastructure which has allowed for active macroeconomic management focusing on the sustainability of large-scale imbalances.

Notes

1. Gratitude is expressed to J. Borowski, M. Gołajewska, Z. Jarczewska, R. Sawinski and P. Sotomska-Krzysztofik (all from the National Bank of Poland) for sharing data and graphs. The usual disclaimer applies.
2. A detailed analysis of Poland's political, social and economic developments of the 1980s can be found in Kaminski (1991).
3. This concept, coined by Kornai (1993), stresses that policies leading to the replacement of a supply constrained economic system (a socialist economy) by a demand constrained economic system (a traditional market economy) must result in a temporary decline in output.
4. These unsuccessful reforms are analysed from the point of view of financial development in Polanski (1991).
5. On socialist banking, in particular as it evolved in Poland, see Podolski (1973).
6. This programme was a relatively small one (it covered less than 5 per cent of industry). It started in the autumn of 1995 and resulted in the establishment of 15 closed-end mutual funds (see Table 5.2).
7. For example, article 128 of the 1997 Banking Law sets the capital adequacy ratio for a newly established bank in its first year of operation at 15 per cent. In the second year the ratio can be lowered to 12 per cent, and only subsequently can it reach the internationally accepted 8 per cent.
8. General Inspectorate of Banking Supervision (2000, pp. 24–8).
9. See Opiela et al. (1999). Banking efficiency is defined here as operational efficiency, i.e. as operating costs to assets ratio.
10. More on the Polish historical experience can be found in Podolski (1973, chapters 6, 8 and 9).
11. An account of this experience can be found in Pinto et al. (1993).
12. Belka (2000).
13. See also Polanski (2000, p. 61).
14. Among others, this was evidenced by the fact that the General Inspectorate of Banking Supervision introduced precise definitions of classified loans in 1992.
15. Polish experience in this respect is quite well-described. See e.g. Borish and Montes-Negret (1998).
16. However, it should be stressed that this is not the case when FDIs are considered on a per capita basis. On this basis, Poland is well behind the Czech Republic and Hungary.
17. For more see Polanski (2000).
18. This is confirmed by two facts. First, government's primary (i.e. excluding interest payments) balances have been positive since 1993, although they declined slightly by the end of the decade. Second, when budgetary expenditures used to cover the deficits of pension systems (the general and

the farmers' one) are deducted, the Polish state budget balance becomes positive (see Wernik 2000).
19. For more details see Polanski (1998).
20. In fact, in August 1998 the Polish monthly current account showed a modest surplus.
21. One should also mention that the Polish 1999 foreign exchange law assumes some emergency measures that can be introduced in the case of a currency crisis (among others, they include such extreme measures as the possibility of a temporary suspension of the convertibility of the zloty).
22. Only imports covered by reserves stabilized; however, one should keep in mind that in 1999 Polish imports (as well as exports) declined. In fact, when measured on a monthly or quarterly basis, this ratio declined in the course of 1999, but by early 2000 it continued to stay above six months.

References

Belka, M. (2000) 'Lessons from Polish Transition', Paper presented at the conference of Polish Academy of Sciences, Warsaw, 7 January.
Borish, M. and Montes-Negret, F. (1998) 'Restructuring Distressed Banks in Transition Economies: Lessons from Central Europe and Ukraine', in G. Caprio Jr., W. C. Hunter, G. G. Kaufman and D. M. Leipziger (eds), *Preventing Bank Crises. Lessons from Recent Global Bank Failures,* Washington DC: World Bank.
General Inspectorate of Banking Supervision (2000) *Sytuacja finansowa banków w 1999 r. Synteza* (summary evaluation of the financial situation of Polish banks in 1999), National Bank of Poland, April.
Kaminski, B. (1991) *The Collapse of State Socialism: The Case of Poland*, Princeton, NJ: Princeton University Press.
Kornai, J. (1993) 'Transformational Recession: A General Phenomenon Examined through the Example of Hungary's Development', *Economie Appliquée* no. 46: 181–227.
Opiela, T. P., Bednarski, P., Gołajewska, M., Józefowska, M. and Nikiel, E. M. (1999) 'Efektywność i ryzyko sektora bankowego w Polsce' (The effectiveness and riskiness of Poland's banking sector), *Materiały i Studia* no. 96, National Bank of Poland, December.
Pinto, B., Belka, M. and Krajewski, S. (1993) 'Transforming State Enterprises in Poland: Evidence on Adjustment by Manufacturing Firms', *Brookings Papers on Economic Activity* no. 1: 213–70.
Podolski, T. M. (1973) *Socialist Banking and Monetary Control. The Experience of Poland*, Cambridge: Cambridge University Press.
Polanski, Z. (1991) 'Inflation and the Monetary System in Poland in the 1980s, and the Stabilization Program 1990', *Osteuropa-Wirtschaft* no. 4: 342–63.
Polanski, Z. (1998) 'Polish Monetary Policy in the 1990s: A Bird's Eye View', in K. S. Vorst and W. Wehmeyer (eds), *Financial Market Restructuring in Selected Central European Countries,* Aldershot: Ashgate, pp. 7–22.
Polanski, Z. (2000) 'Poland and International Financial Turbulences of the Second Half of the 1990s', in J. Hölscher (ed.), *Financial Turbulence and Capital Markets in Transition Countries,* London: Macmillan; New York: St Martin's Press, pp. 53–75.

6
The Financial Sector in Macroeconomic Adjustment Programmes

Gerwin Bell[1]

Introduction

Interest in the macroeconomics of financial sector problems has greatly increased since the Mexican and Asian crises in the second half of the 1990s. While there were certainly financial and banking crises reaching macroeconomic proportions before these episodes – for example, in the Nordic countries in the early 1990s – it is fair to say that these were generally not seen as a genuine complicating or contributing factor to macroeconomic imbalances.[2] This state of affairs, however, has changed drastically since, even to the point that accepted journalistic wisdom mentions the importance of the financial sector in – depending on which newspaper or magazine one happens to read – emphasizing, accelerating, or even triggering macroeconomic problems.

This chapter argues that the recent prominence accorded to the financial sector in discussions on macroeconomic adjustment is indeed appropriate. However, this is not because of inadmissible oversights in earlier discussions, but very much a byproduct of the recent liberalization of financial markets, as well as increased capital convertibility. The chapter also argues that the new, more prominent, role of financial markets in macroeconomic crises has its root cause in fundamental macroeconomic imbalances, which are accentuated by, and tend to become evident first in, the financial sector. That is to say, the financial sector's ability to leverage and mobilize resources for more productive investments may serve to be rather pernicious if fundamental imbalances distort proper incentives.

In examining this role of the financial sector, this chapter first defines some key concepts. In a next step, the theoretical and empirical linkages and feedbacks between the financial sector and the macroeconomy at large are reviewed. It will be seen that the relevant theoretical and empirical literature offers little guidance to policymakers who wish to (a) develop financial markets without running the risk of creating macro-economic imbalances, or (b) develop a macroeconomic adjustment programme which would minimize the adverse impact on financial inter-mediation. The chapter then sets out to suggest some guidance on these questions, and concludes with a brief overview of policy-relevant points.

Some key concepts

Before turning to a more detailed discussion of the issues involved, it is useful briefly to define some of the key concepts. *Macroeconomic imbalances* are meant to describe situations of high inflation and/or balance of payments crises. *Macroeconomic adjustment policies* are policies designed to redress these imbalances, typically stabilization policies that rely on a mix of fiscal consolidation, monetary tightening and exchange rate revaluation. In many practical instances, these immediate policies are supplemented by some more medium-term structural policies, for example in labour markets, financial markets, public enterprises, business regulation and the trade system. While many of these policies have come to be associated with International Monetary Fund- and World Bank-supported programmes, in many cases they are adopted independently by the countries (e.g. Malaysia in 1998 and 1999).

The *financial system* is defined rather broadly as the part in the economy able to affect the intermediation between savers and borrowers, channelling funds from savers to productive uses, notably investments.[3] In the pursuit of this task the financial system has to overcome important transactions costs and informational asymmetries. In practice, financial systems in many less developed countries tend to be dominated by banks (Demirguc-Kunt et al. 1999), likely reflecting the impact of information asymmetries as well.[4]

Linkages between the financial sector and the macroeconomy

Do financial markets have an impact on the macroeconomic performance and, if so, how? Perhaps surprisingly, the answers to these questions have been tenuously debated among economists for quite some time, but a consensus view has only recently begun to emerge on the basis of empirical work.

On a conceptual level, the macroeconomic benefit from a functioning financial system is clear: better resource allocation and provision of funds for growth-enhancing investments. However, the actual merit has been contested. At one end of the spectrum are arguments typically associated with Schumpeter (1912) and Hicks (1969), who viewed the development of the financial system as a *sine qua non* for the advent of technological innovation and growth. At the other end, Lucas (1988) famously argued that the role of financial factors in economic growth had been greatly inflated. Turning to the field of international finance, the above-mentioned debate finds its mirror image in the discussion of the role of international capital market liberalization, with, for example, Bhagwati (1988) arguing that its benefits were grossly overrated, while its risks were downplayed. This view is being contested by, for instance, Rogoff (1999) who stresses that even marginal efficiency gains afforded from such liberalization can be very large.[5]

The empirical resolution of these debates is complicated by the difficulty in assigning the direction of causality between the development/liberalization of a financial system and a country's per capita income. In tandem with the arguments that financial markets spur growth and macroeconomic stability, it also needs to be recognized that low inflation and sustainable rates of economic growth establish an environment in which longer-term planning can go ahead, permitting financial sectors to develop and deepen. Importantly, such an environment mitigates the effects of informational asymmetries (for example, by facilitating the 'signal extraction' of idiosyncratic and systemic shocks).[6] Recent empirical research, which seeks carefully to address the causality problem, appears to be consistent with a positive effect of financial development on long-term economic growth (Levine 1997).

Unfortunately, available empirical work still says little about the *short-run* macroeconomic linkages between the financial sector and macroeconomic performance, yet it is precisely this short-term effect that is crucial for the proper treatment of financial sector issues in macroeconomic adjustment programmes (which are by necessity short term).

Macroeconomic imbalances and financial sector development

In the remainder of the chapter, these short-run linkages will be addressed to obtain a better understanding of the salient issues posed to policymakers who seek to avert a macroeconomic crisis and/or to rapidly develop a financial system. Figure 6.1 is an oversimplified – but expositionally useful – taxonomy providing a roadmap by delineating overall economic outcomes in terms of macroeconomic crisis conditions and development/fragility of the financial sector.[7]

| | | Macroeconomy | |
		No crisis	Crisis
Financial Sector	Developed	I	II
	Underdeveloped/ fragile	III	IV

Figure 6.1   Typology of economic outcomes

- Quadrant I indicates a benchmark situation where no macroeconomic adjustment is required and the financial sector is not a source of concern.
- Quadrant II indicates a rather rare, if historically possible, event (for example, the balance of payments crisis in the United Kingdom in the 1970s). An important component of this situation appears to be the presence of capital controls, which limit the financial contagion from poor macroeconomic policies.
- Quadrant III typifies a situation faced by many emerging markets, which – with stable macroeconomic conditions – would want to harness the benefits of liberalized financial markets. It arguably typifies also the situation of the Asian crisis countries and Mexico prior to the advent of their problems.
- Quadrant IV characterizes a fully-fledged crisis: both the macroeconomy and the financial sector are in need of urgent repair.[8] Importantly, this Quadrant depicts the situation in Mexico and the Asian crisis countries once their respective crises had erupted.

Before proceeding, note that this framework oversimplifies in at least two ways. First, the absence of an obvious crisis does not imply that an economy's fundamentals are correct. This possibility arises in situations where the underlying fundamental weakness is difficult to assess. Cases in point are the Mexican and Asian crises, where a look at the countries' stability in terms of the obvious fundamentals – fiscal deficits, inflation, growth and real exchange rate – tended to miss the point (see Mishkin 1999). Hidden weak fundamentals can take various forms: asset price bubbles; quasi-fiscal or prospective deficits and/or contingent claims on the government (for example, in the form of loan guarantees – explicit or implicit through a pegged rate), or through forward market intervention by central banks.[9] These issues are further discussed below.

Second, a less developed financial sector may not be fragile, whereas a developing one may become increasingly fragile. Fragility depends on the demands being placed on the financial sector, which are, for example, set to increase dramatically with financial liberalization. A banking system that was able to cope under sheltered and non-competitive conditions may very quickly turn into a fragile house of cards if not properly supervised in a more liberalized system. Indeed this is one of the reasons why financial liberalization has come to be associated with the outbreak of recent macroeconomic crises.

With these caveats in mind, this chapter discusses policies and choices pertaining to situations as described in Quadrants III and IV. Two important questions immediately arise: first, for a country with a stable macroeconomy but underdeveloped financial sector (Quadrant III), which type of financial sector development policies should be pursued so as to progress toward the virtuous Quadrant I, and which should be eschewed to avoid a fall into the disastrous Quadrant IV? Second, for a country already in a full-blown crisis situation (Quadrant IV), what implications will macrostabilization have for financial sector development? These questions will now be answered in turn.

Financial sector development and short-run macroeconomic performance

The possibility that a financial system panic can undermine macroperformance has long been established, e.g. in the form of bank runs and bubbles. Similarly, recent crises have shown that entire countries may become subject to such runs – triggered by investors seeking to cut their financial exposure to assets from such countries, all at the same time. Such turmoil in the financial sector regularly translates into credit crunches and attacks on a currency, with both typically resulting in sharply higher real interest rates which trigger/amplify recessions and render otherwise sustainable government debt burdens impossible to service without additional fiscal adjustment.[10] Against this background, what is a country seeking to harness the benefits of comprehensively liberalized financial markets to do, so as to avoid risking the onset of macroeconomic problems?

In the first instance, care has to be taken that the proper macroeconomic fundamentals are in place. While few experts would make the argument that financial market development ought to take precedence over reducing unsustainable current account deficits or taming rampant inflation, the reverse – i.e. to liberalize without any worry if there is no crisis – is not necessarily a good guide for policymakers either. The important additional requirement is that there be no hidden fundamental weaknesses. Such weaknesses lie arguably at the foundation of the Mexican and Asian financial crises.

Hidden fundamental weaknesses and prospective fiscal deficits: the case of pegged exchange rates

By their very nature, *hidden* fundamental macroeconomic weaknesses are not easily discernible. In recent instances, such weaknesses have been associated with the presence of pegged exchange rate regimes, and/or privileged access of a group of creditors to banking system credit based on political criteria, as well as with asset market bubbles.[11] The next paragraphs specify in more detail some of the adverse effects that pegged exchange rates had in contributing to the onset of financial crises, relating to overexposure in unhedged foreign borrowing of the corporate and banking sectors, asset price bubbles, and certain central bank operations in defence of such pegs.

Unhedged foreign borrowing   A pegged exchange rate is often introduced so as to give more policy credibility and better anchor market expectations. It also serves to help compare the cost of domestic finance with the cost of internationally available finance, particularly if the domestic currency risk – the risk of a depreciation – is *perceived* to be insignificant. In such cases, it makes sense to substitute internationally available finance for domestic borrowing if the former is cheaper ('carry trades'). Without the perceived risk of a depreciation, the relevant analysis reduces to a straightforward comparison of interest rates, which, in many emerging market cases, has shown lower international rates, such that significant capital inflows into these economies were mobilized.[12] At this stage, the peg can lead to overexposure in foreign currency debt as a result of the moral hazard that arises in the form of insufficient hedging against foreign currency exposure – after all, the peg is perceived to be credible. Such moral hazard affects not only investors, but also domestic commercial banks, which see a profit opportunity between the domestic currency lending rates and their borrowing cost in international markets. The critical situation arises when unhedged foreign currency borrowing starts to become perceived as being unsustainable, as it will in due course. At this stage, it becomes prudent for lenders and borrowers to reduce their exposure, which if attempted on a comprehensive scale, will quickly give rise to pressures on foreign currency reserves. If the reserves are insufficient to match the thus swelling demand, a devaluation will have to ensue.

Asset price bubbles   Typically, the implicit guarantee provided by pegs becomes aggravated if politically well-connected sectors are able to gain substantial access to such borrowing, and, in many instances, have arguably resulted in unsustainable asset price bubbles, particularly in real estate. The mechanics are very much the same as those that have been evidenced in domestic banking crises when banks were able to accumulate significant amounts of 'bad debt' (non-performing loans), which arise when the value of the assets may fall sharply when banks and/or their borrowers try to sell their collateral/assets and the bubble bursts. Realizing sharply lower collateral values, foreign lenders may also seek to cut their losses, thereby making it harder for domestic borrowers – grown accustomed to easy foreign financing – to raise new funds and/or roll over existing debt, creating additional non-performing loans. In many past instances, the government eventually had to assume these hidden liabilities, as it considered the banks 'too big to fail', thereby sharply increasing its indebtedness.

Forward intervention   Moreover, some central banks have stepped in to further increase prospective deficits by aggressive (uncovered) intervention in the forward foreign exchange market at a point when doubts about the credibility of the peg had already set in and markets had increasingly begun to take positions against the peg. These central banks had become active sellers and market makers in the forward market, thereby running up large 'net open forward positions'. In this way, they were able to secure an appreciated spot market exchange rate by the workings of the interest parity condition (i.e. they established a targeted forward exchange rate through their intervention which, with a given domestic interest rate, determined the spot exchange rate). Such operations have proved especially tempting for central banks lacking sufficient reserves to mount an exchange rate defence in the spot market, as they do not require the use of any reserves in the spot market, and not even in the future spot market if the maturing forward contracts can be rolled over. Moreover, such operations are also off balance sheet, and, thus, at least initially, more easily concealed from financial markets. However, some central banks engaged in such operations assumed substantial contingent liabilities when the support of the spot rate required ever larger forward intervention. These contingent costs became actual when the forward contracts could eventually no longer be rolled over. At that point a steep depreciation ensued – typically more than cumulating the depreciations avoided in the past.

In the ways just described, substantial contingent liabilities can arise in a short time frame and contingent liabilities can quickly turn into actual ones once a depreciation does occur. In the event, investors will scramble to reduce their exposure in the country, as they fear that other investors will do the same, thereby aggravating the depreciation and undermining the viability of additional projects with heavy foreign currency liabilities, i.e., the makings of a financial-cum-macroeconomic crisis. Such an aggravated depreciation will, rationally, occur once the amount of reserves that a government can muster to defend the peg is exceeded by the claim on these reserves in the aftermath of a depreciation (for a formalized version of this mechanism, see Burnside et al. 2000).

An important point to bear in mind in this context is that the sudden onset of these crises owes nothing to cryptic or capricious behaviour of speculators and markets, but instead reflects the ultimate unsustainability of the underlying economic fundamentals. For example, Burnside, Eichenbaum and Rebelo (1999) have estimated that the banking systems in Korea and Thailand had amassed nonperforming loans of 25 and 30 per cent of GDP before the crisis, dwarfing not only their current fiscal deficits but also their outstanding government debt and reserves.

Thus some important lessons to be heeded for financial sector liberalization pertain to economic fundamentals:

- There is no reason to be complacent – especially in pegged or managed-peg countries – even if the fiscal position is comfortable, and inflation and growth performance are satisfactory.
- Even in an apparently calm macroeconomic environment, some – especially politically – painful adjustment may be called for to ensure a smooth financial market liberalization. Notwithstanding the obvious difficulties, it is important to break up politically close relationships between well-connected and favoured enterprises and the banking system. In this context, it is noteworthy that many of the calls for faster and unconditional liberalization will be coming from these well-connected quarters (see below).
- A pegged exchange rate system requires particularly close supervision of the banking system and corporate borrowing. This is not to say that pegged systems are per se inadvisable, but rather,

that they will need to be accompanied by especially close scrutiny of an economy's unhedged foreign exchange position (including that of the monetary authorities) and other such contingent liabilities.[13]

- The domestic banking system is the important transmission channel through which these problems reach systemic proportions.

Development of a financial sector

Turning away now from the question of fundamentals and to financial sector policies, in the first instance, it is important to recall the inherent difficulty of financial sector development. As a financial sector becomes more developed and sophisticated, it is also very likely to become more fragile, when it is called on to perform more complicated and unfamiliar functions which will require a period of acclimatization. This points to the importance of ensuring that sound regulatory and supervisory capacities are in place as new financial markets and instruments emerge.

Policies to develop/liberalize a financial sector have to be guided by this inherent difficulty. In the broadest sense, they may be distinguished into 'active' policies, which seek to establish particular instruments and markets, and 'passive' policies, which rely more on setting up a proper regulatory and supervisory framework within which particular markets and instruments are permitted to develop as the need arises.

Active policies   There are several reasons to be cautious in adopting an 'active' policy stance: first, policymakers or planners are rarely, if ever, ideally placed to predict the best eventual or even transitional structure of the financial sector, which would be most attuned to a country's requirements and comparative advantages. Indeed, since Hayek's (1937) seminal work, it has been recognized that one of the most important features of markets is to deliver information on the otherwise unobservable preferences, such as an economy's desired mix of financial instruments. Second, the financial sector's needed regulation is, at least in its infancy, likely to give rise to some rents and monopoly profits. Policymakers who are in the process of 'picking winners' will make themselves the target of lobbying and other influencing attempts by rent-seeking sectors, and the existing entrenched interests. Finally, proper regulation and supervision are in the first instance likely to slow down the development of the politically desired financial sector structure, especially if such a structure would imply added risk. Regulators and supervisors may thus find themselves at least in the awkward position of slowing financial market progress, and quite possibly even mandating some retrenchment of already existing financial markets.[14] It is very likely that regulators and supervisors would thus come under pressure to 'take it easy', 'exercise restraint', and 'not stand in the way of progress'.[15]

Passive policies   Against this background, a passive approach will in the first instance seek to ensure that the necessary checks and balances within the financial sector are in place, without which enhancing the scope of the financial sector may become highly counterproductive. Supervision and prudential regulation thus assume key importance.[16]

Conceptually, *supervision and regulation* constitute *prima facie* capital controls and an intervention into the market mechanism, and could therefore be chastised.[17] Historically, they arose as the *quid pro quo* for the lender of last resort function, which was established to mitigate the dangers of systemic crises arising from bank runs, i.e. a clear-cut market failure. With recent financial crises sharing many of the attributes of traditional bank runs, the rationale for supervision and regulation in the liberalization of financial markets becomes evident.

Supervision and regulation are not the only tools in the arsenal; it is also important to foster (positive) *competition*:

- The most clear-cut policy in this regard is permitting the entry of reputable *foreign financial institutions*. Admitting foreign banks will bring several benefits. First, *supervision* from their headquarters is imported, which is both often better than local supervision, and can serve as a guideline for domestic supervisors. Second, they are likely to enjoy a *comparative advantage* in more exotic and risky financial operations, with which they will likely already have become familiar.
- The policy implications for easing restrictions on the *entry of domestic private banks and privatizing state-owned banks* require a somewhat more nuanced assessment. On the one hand, these policies provide more competition and efficiency (Claessens 1996). On the other hand, the award of a banking licence may also be seen (especially in conditions of weak prudential regulations and/or supervision) as a licence to exploit a rent, and rent-seeking activities can create substantial problems in a relatively short time (see above). Garber (1998) illustrates the Mexican crisis as a case in point. The successful bank privatization programme was followed by sharp loan growth in subsequent years, and in order to pay off the debt incurred when the banks were privatized, banks needed

high yields from risky lending (e.g. in derivatives which were also frequently off balance sheet).[18] The imminent collapse of these banks was then one of the main propagators of the subsequent crisis.

- Last, but not least, an important element of ensuring positive competition lies in the better *information provision and transparency* to markets. There are several dimensions to this element. Comprehensive information on foreign currency exposure and other contingent liabilities should be provided to international markets so as to help them assess the extent to which they want to be exposed. Domestic investors must be clearly informed about the extent of supervision and (the absence of) guarantees for their investments, while financial sector participants must find a transparent, comprehensive, rules-based framework that they are expected to adopt, the failure of which should trigger transparent sanctions.

To sum up, successful financial sector liberalization requires that economic fundamentals (both evident and hidden) be sustainable. Next, it would be desirable if the financial sector were not made subject to specific plans, but be left instead to develop on its own strengths, provided that proper regulation and supervision are in place. This process can be greatly advanced by fostering positive competition, notably through permitting foreign entry into the financial system and by ensuring transparent and rules-based regulation.

The impact of macroeconomic stabilization on the financial system

Next we look into episodes of macroeconomic distress (Quadrants II and IV in Figure 6.1) and examine the impact and feedback effects of the required stabilization policies on the financial sector. At least in the short term, such policies are shown to have negative effects on the financial markets.

Fiscal policy

Very often, the root causes of a country's macroeconomic imbalances are found in unsustainably large fiscal deficits. The necessary corrective tightening of a country's budgetary position can have an impact on the financial sector in several ways. In the first place, and absent full 'crowding-in', a negative domestic demand effect is likely to prevail. To the extent that this contractionary impulse harms company profitability, banks may see an increase in their non-performing loan portfolio.[19]

On the other hand, of course, the government's borrowing requirement will also have been reduced, now permitting the financial sector to find other profitable uses for savings, facilitated by the reduction in interest rates likely to follow fiscal consolidation.[20] This latter effect, however, is frequently absent in countries with a history of high government deficits and inflation. In such environments, banks have frequently grown accustomed to limiting the scope of intermediation to using their deposits to buy (short-term) Treasury Bills and/or making some extra profit by exploiting the float in the payments system. However, breaking such practices, rather than being seen as simply negative and harmful to banks, should be interpreted as a necessary step along the way to a financial system better attuned to meeting its purpose.

Monetary policy

As in the case of fiscal tightening, the implementation of monetary restraint is likely to result in a contractionary demand impulse to the economy, possibly triggering an increase of non-performing loans on banks' balance sheets. However, in contrast to fiscal policy, interest rates in the economy are also likely to rise, resulting in an additional deterioration in banks' balance sheets, as their short-term liabilities are likely to be rolled over only at higher yields, while their longer-term loan assets (to the extent that they still exist) are likely to have a fixed rate of remuneration. This would suggest that stabilization solely through a tightening of monetary policy will be rather costly in terms of both financial sector health and output cost. It would probably point to an underlying real imbalance – most likely in the fiscal sector – which cannot be solved by the application of nominal variables (see below).

Exchange rate policy

In cases where a substantial real appreciation of the exchange rate has resulted in an adverse expenditure mix between imports and exports, and/or where a run on the domestic currency has set in, a sizeable depreciation is oftentimes the only tool left in the policymaker's arsenal, and past experiences with exchange-rate-based stabilization programmes point to at least initial successes in stabilizing inflation and balance-of-payments pressures at moderate output costs. However, as seen above, the experience of Mexico and some Asian countries has pointed to an unwelcome side-effect of devaluations in cases where banking systems (and/or their corporate clients) have amassed substantial unhedged foreign exchange positions (see Burnside et al. 1999, Wilson et al. 2000). In such instances, a depreciation would increase the value of banks' foreign liabilities (foreign currency deposits and direct foreign lending which are typically of a very short-term nature), while domestic foreign currency assets (typically foreign currency-denominated lending) are likely to sour if overindebted corporations find it hard to raise funds needed to roll them over.[21] As discussed above, the adverse effects of exchange rate depreciation in the concrete instances of the Mexican, Thai, Korean and Indonesian depreciations have reflected an underlying, if hidden, fundamental incentive problem.

Policy mix

An often-overlooked but important component of stabilization programmes concerns the 'real' as opposed to the nominal anchor. For example, an economy's real exchange rate is not generally changed by policies targeting only nominal variables: without a corrective reduction in the fiscal deficit (or real wages) to reduce the real exchange rate, a nominal depreciation may just lead to higher inflation and/or higher interest rates in an attempt to reduce inflation. This would deliver a 'double whammy' to the financial system without really having tackled the macroeconomic problem. The same predicament is possible if monetary policy is exclusively relied on to substitute for fiscal adjustment. In this case, interest rates would have to rise sufficiently high to effect the necessary reduction in domestic demand through 'crowding out'. Even if not undermining the health of banks outright, such a constellation would provide all the incentives for backwards development of financial intermediation, with banks writing off loans to private debtors and engaging in the more profitable and easy government securities market. It is therefore imperative to target the adjustment programme toward the underlying 'real' imbalance so as not to result in unnecessary economic contraction (including that of the financial sector).

However, even recognizing the adverse feedback effects that macro-economic adjustment programmes can have on the health of the financial system, policymakers will not usually find themselves in a position to postpone macroeconomic adjustment policies, if only for the lack of an alternative. Maintaining an overvalued exchange rate and large fiscal deficits will become increasingly difficult to finance, and critics who challenge the logic of arresting the free fall of exchange rates by raising interest rates and/or of bringing a government's financing requirement in line with available resources should specify where the additional financing to avoid these consequences would be generated. Serious critics have at times offered the alternative of a currency board and dollarization, which, however, arguably require even more painful adjustment, especially on the government budget, and may trigger an even larger washout of the financial sector.

Concluding remarks

This chapter has attempted to discuss some of the relevant issues confronting policymakers who wish to liberalize and develop an economy's financial system, without running the risk of creating macro-economic problems, or who have to design macroeconomic adjustment policies and are interested in mitigating the adverse effects on financial intermediation. The starting point is a recognition that the benefits from financial liberalization outweigh the dangers in terms of creating scope for new financial crises, but that a proper regulatory and supervisory framework needs to be in place. Next, the chapter has made the point that financial sector liberalization does not introduce any new and mysterious sets of challenges to policymakers, but that fundamentals are still the determinants for financial crisis and need to be addressed head-on, not only in macroeconomic adjustment programmes, but also in preparation for financial sector liberalization. It has also pointed out that with more sophisticated capital markets, there is no place for complacency with respect to the financial sector in times of capital liberalization. However, it has also recognized that macroeconomic adjustment policies may at times hurt financial sector interests, but there is little scope to avoid these costs. In the longer run there is no divergence between macroeconomic stability and a properly functioning financial system.

Notes

1. The views expressed in this chapter are those of the author, and do not necessarily represent official positions of the International Monetary Fund. The author would like to thank Janet Bungay for helpful comments.
2. See, for example, the list of banking crises studied by Demirguc-Kunt and Detragiache (1998), which includes the US for the entire period 1981–92, i.e. the Latin-American-debt and Savings-and-Loan crises, as well as a long period of domestic economic expansion.
3. For a much more exhaustive list of functions of a financial sector, see Levine (1997).
4. For example, Mishkin (1999) argues that the dominance of banks over securitized financial systems reflects banks' ability to internalize (through private lending) the positive externalities arising from investment in information. If loans were not private, other lenders could take a free-rider

position, waiting to follow an informed lender's lending decisions, thus eroding the latter's incentives to gather information in the first place.

5. Abstracting from arguments relying on efficiency gains, financial markets can also be incorporated into political economy considerations. For example, it could be argued that financial markets may serve as a disciplinary tool for potentially wayward policymakers. One famous – non-economist – exponent of this view is James Carville, an adviser to US President Clinton, who once explained that he wished to be reincarnated as the bond market – no longer as the Pope, as he had wished as a child – because of that market's omnipotence. Krugman (1998) makes a similar argument, postulating that at times policymakers have felt compelled to undertake macroeconomically undesirable policies – for example, interest rate increases during a recession – so as to gain the 'confidence' of financial markets.

6. It is, however, less clear that such an environment also encourages higher volumes of savings, as the relative strength of income and substitution effects is not clear. In this context, it is worthy to note that the 1990s boom in the US coincided with a spectacular drop in the household savings rate.

7. For this exercise, a crisis is considered to encompass a situation where short-term macroeconomic performance is not sustainable. It also needs pointing out that the financial sector's level of development, or its potential fragility would be the relevant parameters, not whether it is in crisis. In crisis, it needs fixing anyway, irrespective of the macroeconomic situation.

8. In this situation, term finance is typically no longer available as all but the most short-term finance has ceased to exist (and even that at huge real interest rates); dollarization has usually taken hold, and the domestic financial system is becoming increasingly demonetized (in real terms).

9. In terms of the previous taxonomy, the question is then whether such cases should not be properly discussed in the second column.

10. This situation becomes particularly acute if the high interest rates undermine the health of banks and require bailing out large state-owned commercial banks through issuance of additional interest-bearing government debt.

11. Hidden fundamentals also arise from other contingent liabilities such as government loan guarantees, or accumulation of bad debt in government-owned banks. In the interest of brevity, however, the discussion in this chapter is limited to problems arising from pegged exchange rate arrangements.

12. Higher domestic interest rates would, for example, result from a higher marginal productivity of investments in emerging countries – a result expected in a neoclassical growth model – but also from an overheating domestic economy, or from Central Bank attempts aiming to sterilize the monetary impact of large capital inflows. It appears that the first reason is usually given while large capital inflows occur, while irrational 'speculators' tend to be assigned the blame if these inflows reverse.

13. In defence of pegs or even tighter bounds on the external value of a domestic currency, it should be pointed out that De Long (2000) showed that financial crises tended to be shorter – i.e. the resumption of critically needed capital flows occurred faster – under the nineteenth-century Gold Standard.

14. It is quite conceivable that in some cases a clear break from past financial sector practices may be called for, instead of the usually favoured

development of existing institutions. The closure of non-viable schemes should be welcomed as a reallocation of resources and will probably avoid the need for higher cost bailouts later on. For example, Denizer et al. (1998) compare large state-owned banks in transition countries which, after liberalization, assumed the role of the previous planning ministry in channelling funds to large public enterprises, and inevitably racked up large losses.

15. Against such calls, it is worthwhile to recall that some of the large prospective deficits identified in the previous section were incurred through politically well-connected sectors which were able to manipulate the course of financial sector development – e.g. by excluding foreign competition and restricting the power of supervisors.

16. Ribakova (1999) makes the point for stricter prudential regulation and standards in liberalizing countries than in countries with a liberal and developed financial system.

17. On the other hand, it is also true that some policymakers favour the adoption of much more restrictive and distortive traditional capital controls (e.g. restrictions on repatriations of earnings) but resist the less intrusive and inefficient extension of better supervision and regulation.

18. It is important to note that foreign bank competition was low in Mexico.

19. If the ensuing non-performing loans problem results in a large-scale need to bail out the banking system, the initial stabilization objective may not be achieved. This argument appears to be at the heart of much of the criticism levelled against macroeconomic stabilization policies in Thailand, Korea and Indonesia.

20. Lower interest rates should make it easier to avoid the adverse selection problems for borrowers which banks likely encounter in high real-interest environments.

21. Garber (1998) even relates instances in Mexico where recorded foreign currency assets (on the basis of derivative products) were wiped out or even turned into liabilities after the Mexican depreciation.

References

Bhagwati, J. (1998) 'The Capital Myth: The Difference Between Trade in Widgets and Trade in Dollars', *Foreign Affairs* 77: 7–12.
Burnside, C., Eichenbaum, M. and Rebelo, S. (1999) 'Prospective Deficits and the Asian Currency Crisis', World Bank Working Paper, available on Burnside's web page: <http://www.worldbank.org/research/bios/burnside.htm>, forthcoming in *Journal of Political Economy*.
Burnside, C., Eichenbaum, M. and Rebelo, S. (2000) 'On the Fundamentals of Self-Fulfilling Speculative Attacks', World Bank Working Paper, available on Burnside's web page: <http://www.worldbank.org/research/bios/burnside.htm>
Claessens, S. (1996) 'Banking Reform in Transition Countries', *World Bank Policy Research Working Papers*, 1642.
Claessens, S., Dooley, M. and Warner, A. (1995) 'Portfolio Capital Flows: Hot or Cold?', *World Bank Economic Review*, Vol. 9, No.1: 153–74.
De Long, J. B. (2000) 'Financial Crises in the 1890s and the 1990s: Must History Repeat?', *Brookings Papers on Economic Activity* No. 1.

Demirguc-Kunt, A. and Detragiache, E. (1998) 'The Determinants of Banking Crises in Developing and Developed Countries', *IMF Staff Papers*, March.

Demirguc-Kunt, A., Levine, R. and Beck, T. (1999) 'A New Database on Financial Development and Structure', *World Bank Policy Research Papers*, No. 2146.

Denizer, C., Desai, R. M. and Gueorguiev, N. (1998) 'The Political Economy of Financial Repression in Transition Economies', *World Bank Policy Research Papers*, No. 2030.

Dooley, M. (1996) 'Capital Controls and Emerging Markets', *International Journal of Finance and Economics*, Vol. 1: 197–205.

Garber, P. (1998) 'Speculative Attacks and Currency Crises', mimeo, Washington DC.

Hayek, F. A. (1937) 'Economics and Knowledge', *Economica*, Vol. 4 (New Series), No. 13.

Hicks, J. R. (1969) *A Theory of Economic History*, Clarendon Press.

Krugman, P. (1998) 'Bubble, Boom, Crash: Theoretical Notes on Asia's Crisis', MIT, unpublished (accessible on Krugman's web page: <http://web.mit.edu.krugman>).

Levine, R. (1997) 'Financial Development and Economic Growth: Views and Agenda', *Journal of Economic Literature*, Vol. 35 (June): 688–726.

Lucas, R. E. (1988) 'On the Mechanics of Economic Development', *Journal of Monetary Economics*, Vol. 32, No. 5 (July): 3–42.

Mishkin, F. S. (1999) 'Global Financial Instability, Framework, Events, Issues', *Journal of Economic Perspectives*, Vol. 13, No. 4: 3–20.

Ribakova, E. (1999) 'Liberalization and Prudential Supervision: Why Sequencing Matters', *IMF Working Paper*, December.

Rogoff, K. (1999) 'International Institutions for Reducing Global Financial Instability', *Journal of Economic Perspectives*, Vol. 13, No. 4 (Fall): 21–42.

Schumpeter, J. (1912) *Theorie der wirtschaftlichen Entwicklung*, Leipzig, Duncker und Humbolt.

Wilson, B., Saunders, A. and Caprio, G. (2000) 'Mexico's Financial Sector Crisis: Propagative Linkages to Devaluation', *Economic Journal*, 110 (January): 292–308.

Part IV

Financial Development in Eastern Europe: Looking Ahead

7
EU Accession Countries: What Path to Successful EMU Membership?

Peter Bofinger and Timo Wollmershäuser

Introduction

After the euro had been launched successfully, the European Central Bank (ECB) and the accession countries began to discuss the processes which would lead to Economic and Monetary Union (EMU) membership of these countries. It is not surprising that at this stage the Helsinki Seminar which brought together central bankers from accession countries and from the ECB on 12 November 1999, has led to rather general conclusions:

> no common path should be prescribed to all 12 accession countries with regard to the orientation of their exchange rate policies prior to accession, the inclusion of their currencies in ERM II or the later adoption of the Euro. Against the background of different starting-points for the economic reform process and the difficulty of ascertaining the lead-time for further headway towards nominal and real convergence, a plurality of approaches should be feasible without compromising equality of treatment ... .[1]

As the topic has many important dimensions,[2] our chapter concentrates on one aspect that plays an increasing role in the discussion on exchange rate regimes: the danger of destabilizing capital inflows.[3] In the last few years several emerging market economies have been threatened by a new generation of currency crises which, in Krugman's (1998) words, is characterized 'by financial excess and then by financial collapse'. Our main question is therefore whether the accession countries can follow exchange rate targets on their path to EMU without incurring the risk of excessive capital inflows which sooner or later would lead to a collapse of their currencies and severe economic disruption. In this context it is also important to discuss whether capital inflow controls, which have been proposed by many economists, would be a useful policy instrument.[4] Of course, any strategy for exchange rate policy can only be successful if the overall macroeconomic policy is stability-oriented. In this chapter, it is assumed that the transition countries are following such policies so that the risk of capital outflows because of inflationary policies is negligible.[5]

While we focus on the five 'lead accession countries' (Czech Republic, Estonia, Hungary, Poland, Slovenia), the main results are to some extent also relevant for the other transition countries and for exchange rate policies of emerging market economies in general.

We begin by presenting a simple roadmap for the path from the present situation to the final aim of monetary union. We then discuss the main options for exchange rate policy in stage I which leaves the accession countries a very broad spectrum for country-specific solutions. Following this, we analyse the mechanics of exchange rate targeting under the specific conditions of a disinflation phase, and then discuss the problems of a fixed nominal exchange rate target. We show that under this arrangement central banks are inclined to follow interest rate policies that are inconsistent with an equilibrium on international financial markets. Only for very small countries and for countries with a rather small inflation differential *vis-à-vis* the anchor currency, a strategy of permanently fixed exchange rates is advisable. For all other countries a flexible exchange rate targeting is recommended. We then explain why such an arrangement is much less prone to excessive capital inflows. These theoretical considerations are supported by the empirical evidence from Asia, Latin America and Eastern and Central Europe. We then present the main lessons for the exchange rate policy of the accession in stage I, where they are compared with the medium-term monetary policy strategies of the Czech Republic, Hungary and Poland. While the strategies of all three countries are flexible enough to avoid the risk of capital inflows, the framework of the Czech National Bank lacks a sufficiently transparent monetary anchor. Finally, we analyse in which way EU accession will change the framework for exchange rate and monetary policy in the new member countries. In our view, stage II still leaves ample leeway for country-specific approaches. This is different in stage III, the two-year period preceding final EMU entry. As the parity that is decided at the beginning of this stage constitutes a ceiling for the final conversion rate, the accession countries should carefully analyse at a very early stage (at best when still in stage I) whether a precautionary devaluation *vis-à-vis* the euro is required.

The roadmap to EMU

Although the concrete institutional frameworks are still open, the overall roadmap from present institutional arrangements to final EMU membership seems quite clear. All accession countries will have to go through three different stages:

- Stage I covers the period from now on until the accession to European Union.
- Stage II extends from EU entry until the two-year period that has to precede the date of final EMU membership.
- Stage III covers the last two years before EMU entry and is identical with the testing period for the criteria of convergence.

During stage I the accession countries have no specific exchange rate relations with the euro and the ECB. Thus, from an institutional point of view they are in the same situation as all other emerging market economies. Stage II implies above all the adoption of the *acquis communautaire*. In addition the institutional framework of ERM (Exchange Rate Mechanism) II is available for the member states from Central and Eastern Europe. It includes intervention support and intervention credits from the ECB and the obligation for the new members to keep their exchange rate *vis-à-vis* the euro within a ± 15 per cent band around the euro parity. In stage III the new members have to comply with the requirements of Article 121 (ex Article 109j) of the Treaty, which defines the four criteria of convergence. For the exchange rate policy of an EMU candidate the relevant criterion stipulates:

> the observance of the normal fluctuation margins provided for by the exchange rate mechanism of the European Monetary System, for at least two years, without devaluing against the currency of any other Member State ... .

In the following we shall concentrate on the first stage as it can be designed with rather different institutional options. Stage II differs relatively little from stage I and stage III leaves little room for country-specific arrangements.

Options in the pre-accession stage (stage I)

For stage I we assume that the five lead accession countries can already be treated as 'normal' market economies. This is widely confirmed by the rankings that the EBRD has given to these countries in its Transition Report (Table 7.1) and by recent econometric studies (Golinelli and Rovelli 1999).[6] Of course, there are still specific problems in the field of financial sector restructuring, but they are of minor importance for the macroeconomic issues that are discussed here.

Table 7.1   Transition Report rankings[*]

	Large-scale privatization	Small-scale privatization	Governance & enterprise restructuring	Trade & foreign exchange system	Banking reform & interest rate liberalizations	Securities markets & non-bank financial institutions
Czech Republic	4	4+	3	4+	3	3
Estonia	4	4+	3	4	3+	3
Hungary	4	4+	3+	4+	4	3+
Poland	3+	4+	3	4+	3+	3+
Slovenia	3+	4+	3–	4+	3	3

[*]   Progress in transition measured on a scale from 1 to 4+ with 4+ signifying standards comparable to advanced industrial economies.

Source: EBRD (1999).

The pre-accession stage prescribes no specific institutional arrangements for the exchange rate policies of prospective member countries. Thus, the accession countries are completely free in choosing an exchange rate strategy that is tailored to the requirements of their economy. In principle, three approaches are possible:

- a *fixed nominal exchange rate target*, either in the form of a currency board or a unilateral peg, e.g. Austria's 'Hartwährungspolitik' *vis-à-vis* the Deutschemark
- a *flexible nominal exchange rate target*, either in the form of a pre-announced crawl or crawling band, of a non-announced crawl

('managed floating') or in the form of a unilateral fixed peg with frequent discrete adjustments
- a *freely floating exchange rate*, which implies that the Central Bank is not aiming at a certain target for the exchange rate. This case can be differentiated from all forms of flexible exchange rate targeting by the criterion of a constant level of foreign exchange reserves.

With this classification we do not make a categorical difference between 'managed floating' and a crawling peg. For the interaction between interest rate and exchange rate policy the public announcement of an exchange rate target is of secondary importance. As the announcement has an important effect on the transparency of monetary policy, we will discuss it in the context of country-specific monetary policy strategies.

In the following, the option of a *freely floating exchange rate* will not be analysed in detail. Above all, the empirical evidence of flexible exchange rates is rather devastating. In the last 25 years countless econometric studies on the determinants of flexible exchange rates have been published. Almost all of them have come to the clear result that 'fundamentals', however defined, have no systematic impact on the exchange rate under a floating system – at least over time horizons of up to four or five years. Isard (1995, p. 138) summarizes the evidence as follows:

> In short, neither the behavioral relationships suggested by theory, nor the information obtained through autoregression, provided a model that could forecast significantly better than a random walk. And furthermore, while the random walk model performed at least as well as other models, it predicted very poorly.

For small open economies a completely unpredictable exchange rate would make it very difficult to achieve macroeconomic stability. In addition, foreign exchange markets in emerging market economies are relatively thin, so that some large transactions could have an even more destabilizing effect. In sum, we agree with the conclusion by Eichengreen and Masson (1998, p. 3):

> For developing and transition countries, as with the smaller industrial countries, there are good reasons why the right exchange rate regime (except perhaps in cases of continuing high inflation) is not something close to an unfettered float.

In fact, with the exception of the exchange rates between the three key currencies (the dollar, the euro and the yen) there are almost no countries that have deliberately refrained from foreign exchange market intervention.[7] From the five lead accession countries Slovenia is regarded as a 'floater', but Figure 7.1 shows that its Central Bank has systematically intervened to keep the tolar/DM rate stable: after a rather short period of constant reserves (September 1992 to April 1994) which had led to a massive depreciation *vis-à-vis* the Deutschemark, strong Deutschemark purchases prevented a subsequent appreciation of the tolar.

Besides the definition of the target, a comprehensive strategy for exchange rate policy has to determine the *width of the band* around the exchange rate target and the anchor currency and it has to decide whether *capital controls* for short-term capital flows will be imposed.

The mechanics of exchange rate targeting in a disinflation phase

For all small open economies which conduct a monetary policy aimed at achieving price stability it is important to differentiate between two main transmission channels of monetary impulses: the exchange rate channel and the interest rate channel. With the latter, monetary policy affects aggregate demand via its effect on the short-term real interest rate (and possibly on the availability of credit). Subsequently, aggregate demand affects inflation via the supply-side of an economy which is often described by a Phillips curve relation (see Svensson 1998). The exchange rate channel can be divided into a direct and an indirect channel. The direct channel explains domestic inflation fluctuations via the pass-through of exchange rate fluctuations to import prices. Indirectly, the real exchange rate affects the relative price between domestic and foreign goods, which in turn has an impact on both, domestic and foreign demand for domestic goods, and hence contributes to the aggregate demand channel for the transmission of monetary policy.

A comprehensive measure of the restrictiveness of the Central Bank's two operating targets, real interest rate and real exchange rate, is provided by the so-called Monetary Conditions Index (MCI) which can be defined in its simplest form as follows:

$$MCI = \delta_1 r - \delta_2 \Delta q$$

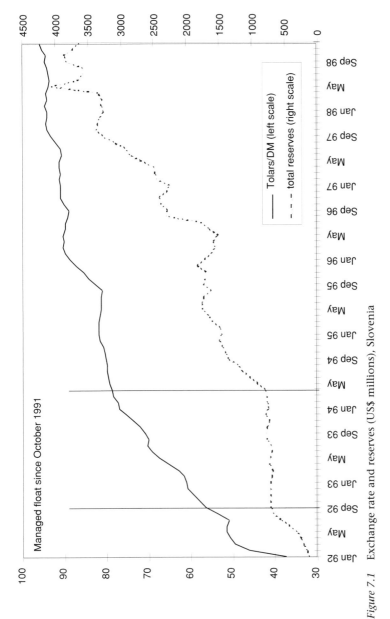

Figure 7.1 Exchange rate and reserves (US$ millions), Slovenia

Source: IFS.

The index is a linear combination of the real short-term interest rate r and the change in the real exchange rate Δq, both measured with respect to a reference period. The coefficients are equal to the estimated effects of these two financial variables on aggregate demand, and thus, on inflation. For the purpose of this chapter, the weighting of the two operating targets will play an important role since δ_1 and δ_2 are determined by the structural characteristics of an economy.

This coexistence of an internal and external lever of monetary policy is particularly relevant if a policy of exchange rate targeting is conducted in a period of disinflation. It is obvious that any form of exchange rate targeting has to observe two important constraints. From the real side, a constraint is set by *purchasing power parity*. If a policy of exchange rate targeting leads to a substantial real appreciation, it undermines the competitiveness of domestic producers, increases unemployment and leads to growing current account deficits. Kaminsky et al. (1998) show that a real appreciation is a very serious warning signal for a currency crisis. From the financial side, an important constraint is set by the *uncovered interest parity* (UIP) condition. This chapter concentrates on this constraint, because it provides an important explanation for the problem of speculative capital inflows.

Applied to a policy of exchange rate targeting, the uncovered interest parity condition can be written as

$$\Delta s^T + \alpha = i - i^*$$

The targeted depreciation of the logarithm of the domestic currency Δs^T plus a risk premium α on the expected depreciation[8] has to equal the difference between the domestic nominal interest rate i and the interest rate of the anchor country i*.

In principle, exchange rate targeting means nothing other than targeting the domestic interest rate together with the exchange rate. This is clearly reflected in the construction of the MCI which brings together these two operating targets to one measure indicating the overall policy stance. We assume that the short-term nominal interest rate and the nominal exchange rate can be perfectly controlled by the Central Bank either by intervening in the domestic money market through the use of efficient money market instruments and/or by intervening in the foreign exchange market, i.e. sales and purchases of foreign reserves.

The real interest rate can be derived from the nominal interest rate by applying the well-known Fisher equation. Since money market interest rates are of very short-term nature, not exceeding a term of maturity of three months in general, the equation can be formulated as follows:

$$r = i - \pi$$

Thus, by assuming a certain rigidity in the movement of prices, the short-term real interest rate can directly be controlled through the nominal money market rate.

The real and the nominal exchange rate are linked together by the following equation:

$$\Delta q^{(T)} = \Delta s^{(T)} + \pi^* - \pi$$

where π and π^* reflect the inflation rate in the domestic and in the foreign country. By deciding on the degree of flexibility of the nominal exchange rate, the Central Bank determines the restrictiveness of its monetary policy exerted by the exchange rate channel. This leads us to distinguish between three different macroeconomic strategies:

- The most abrupt disinflation via the exchange rate channel is achieved if the Central Bank keeps the nominal exchange rate *constant*, i.e. $\Delta s^T = 0$. The initial real appreciation is then given by the inflation differential. This approach has been followed by Estonia and by the Czech Republic (until the May 1997 crisis).
- An intermediate solution can be characterized by an exchange rate target that aims at a depreciation that equals the difference between the targeted inflation rate and the foreign inflation rate, i.e. $\Delta s^T = \pi^T - \pi^*$ (in the case of a disinflation strategy it is assumed that $\pi^T < \pi$; otherwise see third variant). Such an *active crawl* has been followed by Poland and Hungary.
- A third, least restrictive variant is an exchange rate target which simply compensates for the existing inflation differential, i.e. $\Delta s^T = \pi - \pi^*$. Chile's crawling band system and the exchange rate policy of Brazil and Indonesia (until the crisis) are examples for such a *passive* (or backward-looking) exchange rate strategy.[9]

With the imputed time horizon of a maximum of three months the UIP condition allows an analysis of the interrelationship between the foreign and the domestic levers of monetary policy. The crucial question that has to be answered is how the policy mix between exchange rate targeting and interest rate targeting can avoid imbalances on the international financial markets. The best indicator for an interest rate policy that is incompatible with UIP is high short-term capital inflows or outflows. Thus, the problem of excessive capital inflows simply shows a persistent violation of this equilibrium condition, and all proposals to impose capital controls mean nothing else but to suspend this condition so that countries can follow interest rate policies that are incompatible with UIP. If a disequilibrium leads to capital inflows, the increase in reserves has to be sterilized, at least partially. The coexistence of strong capital inflows with a constant or sometimes increasing interest rate differential indicates that sterilized interventions can be much more efficient than is recognized by the literature. As Table 7.2 shows, the ratio of domestic assets to total assets declined considerably in almost all cases.

The intuition of the equilibrium condition is quite simple: in the case of a fixed exchange rate ($\Delta s^T = 0$) a Central Bank can use domestic interest rates for disinflation only to the extent that the foreign exchange market demands a sufficiently high risk premium for the domestic currency, $i = i^* + \alpha$. If the Central Bank conducts a more restrictive interest rate policy, strong capital inflows are induced which lead to a substantial real appreciation of the domestic currency and create the expectations of an upcoming nominal devaluation and therefore the abandonment of the fixed exchange rate. Thus, strong capital inflows are a signal that a Central Bank is following a restrictive interest policy which is incompatible with an equilibrium on international financial markets. The strategy of disinflation under a constant nominal exchange rate target will be discussed below. It will be shown that this strategy mainly has to rely on the external lever of monetary policy, i.e. the exchange rate channel.

The situation is somewhat inverse under a strategy of flexible exchange rate targeting ($\Delta s^T > 0$), which will be discussed later in this chapter. The weighting of the exchange rate channel is reduced in favour of the interest rate channel. Once again, this strategy has to be compatible with our UIP condition: $i = i^* + \alpha + \Delta s^T$. In comparison to the strategy of a fixed exchange rate, it is obvious that, with a given i^* and α, the domestic interest can be higher. Thus, monetary contraction stems above all from the interest rate channel and follows a quite simple rule: the higher the rate of nominal depreciation (i.e. the more inflation-compensatory the exchange rate strategy and the less monetary pressure through real appreciation), the more monetary policy can exert pressure via domestic interest rates.

Table 7.2 Exchange rate targeting and changes in Central Bank portfolios

	Period with a fixed rate	Average interest rate differential vis-à-vis the dollar	Increase in reserves (US$ millions)	Share of domestic to total Central Bank assets at the beginning	Share of domestic to total Central Bank assets at the end
Indonesia	1987–96 (avg. crawl: 4.0% p.a.)	7.0	14,200	67.9	24.0
Korea	1992–6	8.4	20,336	69.3	48.9
Thailand	1987–96	3.1	34,927	60.0	15.6
Malaysia	1986–96 (almost fixed, 2.8% total appr.)	–0.3 1.9 (92–6)	22,097 16,123 (92–6)	16.5	21.7
Czech Republic	1991–6	7.4 (DM and US$)	8563	40.4	29.5
Italy	1987–90	7.1 (DM)	52,990	68.2	59.6
Argentina	1991–8	11.3 (91–8) 2,3 (93–8)	20,160	82.8	26.0
Brazil	1994–8 (avg. crawl: 0.0002 reais/day)	28.4	11,976		
Mexico	1990–3	19.2	18,781	69.3	30.3

Source: IFS.

The strategy of a constant nominal exchange rate target

We have already made clear that the strategy of a constant nominal exchange rate leaves relatively little scope for a restrictive interest rate policy in the sense of a positive interest differential with respect to the anchor country. A restrictive, disinflationary monetary policy stance can avoid high capital inflows only under three conditions:

- if a country is so small that it suffices to rely on the exchange rate channel, i.e. δ_1 is relatively small compared to δ_2
- if the inflation differential *vis-à-vis* the anchor currency $(\pi - \pi^*)$ is rather small and if at the same time the need to disinflate is not very high $(\pi^T \approx \pi)$
- if the risk premium is very high

Fixing the exchange rate in order to disinflate

The first condition is compatible with the observation that most countries which were able to maintain a fixed nominal exchange for longer periods of time are typically very small and very open countries (Jadresic et al. 1999, p. 24). As a great part of the demand for domestic goods depends on exports, and as the pass-through from import prices to the domestic inflation is very high, the weighting of the exchange rate channel in our MCI increases. An alternative explanation for the reduced importance of the interest rate channel is delivered by a low degree of monetization which measures the share of M2 as a percentage of GDP. The ratio of this relationship can be demonstrated with the help of an extreme case. If one considers an economy where no domestic money circulates, it is obvious that the domestic lever of monetary policy via changements in the short-term interest rate has no effects on aggregate demand. Thus, the lower the degree of monetization, the higher the importance of the exchange rate channel. Table 7.3 confirms these considerations. With the remarkable exception of the Latin American countries, all countries in our sample that introduced a currency board or fixed their exchange rates were very open at the beginning of the stabilization phase. In contrast, the Latin American economies were characterized by a very low monetization. The figures for the euro area can be viewed as reference values for a relatively close and highly monetized economy.

Table 7.3 Currency boards and fixed exchange rates: inflation, openness and monetization

	Date of introduction	Inflation rate in the year of introduction	Degree of openness	Monetization
Currency Boards				
Argentina	03/91	172%	5%	11%
Estonia	06/92	1076%	41%	30%
Lithuania	04/94	72%	52%	26%
Bulgaria	07/97	1082%	48%	34%
Fixers				
Czech Republic	12/90	57% (91)	42% (93)	70% (93)
Mexico	11/91	23%	10%	25%
Euro area			*13% (99)*	*70% (99)*

Sources: IFS ; EBRD (1999).

If the domestic Central Bank completely refrains from an autonomous interest rate policy, the domestic interest rate is only determined by the interest rate of the anchor country and the risk premium and there is always an equilibrium for short-term capital flows. Given the basic requirement for an anchor country of having stable prices it clearly follows that the resulting interest rate cannot be very restrictive given the very high inflation rates at the time of the introduction of the fixed rate. In many cases, especially when the initial risk premium was not very high, countries started their stabilization phase with negative real interest rates. Thus, restrictive monetary policy can only be exerted via a substantial real appreciation of the domestic currency (see Figure 7.2). This situation is most typical for a *currency board*, where traditional instruments for targeting domestic short-term rates are not available. Figure 7.3 shows that the money markets rates in Estonia remained remarkably close to German money market rates until the outbreak of the Asian crisis. Thus, the decisive feature of a currency board is a completely endogenous domestic interest rate. The substantial deviations from German interest rates following the crisis reflect the risk premium that was demanded by international investors, compensating for the probability of an abandonment of the fixed exchange rate and a subsequent devaluation of the kroon.

The currency board arrangements all survived up to the present, whereas Mexico and the Czech Republic abandoned their fixed exchange rates in end-1994 respectively in mid-1997, and both officially adopted a system of freely respectively managed floating rates. The critical

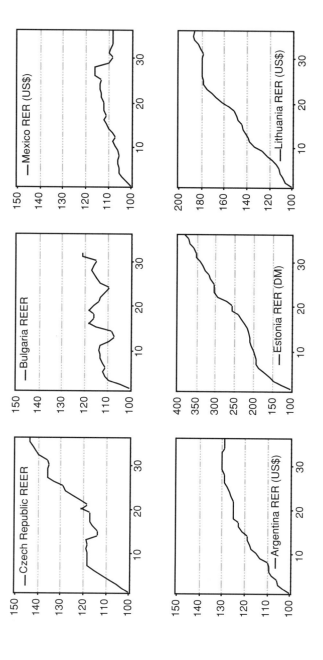

Source: IFS.

Figure 7.2   Real appreciation in the first three years of disinflation (fixed exchange rates)

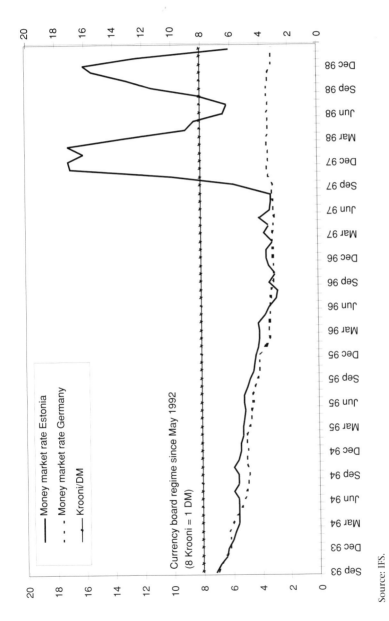

Source: IFS.

Figure 7.3   Interest differential and exchange rate, Estonia

difference between the fixers and the currency boards can be found in the degree of autonomy when setting domestic interest rates. The standard textbook in international macroeconomics teaches us about the impossibility of combining an autonomous interest rate policy with rigidly fixed exchange rates in an environment of unrestricted capital movements which is often called the inconsistency triangle (see Padoa-Schioppa 1987). Applied to our UIP condition it follows that the domestic interest rates are set in accordance with the exogenous interest rate of the anchor currency adjusted by a potential risk premium. As this condition always holds within a currency board arrangement where the interest rate is totally endogenous, in all other systems of fixed exchange rates monetary authorities can deviate from this rule and set their interest rates with a certain degree of discretion. Thus, if a Central Bank tries to reinforce its disinflationary monetary policy stance by raising the nominal interest rates above the UIP equilibrium level, an unsustainable imbalance on the international financial markets is created, leading to speculative capital inflows and a subsequent breakdown of the fixed exchange rate, as described earlier.

Fixing the exchange rate in order to stabilize

In the case of low inflation differentials the situation is somewhat different. Good examples are the stable long-run pegs of Austria and the several ERM I countries against the Deutschemark. Table 7.4 shows that these countries had an inflation differential of almost zero at the time they fixed their exchange rates. In contrast to the previous discussion, in this case the major objective of the constant nominal exchange rate was not to bring down inflation from at least double-digit rates but to stabilize the erratic movements in the exchange rates and, closely related to this, to alleviate the danger of prolonged misalignments. Both the high volatility and the misalignments turned out to be very harmful to a small, open and highly trade-integrated economy whose primary goal in the field of monetary policy is to guarantee stable prices. From the experience of the ERM I the critical inflation differential seems to lie in the range of 3.75 percentage points. Subtracting a certain safety margin, the critical value could be established at 3 per cent. According to this criterion Estonia and Slovenia would already qualify for a fixed nominal exchange rate target *vis-à-vis* the euro.

If the inflation differential is higher, a constant nominal exchange rate target cannot be maintained. This is not only confirmed by those ERM I countries which had to adjust their parities after 1987 or even left the system (United Kingdom), but also by the failed attempt of the Czech

Republic and Mexico to maintain the fixed rate. The experience of the Asian countries is more difficult to interpret. On the one hand, the long periods of a stable dollar rate in Malaysia and Thailand fit the observation that a fixed rate can be sustainable if the inflation differentials are very low. In the second half of the 1980s both countries had lower inflation rates than the US. In this area the crises were initiated by the very low short-term dollar rates in 1994/5 combined with a substantial dollar depreciation *vis-à-vis* the yen. Thus, the external and the internal channels of monetary policy were too expansionary. As a result the Asian countries tried to dampen the domestic economy with a restrictive interest policy in the years 1994/5.

Table 7.4   ERM I experience

	Date of realignment (entry)	*Inflation differential to Germany (averages of 6 months before and 6 months after realignment)*	*Interest differential to Germany (averages of 6 months before and 6 months after realignment)*	*Last realignment?*
Netherlands	21.03.83	−0.49	0.30	yes
Denmark	12.01.87	3.79	5.84	yes
Belgium	12.01.87	1.48	1.87	yes
France	12.01.87	3.15	3.56	yes
Italy	12.01.87	*4.25*	7.33	*no*
	08.01.90	*3.53*	5.09	*no*
	25.11.96	1.50	4.71	yes
Spain	19.06.89 (entry)	*3.86*	7.78	*no*
	06.03.95	2.56	3.68	yes
Portugal	06.04.92 (entry)	*4.25*	8.26	*no*
	06.03.95	2.17	4.28	yes
Greece	16.03.98 (entry)	3.60	–	yes
Sweden	17.05.91 (peg)[a]	*8.10*	3.27	*no*
Finland	14.10.96 (entry)	−0.84	0.14	yes
United Kingdom	08.10.90 (entry)	*7.43*	6.07	*no*
Austria	December 81 (peg)[b]	0.12	−0.76	yes

Notes:

[a] Sweden pegged its currency to the ECU from 17 May 1991 until 19 November 1992.

[b] The last significant change of the schilling/DM exchange rate took place between September 79 and the end of 81 (an appreciation of the schilling of about 4.5 per cent).

Source: IFS.

But this restrictive interest rate policy turned out to be completely ineffective in a situation where a kind of 'currency illusion' prevailed. To describe this we distinguish between two channels for capital flows. If domestic firms can borrow abroad and if they believe in a short-term stability of the fixed exchange rate, they will be tempted to *borrow in the currency of the anchor country*. Whatever domestic interest rate a central bank targets, the monetary pressure remains unchanged. Instead of dampening the economy a restrictive interest rate policy simply drives the enterprise sector into foreign currency lending. Additional counter-productive effects are produced by a second channel: higher domestic interest rates *attract foreign investors* that want to profit from the short-term stability of the domestic currency even if they know that it is not sustainable. Their lending to domestic banks in the domestic currency has the effect that it weakens the credit rationing by domestic banks. This destabilizing effect of higher interest rates is described by Froot et al. (1998, p. 3):

> international investors are 'trend chasers'. Indeed, trend chasing – interpreted to mean that an increase in today's returns leads to an increase in future flows, without holding current and past inflows constant – seems to explain 60–85 percent of the quarterly covariance between emerging market inflows and returns.

As it was not possible to exert a sufficiently strong pressure on the domestic sectors under fixed rates, a depreciation should have been targeted combined with higher nominal rates. This is one of the main reasons for us to support the alternative strategy of adjustable or crawling nominal exchange rates which will be discussed later.

In fact, all accession countries still have inflation rates that are higher than the actual Harmonised Index of Consumer Prices (HICP) inflation rate of the euro area which is currently below 2 per cent (see Figure 7.4). In this regard they are in a similar situation as most ERM I countries in 1979 when their inflation rates exceeded the German rate considerably. According to our criterion of an inflation differential of maximum 3 per cent, only the Czech Republic and Estonia would already qualify for a fixed exchange rate target *vis-à-vis* the euro.

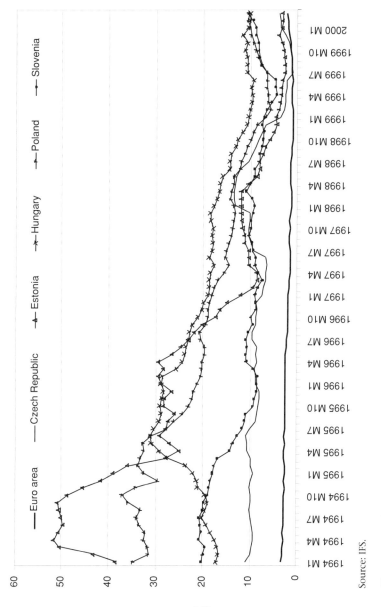

Source: IFS.

Figure 7.4   Inflation rates in the accession countries and the euro area, 1994–2000

163

Risk premiums and imbalances on the international financial markets

Finally, the existence of high risk premiums explains why a constant exchange rate target can be a useful policy tool in the early stages of a macroeconomic stabilization strategy (Bofinger 1996). After a period of very high and volatile inflation and a low credibility of policymakers, the markets will not immediately be convinced that the new regime is sustainable. Thus, the risk premium can be very high. But as soon as the risk premium declines, an exit strategy is needed (Eichengreen and Masson 1998).

This illustrates a specific problem of all constant exchange rate targets. The risk premium for short time horizons (one to three months) can be very unstable over time. If a fixed peg is introduced in a period of very high inflation, the risk premium will initially be very high, then go down to almost zero and after some time increase again. In countries with lower inflation differentials *vis-à-vis* the anchor currency, investors will normally expect that the exchange rate will remain constant for the time being even if they do not believe in the sustainability of an announced exchange rate target in the longer run. Over time, especially if a constant nominal rate is associated with a real appreciation, the risk premium increases sharply.

For policymakers in fixed exchange rate regimes the quantitative determination of the risk premium is not an easy task. In principle, at the time they set their nominal interest rates, they should be aware of the major components of their interest rates. To a hypothetical risk-free nominal rate one has to add the risk premium which itself consists of two components: the country premium and the currency premium. As the currency premium which is required by international investors as a compensation for foreign exchange variability risk and the probability of a currency devaluation are hard to estimate *ex post*, Central Banks often run the risk of setting their interest rates too high, especially in situations where the inflation rates are still pronounced and the need to disinflate is still high. Therefore, the best indicator for a UIP inconsistent interest rate policy is the volume of short-term capital flows (for the empirical results see below, 'Evidence'). Since in a currency board arrangement the interest rate is totally endogenous, i.e. market-driven, time-varying risk premiums are always reflected in the actual interest rate in a way that guarantees an equilibrium on the international financial markets. The two peaks of the Estonian money market rate in Figure 7.3 were triggered by the fear of contagion from the Asian crises (October 1997) and the Russian devaluation (August 1998), hindering international investors from withdrawing all capital.

Thus, if a Central Bank wants to maintain an equilibrium on the foreign exchange market while it targets a constant nominal exchange rate, it can cause very unstable domestic monetary conditions when risk premiums are declining. Therefore, it is not surprising that Central Banks have tried to avoid the too lax monetary policy by setting domestic interest rates higher. As this was associated with a disequilibrium of the international financial market, high capital inflows were the consequence.

The strategy of an adjustable nominal exchange rate target

Characteristics

Above, one of the main conclusions was that for countries which have an inflation differential of more than 3 to 4 percentage points, an adjustable exchange target seems the preferable solution. Of course, an adjustable exchange rate target also requires a consistent interest rate policy, if excessive capital inflows are to be avoided. But for situations with a substantial inflation differential or a strong asset-price inflation this approach offers many advantages compared with a fixed rate. For the real sector of the economy, the risk of a real appreciation due to inflation inertia can be avoided. For financial markets an adjustable exchange rate target makes it much easier to cope with the problems of *capital inflows*.

For a given risk premium we already showed that domestic interest rates can be much higher without jeopardizing the equilibrium on foreign exchange markets: $i = i^* + \alpha + \Delta s^T$. Due to the *higher weighting of the interest rate channel*, this approach can be advised to economies that are less open and/or already have a higher degree of monetization. Applied to our country sample, Figure 7.5 shows that the initial real appreciation was less pronounced within the crawlers than within groups of countries with a fixed exchange rate or a currency board (see Figure 7.2). Brazil, which had almost no real appreciation, confirms the idea of a passive crawl.

If the exchange rate adjustment is made in the form of a permanent depreciation ('crawling peg'), the problem of *shifting risk premiums* can also be reduced, as one-way bets are no longer possible. A more constant risk premium avoids the threat of unstable interest rates for domestic firms.

In addition, a Central Bank can always *increase a risk premium* which it regards as too low. While this is possible under a fixed and a flexible exchange rate target, a flexible target with a wide band avoids that such a policy of 'causing ripples' is limited by reaching the limit of the band.

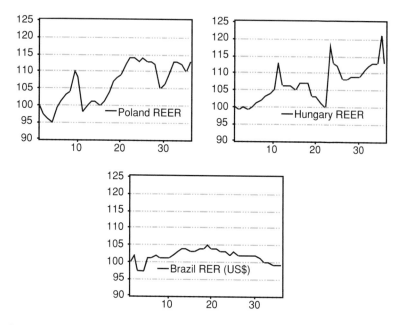

Source: IFS.

Figure 7.5   Real appreciation in the first three years of disinflation (crawling pegs)

If the targeted depreciation and the interest rate are *substitutes* for monetary restriction, which the construction of our MCI assumes, a Central Bank can react to shifting risk premiums by adjusting the policy mix.

An additional advantage of an adjustable exchange rate is related to the *sterilization of interventions*. In principle, a Central Bank is able to avoid a nominal appreciation of its own currency (caused by strong capital inflows) simply by interventions on the foreign exchange market. The subsequent depreciation reduces or even eliminates any potential speculative pressure and stops the capital inflows. In order to maintain a certain level of domestic interest rates, the liquidity impact of interventions has to be sterilized with domestic monetary policy instruments (reduction of domestic credits or even offering some kind of deposit facility). While domestic assets are in principle available without any limitation and in the case of a deposit facility the sterilization potential is also unlimited, a hard budget constraint can be created by the costs of intervention. With a constant exchange rate, these costs are determined by the difference between the domestic interest rate and the interest rate in the anchor country. With a positive interest rate differential to the anchor currency, a prolonged policy of sterilized intervention can become very costly. If a central bank follows a flexible exchange rate target, sterilization can be made without any costs. Thus, sterilized intervention provides an additional degree of freedom to monetary policy. It can simultaneously target the domestic interest rate and a floor for an exchange rate path.

This is illustrated in Figure 7.6. Let us assume that the Central Bank targets an annual (t_0 to t_1) nominal depreciation of 5 per cent. At the time, when the exchange rate reaches the lower limit A of the band (say, –1 per

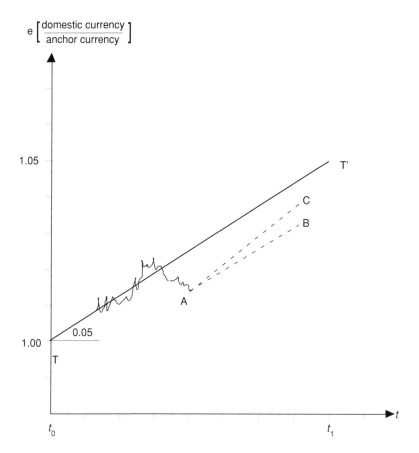

Figure 7.6   Intervention policy in the case of capital inflows

cent from the target path TT'), the Central Bank starts to intervene in the foreign exchange market. The two dotted lines AB and AC represent the 'no-loss-paths', which means that along these lines the loss from the interest rate differential (i – i* = 5 per cent on line AB and i – i* = 5 per cent + α on line AC when there is a risk premium)[10] is compensated by the increase of the value of the foreign exchange reserves caused by a successful depreciation of the domestic currency. Costs are only created if the exchange rate moves below the no-loss-path despite the intervention of the Central Bank. But this situation will never occur provided that the Central Bank has an unlimited sterilization potential.

The situation turns out to be much more different in the case of *capital outflows*. There is a clear budget constraint for a Central Bank trying to defend its currency against a devaluation. Nevertheless, by avoiding speculative inflows, a Central Bank can reduce the risk of excessive outflows.

Evidence

The experience with flexible exchange rate targets shows that in most cases speculative capital inflows have not been a major problem. In the ERM I from 1979 to 1986 Italy has followed a policy of infrequent depreciations (seven realignments with a first adjustment only six months after the start of the system) within a ±6 per cent band. Figure 7.7 shows that during this period capital inflows remained rather limited. The situation changed significantly in the five and a half years of the 'stable' ERM where the lira was devalued only once (3.68 per cent) and where the fluctuation band was reduced to ±2.25 per cent.

The experience of the five lead accession countries also confirms that capital inflows are mainly a problem of fixed exchange rates combined with inconsistent interest policies.

Table 7.5   Cumulative direct investment and other financial inflows (net) to the lead accession countries, 1993–6

Country	Other financial inflows (net) in % of GDP	Direct investment inflows in % of GDP
Czech Republic	28.3	9.8
Estonia	9.2	16.7
Hungary	9.9	22.2
Poland	–2.0	8.7
Slovenia	2.2	3.1

Source: IFS.

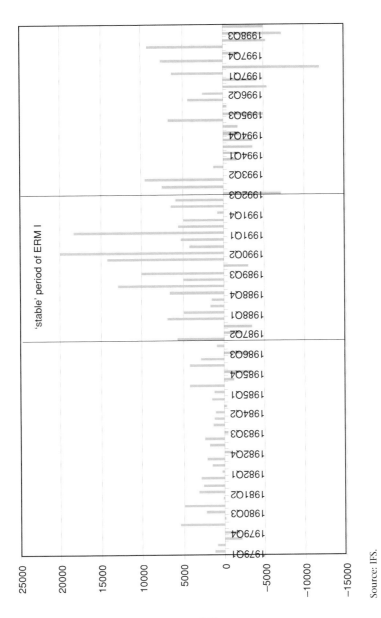

Figure 7.7   Financial inflows (net) minus FDI (US$ millions), Italy

Source: IFS.

As Table 7.7 shows, the only country with excessive capital inflows was the Czech Republic. In all other countries direct investment inflows were higher than the other financial inflows which remained relatively small.

In the Asian region, Indonesia with its *de facto* crawl received much fewer currency inflows than Korea, Thailand and Malaysia (Table 7.8). The fact that the Asian crisis started in Thailand fits with its extremely high exposure to capital inflows. But because of a strong contagion effect (Ito 1999, p. 28) Indonesia was also hit by the crisis.

> Indonesia appears to be the clearest case of contagion in the region ... By most, Indonesia's imbalances were among the least severe in the region, and clearly much less dramatic than in Thailand. (Radelet and Sachs 1998a, p. 37)[11]

As above, the example of France in the ERM crises of 1992/3 shows that currency crises tend to affect countries in the same region even if their fundamentals are solid and if they have been able to avoid excessive currency inflows.

Table 7.6   Cumulative direct investment and other financial inflows (net) to selected Asian countries, 1993–6

Country	Other financial inflows (net) in % of GDP	Direct investment inflows in % of GDP
Indonesia	7.6	8.6
Korea	13.5	1.2
Malaysia	12.1	21.3
Thailand	35.1	4.5

Source: IFS.

In Latin America, a similar picture as in the five lead transition countries emerges. Mexico, which *de facto* followed a fixed peg, received by far the highest capital inflows, while the inflows were rather limited in Argentina (currency board) and Brazil (crawling peg).

In sum, a flexible exchange rate targeting has the important advantage that it considerably reduces the risk of destabilizing capital inflows. In this respect it is identical with a currency board. In both cases, interest rate policies that are incompatible with UIP can be avoided.

Thus, flexible exchange rate targeting provides a limited solution to the inconsistency triangle. Instead of choosing one of the two corner solutions (perfectly fixed exchange rates or an autonomous monetary policy with freely floating exchange rates) a dynamic interpretation of the triangle allows the combination of free capital movements with an autonomous interest policy and a stable floor for an exchange rate path. The notion dynamic refers to a time *path* for the exchange rate which at the given interest rate differential has to ensure a permanent UIP equilibrium.

Table 7.7   Cumulative direct investment and other financial inflows (net) in Latin America (selected four-year periods)

Country	Other financial inflows (net) in % of GDP	Direct investment inflows in% of GDP
Argentina (1995–8)	8.5	8.7
Brazil (1995–8)	5.1	8.7
Mexico (1991–4)	19.1	6.1

Source: IFS.

While such a policy is a good recipe against a currency crisis, it does not completely rule it out. The examples of France, Indonesia and Brazil show that contagion effects can play an important role. In these cases the risk premium increases to levels which would require an overly restrictive monetary policy stance. Therefore, if countries are obliged to support an exchange rate target without external support, in the short run a major devaluation is the only solution. As such an exit can have disastrous consequences; an international framework for stabilizing such currencies would urgently be needed.

Implications for the lead accession countries in stage I

The main lessons

The experience with different exchange rate arrangements in the last two decades provides relatively clear implications for the exchange rate policy of the accession countries during the period until their EU membership:

- A complete neglect of exchange rate policy, i.e. *flexible exchange rates* in the pure sense that the Central Bank refrains from foreign exchange market interventions, should be ruled out. In the past this arrangement has been practised only between the three key currencies (the dollar, the euro and the yen) and has led to excessive exchange rate fluctuations. The experience of all three areas (Asia, Latin America, and Central and Eastern Europe) does not support the popular view that a flexible exchange rate regime is required because 'pegged exchange rate regimes are a very dangerous strategy for emerging market economies and make financial crises more likely' (Mishkin 1999, p. 22).[12]

- A *fixed nominal exchange rate target* can be adopted only if the disinflation process and the process of price liberalization is completed. For such a step the inflation differential between the domestic currency and the euro should not exceed 3 percentage points.

- A *currency board* is only advisable for countries which have a very open economy. Under this condition it can be sufficient to rely on the external lever of monetary policy only. The risks of this strategy have been extensively discussed in the literature on monetary unions. However, in contrast to a monetary union, a currency board does not protect a country against the risks of excessive interest rates due to speculative pressure. In addition, it lacks a lender of last resort.

- A *flexible exchange rate target* with a relatively wide band is the safest policy option. The findings of this chapter confirm Williamson's (1996) analyses of the experience with crawling bands in Chile, Colombia and Israel.[13] Hungary and Poland have practised this strategy successfully. This approach avoids above all the risk of destabilizing capital inflows. Flexible exchange rate targeting can be practiced in different forms. A Central Bank has to decide whether it announces the target ('crawling peg') or not. In addition, the crawl can be active (not fully compensating for the inflation differential) or purely accommodating. A nominal anchor is provided only by a publicly announced active crawl.

- If the exchange rate target is not announced, the nominal anchor has to be provided by a publicly announced inflation target. Such an *inflation targeting* would signal to the public that the inflation target has priority but it would also make clear that the exchange rate will not be allowed to fluctuate in an uncontrolled way. Thus, 'a nominal (non-fixed) exchange rate target could coexist with an inflation target' (Masson et al. 1997, p. 9). If a policy of inflation targeting is combined 'with greater exchange rate flexibility' (ibid., p. 17), the risk of missing the inflation target because of erratic exchange rate fluctuations is high.

- *Capital controls* for short-term capital flows can be avoided if the framework for exchange rate policy is compatible with the requirements of domestic interest rate policy. In addition the exchange rate target should be surrounded by a 'wide' band. Williamson (1996, p. 110) recommends a band width of ±7–10 per cent. The experience of ERM I shows that Italy had been able to manage a substantial disinflation with a ±6 per cent band.

The monetary policy strategies of the Czech Republic, Hungary and Poland

Of the five lead accession countries, the Central Banks of the Czech Republic, Hungary and Poland have developed comprehensive monetary policy strategies for the period until their EU accession.

The strategies of *Poland* and the *Czech Republic* rely on *inflation targets* as a nominal anchor. Poland implemented this approach with a 'freely floating exchange rate' (Monetary Policy Council 1999, p. 14),[14] while the Czech Republic completely neglects the role of exchange rate policy in its monetary strategy (Czech National Bank 1999). This is rather astonishing because the Bank is aware of the fact that the 'Czech economy is a small, very open economy, both in terms of trade and finance, with liberalized capital flows' (ibid., p. 3). Nevertheless, the Czech National Bank intervened heavily in the foreign exchange market in the end of 1999 and the beginning of 2000.[15] The main difference between the strategies of these two countries concerns the definition of the inflation target. The Polish Central Bank sets the target for the consumer price index because 'it is deeply rooted in the public perception as the underlying measure of inflation' (Monetary Policy Council 1999, p. 119). The Czech National Bank favours 'net inflation' which excludes all price changes of 'regulated prices'.[16] The main problems of this approach are clearly discussed by the Polish Monetary Policy Council:

> Application of core inflation as the official policy target would require eliminating from CPI the prices of goods and services that strongly influence the public perception of inflationary developments. (ibid., p. 11)

Hungary has decided on the opposite strategy. It avoids an announcement of an inflation target:

The Bank, as in the past, cannot set an inflation target on its own. It can make significant progress in reducing inflation only together with the government and the other sectors of the economy, provided that unforeseen external developments do not impede monetary policy in pursuing these objectives with regard to inflation and external balance. (National Bank of Hungary 1999, p. 6)

As a consequence it uses 'the pre-announced course of the exchange rate' as its main nominal anchor. On 1 January 2000 the National Bank of Hungary abandoned its currency basket and fixed the forint solely against the euro. Since April 2000 the monthly crawl is 0.3 per cent, which means an annual depreciation of 3.6 per cent. With an inflation rate of 10 per cent in 1999 and a euro area inflation of between 1 and 2 per cent, this crawl can be regarded as an 'active crawl' which clearly contributes to a further reduction of inflation.

Estonia has not presented a medium-term strategy for its EMU entry, but it seems set on maintaining the currency board for all intermediate stages:

The fixed exchange rate and the currency board system form a suitable platform for Estonian monetary policy in its approximation to the Euro zone. (Kraft 1999)

Concerning the current debate on a full euroisation of the Estonian economy, the Eesti Pank also has a well-defined position:

becoming a member of the eurosystem is something more than adopting the euro unilaterally. The latter we clearly oppose. We are of the opinion that accession to the eurosystem can only be a part of the general development in Estonia. (Kraft 2000)

As the *Slovenian* Central Bank has not published a medium-term monetary policy strategy it cannot be discussed in this chapter.

Assessment

The strategies of the four lead accession countries with a clearly defined monetary policy framework are compatible with the implications that can be drawn from the currency experience of the last two decades. Above all, the risk of destabilizing capital inflows can be ruled out. Therefore, it is consequent that in all four countries capital controls are not regarded as a relevant policy instrument.

A major problem is the Polish preference for 'freely floating exchange rates' and the complete disregard of exchange rate targeting in the Czech approach. After the experience with freely floating rates, especially with the yen/dollar rate in the 1990s, it sounds somewhat naive when the Polish Monetary Policy Council (1999, p. 14) states:

> This arrangement [freely floating exchange rates] will help to bring the market rate closer to the equilibrium rate.

However, at the same time it emphasizes:

> Both within the present exchange rate system and after the introduction of a fully floating rate, the National Bank of Poland will maintain the right to intervene in foreign exchange markets when it recognizes a need to do so for monetary policy reasons. (ibid., p. 14)

Such contradictory statements do not contribute to the transparency and credibility of monetary policy. A similar lack of transparency is created by the Czech strategy which creates the impression that the Central Bank no longer takes an active interest in the exchange rate of the koruna. While in both countries it would not be necessary to announce explicit targets for the exchange rate, it is misleading to pretend a strategy of 'free floating' or of a 'benign neglect'. Poland and especially the Czech Republic are very open economies which could not afford to live with a strongly fluctuating exchange rate. Table 7.8 shows that there was a substantial increase in the volatility of daily exchange rate changes, and that the volatility of the zloty even surmounted that of the euro and the Deutschemark *vis-à-vis* the dollar. Therefore, a general commitment of the Central Bank to a stable exchange rate path would help to stabilize the expectations of investors during the process to EU accession. In this respect the Hungarian approach provides much more transparency.

Because of its focus on 'net inflation' the Czech approach provides a less visible monetary anchor than the strategies of Poland and Hungary. An inflation target that differs considerably from CPI inflation is not an ideal focal point for trade unions and all other agents that have to fix nominal values for future dates. In the words of the Czech National Bank (1999, p. 7):

> The fall in the consumer price and net inflation indices have not yet been adequately reflected in inflationary expectations or in the

Table 7.8   Volatility of daily exchange rate changes, 1993–2000

	Zloty/basket	Zloty/DM respectively zloty/euro (1999–)	Zloty/US$	DM/US$ respectively euro/US$ (1999–)	Franc/DM
1993*	0.07	0.32	0.38	0.70	0.28
1994	0.07	0.30	0.32	0.61	0.12
1995*	0.17	0.44	0.41	0.82	0.31
1996	0.16	0.26	0.30	0.44	0.14
1997	0.54	0.56	0.68	0.61	0.10
1998	0.64	0.66	0.72	0.57	0.09
1999	0.65	0.69	0.75	0.57	
2000 (to 12 April)	0.64	0.75	0.61	0.66	

*   Because of discrete jumps in the exchange rate (devaluations and revaluations) the figures are adjusted.

Source: National Bank of Poland; authors' calculations.

decision making of economic agents. This is illustrated, among other things, by the results of wage bargaining for 1999.

In sum, it should be clear that in all arrangements with a flexible exchange rate target, monetary policy has to be conducted on the basis of an inflation target. Such a target should be comprehensive. It should reflect the degree of price rigidities, a potential productivity bias and the remaining necessities to adjust administered prices. The inflation target does not necessarily have to be published. But if this is the case, the exchange rate target has to be made public in order to provide at least one nominal anchor for private expectations. The inflation target has to be implemented through an exchange rate target *vis-à-vis* the euro and a target level for domestic short-term rates. Both levers of monetary policy have to conform to the requirements of UIP at a given risk premium. Thus, the crawl cannot be simply calculated by a formula 'target for domestic inflation minus expected foreign inflation minus expected productivity bias' (Williamson 1996, p. 111). A macroeconomic strategy without an exchange rate target ('freely floating exchange rate') runs the risk of missing the inflation target because of short-term exchange rate variations. This risk is especially high in the very open accession countries (Czech Republic, Estonia and Slovenia).

Stage II: no major regime change compared with stage I

After EU accession, the new member states will have to adopt the so-called *acquis communautaire* (the set of obligations deriving from the treaties, secondary EU legislation and jurisprudence of the Court of Justice). For monetary and exchange rate policy this includes above all the following obligations:

- to regard their economic policies as a matter of common concern and to coordinate them with the Council (Article 99, ex Article 103)
- to exclude all central bank credits to the government (Article 101, ex Article 104)
- to avoid excessive deficits (Article 104, ex Article 104c)
- to treat exchange rate policy as a matter of common interest (Article 124, ex Article 109m)
- to submit annually medium-term convergence programmes, subject to surveillance by the Council (Article 7, Stability and Growth Pact)

In addition, the new members are expected to participate in the ERM II sooner or later.

For the field of exchange rate and monetary policy these obligations do not require major changes compared to stage I. With its ±15 per cent band and the option to adjust parities at infrequent intervals ERM II leaves a wide scope for a rather flexible exchange rate policy. Even the present crawl rate of the forint could easily be combined with a fixed parity that is adjusted at an annual basis ('crawling snake within the tunnel'). Estonia would not need a formal ERM II membership.

The main advantage of ERM II over the present situation is the access to the unlimited short-term intervention credits of the ECB ('very short-term financing'). This strengthens a Central Bank's position in the situation of a speculative attack. However, as all intervention credits have to be paid back with foreign exchange reserves by the country with the weak currency, the support by such credit lines is rather limited. The experience of the ERM crises in 1992/3 shows that even France as a country with sound fundamentals was unable to defend the Franc within the ±2.25 per cent band. In addition, in the ERM II the ECB can unilaterally suspend intervention credits if they endanger the target of price stability. In ERM I such an opt-out clause was not explicitly agreed.

In sum, stage II will not imply a major regime change compared with stage I. The only major change is that countries can no longer determine their euro exchange rate independently. Thus, if an accession country feels a need for a major adjustment of its euro rate, it would be well-advised to do this before EU accession.

Stage III: limiting the risks of the endgame

Stage III covers the last two years before EMU membership. It leaves the accession countries relatively little room for country-specific arrangements as ERM II membership is a mandatory criterion of convergence. The most important decision at the beginning of the stage is the determination of the parity which according to Article 121 of the Treaty is a identical with a *ceiling*[17] for its final conversion rate for EMU membership. As the wording of the Treaty does not prohibit an appreciation, a country could start the two-year transition period with a somewhat undervalued currency and adjust downwards if necessary.

With the ERM II fluctuation margins, relatively large deviations from that midpoint are possible without violating this specific criterion for convergence. The experience with the last nine months of the ERM I shows that the announcement of the final conversion rates can act as a very firm anchor for the actual exchange rate. If the markets regard the conversion rate as *credible*, it will be identical with the expected exchange rate for the entry date. Because of the uncovered interest parity, the spot rates during the ERM II period will be very closely determined by the interest rate differential between the accession country and the euro interest rate. Thus, as soon as an accession country determines the parity for ERM II, it automatically defines the path for the spot rate by the prevailing interest rate differential.

This scenario has the attractive feature that an accession country can still use the national interest rate instrument for a fine-tuning of the economy in the very sensitive transition period. Above all, a restrictive monetary policy could be pursued if there are signs that the inflation criterion might not be met. Over time, the impact of national monetary policy is reduced because the interest rates for periods that go beyond the entry date are an average of the national and the euro rate with a declining weight of the national rate. In addition, as long as the exchange rate path follows the interest rate differentials, the risk of speculative capital inflows would be very limited. There is nothing foreign investors could gain by holding short-term assets denominated in such a currency.

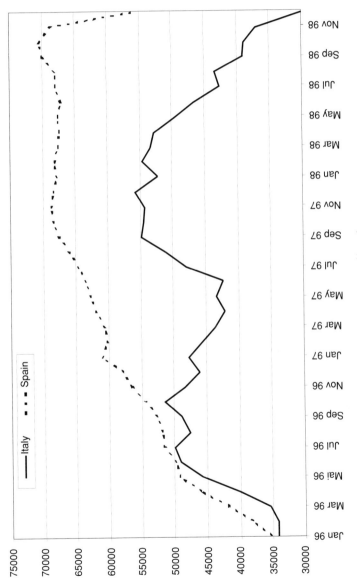

Figure 7.8 Exchange reserves: Italy and Spain, 1996–8 (US$ millions)

Source: IFS.

179

The situation gets more complicated if the markets regard the final conversion rate as *not credible*. In the case of an expected conversion rate that is *higher* than the announced rate, the distrust of the markets would be immediately reflected by a spot rate that diverges from the conversion rate *by more* than the interest rate differential. In order to avoid such a destabilizing process the domestic Central Bank has to intervene on the foreign exchange market. The exchange reserves of Italy and Spain show that both countries have bought and sold major quantities of their own currency in the last three years of ERM I (Figure 7.8). As the foreign exchange reserves are limited and the ECB is not obliged under ERM II to intervene without limits, the risk of a non-credible conversion rate shows how important it is to start the two-year transition period with a sustainable exchange rate.

The case of a somewhat *undervalued conversion rate* would be less problematic. Again the markets could regard the announced rate as not credible, but now they would expect the actual conversion rate to be lower than the announced conversion rate. This would become visible in a spot rate that diverges from the conversion rate *by less* than the interest rate differential. It seems unlikely that such a divergence would lead to destabilizing processes.

Given the huge analytical difficulties in determining equilibrium exchange rates, the strategy of entering the transition period with a somewhat undervalued currency looks quite attractive. However, if the undervaluation is reached by a depreciation at the beginning of the two-year qualification period, it bears the risk of stimulating inflation, which could lead to a violation of the inflation rate criterion. Therefore, already at an early stage of accession or even before accession, the accession countries should carefully analyse whether a precautionary depreciation of their currency might be required.

Summary

Assuming that the five lead accession countries are strongly committed to stability-oriented macroeconomic policies, the choice of an adequate exchange rate policy for their path towards EMU membership is not too difficult. The experience of the ERM I countries shows that a fixed euro exchange rate should only be adopted if the inflation differential is lower than 3 per cent. In the meantime, a flexible exchange rate targeting should be followed under the overall framework of an inflation targeting. The target values for the inflation rate, the exchange rate and the domestic interest rate have to be derived in a way that guarantees a UIP equilibrium. The experience with flexible exchange rate targeting shows that such regimes do not give rise to excessive currency inflows. Thus, capital inflow controls are not needed in the whole transition period to EMU. With the EU accession and even an ERM II membership, the overall framework for monetary and exchange rate policy in the new member countries does not change very much. This is different in the two-year qualification period preceding final EMU entry which sets clear limits for the path of the spot rate. Nevertheless, it still leaves some scope for an autonomous interest policy. As an overvalued entry rate is a major risk for the qualification period and for EMU membership, the accession countries should target a somewhat undervalued rate already in the pre-accession phase.

Notes

1. ECB Press Release <www.ecb.de/press/pr91112.htm>
2. A very important topic which we do not discuss is the identification of equilibrium exchange rates. For a comprehensive analysis see Begg et al. (1999).
3. See Council on Foreign Relations (1999).
4. See ibid., p. 3: 'Emerging market economies with fragile financial systems should take transparent and non-discriminatory tax measures to discourage short-term capital inflows and encourage less crisis-prone, longer-term-ones, like foreign direct investment.' See also Begg et al. (1999, p. 7), Reisen (1998) and Radelet and Sachs (1998b, p. 71).
5. For a comprehensive discussion of the requirements in other fields of macro-economic policy see Kopits (1999).
6. See also Begg et al. (1999, p. 1): 'In fact, to a surprising extent general principles apply to the transition countries.'
7. See Jadresic et al. (1999, p. 9): 'Indeed, while an increasing number of these countries (together with the emerging market economies) officially describe their exchange rate regimes as "managed float" or "independent floating" ... the fact is that most of these countries do maintain some form of de jure or de facto exchange rate peg or otherwise narrowly limit fluctuations of the exchange rate.'
8. The term 'risk premium' as it is used here and in the literature (see Isard 1995, p. 84) is defined as a risk premium on the expected exchange rate change. Thus it is different from the literature on financial markets where risk premia are added to a risk-free interest rate.
9. See Eichengreen and Masson (1998, p. 32).
10. Remember that we are considering sterilized interventions. An increase in low interest bearing foreign assets yields to this loss when we reduce the higher interest bearing domestic credits at the same time.
11. Above all Radelet and Sachs (1998b, p. 38) show that there was no evidence for a 'boom-bust pattern in Indonesia'.
12. See also Blöndal and Christiansen (1999).

13. '[A] crawling band is capable of achieving a reasonable trade-off between the conflicting objectives of reducing inflation and maintaining export growth. Furthermore crawling bands appear to perform quite well in limiting both exchange rate and reserve volatility; fixed rates perform better in the former dimension, as long as they really remain fixed, but the crawling band outperforms (although not significantly) an average of fixed rates and the adjustable peg' (Williamson 1996, p. 101).

14. 'The floating exchange rate system will be introduced following a period of the gradual expansion of the band of permitted exchange rate fluctuations and the gradual reduction the crawling devaluation within the framework of the present exchange rate system' (Monetary Policy Council 1999, p. 14). The band was widened from ±10 per cent (February 1998) over ±12.5 per cent (October 1998) to ±15 per cent (March 1999), and on 12 April 2000 the Bank of Poland finally introduced the free float of the zloty.

15. 'The CNB used foreign exchange intervention to prevent a continuing strengthening of the exchange rate, which could have an adverse effect on the real economy. In keeping with both the current and the expected price trend, the foreign exchange interventions were perceived as being consistent with the CNB's inflation target.' Also, 'The monetary policy decisions in 2000 Q1 were affected by the exchange rate' (Czech National Bank 2000).

16. 'Regulated prices include maximum prices, limited prices (both can be set on the central as well as on the local levels) and administratively fixed fees' (Czech National Bank 1998).

17. Price quotation for the exchange rate, i.e. the exchange rate is expressed in units of the domestic currency per one unit of the foreign currency.

References

Begg, D., Halpern, L. and Wyplosz, C. (1999) *Monetary and Exchange Rate Policies*, EMU and Central and Eastern Europe, Forum report of the Economic Policy Initiative no. 5, CEPR, London.

Blöndal, S. and Christiansen, H. (1999) *The Recent Experience with Capital Inflows to Emerging Market Economies*, OECD Economics Department Working Papers No. 211, Paris.

Bofinger, P. (1996) 'The Economics of Orthodox Money-based Stabilizations (OMBS): The Recent Experience of Kazakhstan, Russia and the Ukraine', in *European Economic Review*, No. 40: 663–71.

Council on Foreign Relations (1999) 'Safeguarding Prosperity in a Global Financial System'. The future international financial architecture report by an independent task force: <www.foreignrelations.org.public/pubs/IFATaskForce.html>

Czech National Bank (1998) 'Net Inflation – The CNB Inflation Target': <www.cnb.cz/en/archiv/bulletin/9801/str3.htm>

Czech National Bank (1999) 'CNB Monetary Strategy', document approved by the Board of the CNB on 8 April 1999: <www.cnb.cz/en/archiv/dms.htm>

Czech National Bank (2000) 'Inflation Report – April 2000': <www.cnb.cz/en/_mpolitika/inflace0004/docs/04.htm>

Deutsche Bundesbank (1999) 'Taylor Interest Rate and Monetary Conditions Index', *Monthly Report*, April.

EBRD (1999) *Transition Report*, European Bank of Reconstruction and Development, London.

Eichengreen, B. and Masson, P. (1998) *Exit Strategies, Policy Options for Countries Seeking Greater Exchange Rate Flexibility*, International Monetary Fund, Occasional Paper No. 168, Washington DC.

Froot, K., O'Connell, P. and Seasholes, M. (1998) *The Portfolio Flows of International Investors, I*, NBER Working Paper Series No. 6687.

Golinelli, R. and Rovelli, R. (1999) 'Monetary Policy and the Convergence to Low Inflation: A Small Macro Model for Hungary and Poland, 1991–1998', Paper for the Phare-ACE Programme 'Central Banks, Financial Structure and Monetary Policy in the Economies in Transition in Central and Eastern Europe', Bologna.

Isard, P. (1995) *Exchange Rate Economics*, Cambridge Surveys of Economic Literature, Cambridge.

Ito, T. (1999) *Capital Flows in Asia*, NBER Working Paper Series, No. 7134.

Jadresic, E., Masson, P. and Mauro, P. (1999) 'Exchange Rate Regimes of Developing Countries: Global Context and Individual Choices', mimeo.

Kaminsky, G., Lizondo, S. and Reinhart, C. M. (1998) 'Leading Indicators of Currency Crises', IMF Staff Papers, Vol. 45, No. 1: 1–49.

Kopits, G. (1999) *Implications of EMU for Exchange Rate Policy in Central and Eastern Europe*, IMF Working Paper No. 99/9, Washington DC.

Kraft, V. (1999) 'Keynote Speech', Conference dedicated to the 80th anniversary of the Eesti Pank: <www.ee/epbe/en_ep_80_conference/vahur_kraft.html>

Kraft, V. (2000) 'Estonia on its Way to the Eurozone: The Position of the Central Bank', Briefing of the monetary policy overview on 27 January: <www.ee/epbe/en/release/20000127.html>

Krugman, P. (1998) 'What Happened to Asia?': <www.web.mit.edu/krugman/www/DISINTER.html>

Masson, P. (1999) *Monetary and Exchange Rate Policy of Transition Economies of Central and Eastern Europe after the Launch of EMU*, IMF Policy Discussion Paper PDP/99/5, Washington DC.

Masson, P., Savastano, M. and Sharma, S. (1997) *The Scope for Inflation Targeting in Developing Countries*, IMF Working Paper, WP/97/130, Washington DC.

Mishkin, F. (1999) *Lessons from the Asian Crises*, NBER Working Paper Series No. 7102.

Monetary Policy Council (1999) 'Medium-term Strategy for Monetary Policy (1999–2003)', September: <www.pnb.pl>

National Bank of Hungary (1999) 'Monetary Policy Guidelines for 2000', October: <www.mnb.hu>

Padoa-Schioppa, T. (1987) *Efficiency, Stability, and Equity: A Strategy for the Evolution of the Economic System of the European Community*, Oxford University Press, Oxford.

Radelet, S. and Sachs, J. (1998a) *The Onset of the Asian Financial Crisis*, NBER Working Paper Series, No. 6680.

Radelet, S. and Sachs, J. (1998b) 'The East Asian Financial Crisis: Diagnosis, Remedies, Prospects', *Brookings Papers on Economic Activity*, 1: 1–74.

Reisen, H. (1998) *Domestic Causes of Currency Crises: Policy Lessons for Crisis Avoidance*, OECD Development Centre, Technical Papers No. 136, Paris: <www.oecd.org/dev/pub/tp1a.htm>

Svensson, L. E. O. (1998) *Open-Economy Inflation Targeting*: <www.iies.su.se/~leosven/>

Williamson, J. (1996) *The Crawling Band as an Exchange Rate Regime, Lessons from Chile, Colombia and Israel*, Institute for International Economics, Washington DC.

8
Financial Institution-Building in Eastern Europe

Claus-Peter Zeitinger

Introduction

This chapter deals with experience gathered in introducing the idea of 'New Development Finance' to the countries of transition in Central and Eastern Europe. In particular, the goal is to improve the access of micro and small enterprises, small farmers and other comparatively weak economic units – the so-called target groups – to credit, deposit facilities and payment services.

The positive correlation between financial development and economic growth has for a long time been recognized as a fact, proven both empirically and theoretically.[1] Development finance, i.e. efforts that are undertaken in the framework of development assistance to support the growth and modernization of financial systems in developing and transition countries, have also been under way for a long time.[2] The distinctive characteristic of the approach referred to as New Development Finance is the insight that the key to improving financial systems lies in building stable and efficient financial institutions which tailor their services specifically to target groups, like micro, small and medium-sized enterprises, rather than merely channelling foreign capital to these groups.[3]

The chapter is structured as follows: following this introduction, I analyse some key characteristics of financial institutions in transition economies, with the conclusion that there is indeed a need for financial institution-building. I then highlight special features of this particular approach to development finance, and explain the rationale behind the 'greenfield approach' to institution-building which has been chosen for a number of countries, i.e. the establishment of a new target group-oriented financial institution. The implementation of this approach and the results obtained with it to date are then described with reference to three examples: the FEFAD Bank in Albania, the Micro Enterprise Bank (MEB) in Bosnia-Herzegovina, and the Microfinance Bank of Georgia (MBG). I then consider the question of the extent to which this form of development finance contributes to the development of local financial systems. The chapter concludes with a summary and some tentative assessments.

Characteristics of financial institutions in transition economies

Financial institutions, i.e. banks, are the core of financial development.[4] Their importance derives from the fact that they have the potential to overcome the functional deficiencies of financial markets which are caused by underlying informational and incentive problems.[5] This is particularly relevant to transition countries, where these problems occur in a particularly acute form. Most enterprises do not have a long track record, nor do they have audited financial statements that they could publish in order to demonstrate their financial solidity to the capital markets and thereby obtain outside financing. This makes it all the more likely that financial institutions, through their screening and monitoring activities, could help to create a situation in which large segments of the population can realize more of their economic potential and improve their living conditions.

However, as various commentators have shown – not least of all, Bokros (this volume)[6] – it has been wrong to assume that banks with the ability to play this role will evolve automatically under the conditions prevailing in most transition countries.[7] Poor governance in the case of state-owned and private banks, which were more often than not set up in order secure cheap financing for the companies or individuals who founded them,[8] and a lack of experience in assessing and managing credit risk, the use of loan security, credit monitoring and other key elements of financial intermediation led to a situation in which non-performing loans soared, ranging between 10 and 40 per cent of the banking system's total portfolio. Under these circumstances it is not surprising that a series of banking crises have occurred since the start of the transition process. The consolidation that followed these crises was usually accompanied by the liquidation of those banks with the worst governance performance. However, it did not bolster high-quality lending to the private sector. Rather, it initiated a flight to highly liquid, safe assets like treasury bills and deposits with banks abroad. Accordingly, the ratio of private sector credit to GDP is in many transition countries negligibly low, even if allowance is made for the low level of incomes (EBRD 1999, p. 94). This implies, conversely, that most enterprises, especially those in the newly emerging private sector, have no access to credit from the formal financial system, although these are precisely the enterprises that form the basis for growth and employment creation in the transition countries (ibid., pp. 92 and 137).

In many transition economies, therefore, the task at hand is to create a basic supply of financial services for the new private sector. That is why assistance in the form of systematic 'financial institution-building' is needed. Successful institution-building creates incentives to save, repay loans and keep financial institutions viable, thereby giving an ever-expanding proportion of the economically weak segments of the population lasting access to financial services that are useful to them. In particular, this task involves devising efficient methods of providing financial services tailored to private micro, small and medium-sized businesses. Of paramount importance in this context is the introduction of an appropriate lending technology,[9] i.e. a technology that takes account not only of the specific characteristics of micro, small and medium-sized enterprises but also the specific lending environment in the countries in which they operate. In practical terms, this means that the information and incentive problems of external financing must be resolved largely without recourse to formal signalling and self-selection instruments, especially collateral. This is because the enterprises generally lack the kinds of collateral normally required by banks, and also because the legal environment – both the laws themselves and enforcement practices – is not conducive to successful collateral-based lending. Consequently, the credit technology focuses on loan analysis, screening and monitoring, and the application of the 'graduation principle', i.e. the principle of granting borrowers who repay on time the entitlement to borrow larger amounts with longer terms, thus creating an incentive for them to keep to the payment plan.

The second key component of the institution building approach is the design of organizational structures and concepts of organizational development that lead to the establishment of formal full-service banks. This aspect, which is often underestimated because it is less tangible, and not at all quantifiable, automatically raises questions about the governance and ownership of the partner institutions. After all, micro and small loans are not granted in an institutional vacuum, a fact that is often overlooked when SME credit lines are designed.[10] On the contrary, small and micro lending has to fit in with the partner institution's overall business operations. For one thing, this means that the work of a new SME lending department has to be coordinated with other departments. If the partner institution is a commercial bank, this means the legal, collateral, liquidity management (treasury), marketing and accounting departments. The success of the institution-building process can depend to a large degree on how well this 'interface management' functions. However, the most important factor is the quality of the dialogue between the project staff and the institution's management and owners regarding the status of the micro, small and medium-sized enterprise lending operation. After all, the goal of the institution-building process is to enable the target group to develop a lasting relationship with the partner banks which continues after the project has ended.

Special features of financial institution-building in the countries of Central and Eastern Europe

There are several approaches to financial institution-building. They differ in their response to the question of which type of partner institution offers the best prospects for establishing a formal full-service bank. Based on experiences in developing countries, particularly in Latin America, two main approaches have evolved: downscaling and upgrading.[11] In the transition countries, downscaling is the one primarily used.[12] The upgrading approach, which involves cooperating with credit institutions that are not subject to regulation by the local banking supervisory authority with the aim of transforming them into formal financial institutions, is of much less practical relevance in the transition economies than in developing countries. This is so for two reasons: one is that – apart from a very few exceptions – there are no credit-granting NGOs in the transition countries with a significant number of clients and significant loan portfolio volume. The other is that the banking laws of many countries in the region do not (or no longer) allow non-bank financial institutions to conduct lending operations – at least, not in their own name. Following a series of financial scandals and crises which originated in the informal financial sector, the banking laws were worded such that not only the collection of deposits but also lending was defined as a banking activity which could therefore not be pursued without a banking licence.[13]

This is why in transition economies a second alternative to the downscaling approach has gained favour, the one that I referred to earlier as the 'greenfield approach'.[14] It is grounded in the idea that Internationale Projekt Consult (IPC), in close consultation with several important donor and investor institutions such as the International Finance Corporation (IFC), Kreditanstalt für Wiederaufbau (KfW), the Deutsche Entwicklungsgesellschaft (DEG), the European Bank for Reconstruction and Development (EBRD), and the Dutch institutions, FMO and DOEN Foundation, has developed. That idea is that, while it is generally advisable to have a local partner at the outset, under certain circumstances it may better serve the interests of micro, small and medium-sized enterprises, and contribute more to the development of the financial sector, if a new institution is created from scratch.

These circumstances can be described as follows:

1. The existing commercial banks are too weak financially, are unwilling to serve the target group on a significant scale and/or have such a poor governance structure that lending to the target group via these institutions and investing sizeable amounts of technical assistance in these banks would be either too risky or too time-consuming, i.e. cost-inefficient.
2. The credit-granting NGOs, if they exist at all, are either too small and/or unwilling to shift their overall orientation to one that would enable them to cover their costs and ensure economic survival. In other words, there is no prospect of their becoming self-sustaining, stable, efficient and ultimately formalized financial institutions.[15]

Next, I shall illustrate how this approach is applied in practice by describing three examples: the FEFAD Bank in Albania, the Micro Enterprise Bank (MEB) in Bosnia-Herzegovina, and the Microfinance Bank of Georgia (MBG).

The greenfield approach in Practice: Albania, Bosnia-Herzegovina and Georgia as case studies

Every financial institution-building project starts with a detailed financial sector study. The twofold purpose of such studies is to ascertain whether there is an adequate supply of financial services available to micro, small and medium-sized enterprises in the respective country, and if not, to identify local partners for a possible internationally financed project to close the supply gap. Table 8.1 summarizes the main characteristics of the local financial sectors at the time when the preparatory financial sector studies were conducted.

Table 8.1 contains, in a nutshell, all of the arguments in favour of the greenfield approach as the best option for a financial institution-building project in each of these countries:

- the level of lending to the private sector is extremely low, both in relation to GDP and in relation to the level of monetization, the broad money/GDP ratio;
- the financial sector is dominated by state-owned banks with a poor governance structure, a high degree of political interference and severe technological deficiencies leading to a high level of bad loans (Albania, Bosnia-Herzegovina);
- a huge number of small local banks, most of them financially weak, operate as agent banks and/or are unwilling to serve micro and small businesses with no connection to the banks' management and owners (Bosnia-Herzegovina, Georgia);
- foreign private banks invest in transition countries in order to serve non-financial firms from their own countries that are active in transition countries, or that cooperate with local enterprises. Accordingly, these banks focus on areas that generate fees and commissions, e.g. international payment transactions, short-term trade credits, and the issuance of securities, whereas retail banking is largely avoided (Albania).[16]

Under these circumstances, pursuing the downscaling approach to financial institution-building would have been extremely risky. Not only would there have been a high risk of losing the funds invested due to the financially weak position of many banks and the uncertain status of their ownership and governance structures. It would also have been impossible – at least within a reasonably short period – to carry out the changes to the banks' operating procedures that would have been necessary in order to facilitate efficient lending to micro, small and medium-sized enterprises. Another point to bear in mind is that the legal environment for lending was extremely difficult in these three countries. Table 8.2 compares the three countries with the average for all 26 transition countries in terms of various legal transition indicators, as reported by the EBRD.

Table 8.1 Selected characteristics of the financial sectors of Albania, Bosnia-Herzegovina and Georgia at the time of the respective project-oriented financial sector study

Characteristics	Albania (1995)	Bosnia-Herzegovina (1996)	Georgia (1997)
Broad money/GDP	47.8	19.0	5.5
Private sector credit to GDP	3.7	n.a.	2.7[a]
Number of banks (foreign owned)	6 (3)	41 (5)[b]	53 (8)
Asset share of state-owned banks	84.8	78.7[b]	0.0[c]
Bad loans (% of total loans)	34.9	n.a.	6.6[d]
Qualitative Assessment	• State banks with major corporate governance problems and technological deficiencies leading to high default levels • Joint-venture and foreign private banks that are not interested in serving the target group, concentrating instead on fee income-generating business	• State banks with major corporate governance problems and technological deficiencies • Many small, financially weak private banks as a consequence of a *laissez-faire* licensing policy • High degree of connected lending, both by state-owned as well as private banks	• Following financial crisis of 1994/5, financial sector in process of consolidation: No. of banks down from 229 to 53; further reduction expected • Former state banks formally privatized • Many small, financially weak private banks; predominantly with agent bank character

Notes:
a 1996.
b Federation.
c Privatization of the state-owned banks in this year. In 1995 these banks still accounted for a 45.8 per cent market share.
d Before the outbreak of the financial crisis in 1995, bad loans accounted for 45 per cent.

Source: EBRD (1999).

Table 8.2   Legal transition indicators: Albania, Bosnia-Herzegovina, Georgia and transition country average, 1999*

	Albania	*Bosnia-Herzegovina*	*Georgia*	*Transition country average*
Commercial law	2	2–	2	3
Financial Regulations	2+	1	1	2+/3–
Bankruptcy law	1	1	2–	3–

* The lowest ranking is 1, the highest ranking 4+.

Sources: EBRD (1999, pp. 44, 46, 164); author's calculations.

These index values are a strong argument in favour of using the non-asset-based credit technology outlined above. However, the large percentage of liquid assets in the banking systems' total assets indicates, and the experience of many downscaling projects confirms, that banks in this environment will generally prefer to avoid lending to a target group that they do not regard as a priority clientele, rather than applying a credit technology that is new and untried. It was therefore concluded that, even with a substantial input of technical assistance, it would not have been possible to persuade the existing banks to issue credit to the target group on any significant scale, or to make the organisational changes that would allow them to pursue that goal.

This assessment was shared by donors and financial investors,[17] which therefore decided to set up a new target group-oriented bank in each of these countries (see Table 8.3).[18] Common to all three institutions are business policies based on the following principles:

- The target group for the banks' range of financial services consists of the 'lower end' of the market, i.e. micro and small enterprises and private households.
- The owners do not measure the success and significance of the banks merely in terms of business volume and profits but above all in terms of the number of customers reached.
- The banks are profit-oriented, but do not aim for short-term profit maximization. They seek a reasonable balance between social and economic goals. In this respect, they are following in the continental European tradition of savings and cooperative banks.

Table 8.3 Selected Indicators of the FEFAD Bank, the MEB and the MBG, 1996–2000

	Total assets[a]	Gross loan portfolio[a] (arrears >30 days)	No. of loans outstanding	Employment[c]	Deposits[a]	Liabilities to financial institutions[a]	Equity[a]	Return on equity (after taxes)
MEB								
Dec. 97	1,980	450 (0.0%)	110		–	–	1,980	–5%
Dec. 98	4,368	3152 (0.6%)	937		180	2,094	1,956	0%
Dec. 99	9,207	7137 (0.3%)	2,171	2.7	570	5,438	2,763	9%
FEFAD								
Dec. 96	4,624	1707 (1.2%)	273		–	2,573	1,901	–
Dec. 97	3,713	1417 (9.3%)	315		–	2,232	1,431	7%
Dec. 98	8,230	4502 (2.8%)	607		–	6,095	1,526	35%
Dec. 99	18,157	7317 (1.2%)	1,007	3.1	8,631	4,849	3,709	2%
MBG								
Jun. 99	2,599	1140 (0.0%)	218	–	–	–	2,577	–
Dec. 99	5,513	3125 (1.1%)	1,635[b]	9.4	149	2,907	2,526	–2.5%

Notes:
[a] In US$ 000s.
[b] Including gold pawn loans.
[c] Average number of people employed by clients.

Sources: MEB, FEFAD BANK, MBG.

- As universal banks they are able to perform every kind of banking operation, and indeed they do provide all kinds of services as long as these do not conflict with the interests of the target group.

Table 8.3 shows how key parameters for the FEFAD Bank, the MEB and the MBG have evolved since the institutions were first set up.[19]
From the above, the following conclusions can be drawn:

- Lending to the lower end of the market is not only possible, but can be very successful: from when they were first set up until the end of 1999 the three banks disbursed about 6200 loans worth a total of roughly US$35 million. The outstanding portfolio of the banks at the end of 1999 consisted of 4813 loans with a total volume of US$17.57 million.
- The FEFAD Bank and the MEB are operating at a profit; only the more recently established MBG reported a small loss at the end of its first nine months of operation.
- Micro and small loans have created, and continue to create, employment opportunities in the most dynamic sector of the region, the new private sector of micro, small and medium-sized enterprises.
- The banks themselves provide employment for around 150 people, and are making a decisive contribution to the transfer of know-how to the region regarding sound banking practices, with special emphasis on the lending technology.

In other words, the micro banks have achieved their overriding goal: to provided on a sustainable basis the kind of financial services which the target group demands.

The contribution of financial institution-building to financial sector development

Micro banks: source of credit for the nascent private sector

As implied by the term 'micro banks', and as indicated by the figures for total assets and gross portfolio presented in Table 8.3, these institutions are comparatively small. It is therefore not surprising that they account for only a very small percentage of the total assets of their respective local banking systems (see Table 8.4). Even the FEFAD Bank, which, if its time as the credit-granting foundation FEFAD is taken into account, had already been in business for four years by the end of 1999, holds a mere 1 per cent of the combined total assets in the Albanian banking system.

Table 8.4 The position of micro banks in the local banking systems, December 1999

	FEFAD Bank	*MEB*	*MBG*
Share of Total Assets	1.0	0.6	1.7
Share of Private Sector Credit	9.2	4.6	2.1
Memo: Months of operation	48	26	7

Sources: Bank of Albania, FEFAD Bank, MEB; author's calculations.

However, a quite different view of the significance of the micro banks emerges if their importance is measured in terms of their share in private sector lending. Even if the entire banking system is taken into account, i.e. including the still large portfolios of the (former) state banks, the micro banks, apart from the young Georgian institution, make up a percentage of total lending to the private sector that can no longer be considered negligible. At just under 10 per cent of total outstanding loans to the private sector in Albania and nearly 5 per cent in Bosnia-Herzegovina in volume terms, the micro banks are clearly an important source of credit, despite the fact that the average size of the loans is small.

In view of the large number of borrowers that have received credit from these institutions (see Table 8.3, column 4), the market share of the micro banks in terms of numbers of loans is probably even larger – indeed, significantly larger – than it is in volume terms. However, since there are no data on the total number of borrowers in the countries concerned,[20] this market share can only be gauged against the background of anecdotal evidence. On this basis, the figures even for Georgia, where the MBG had been operating for only seven months at the end of 1999, are probably around 5–10 per cent.

A closer look: the case of FEFAD Bank, Albania

Here I analyse in somewhat greater depth the contribution of the micro banks to financial development, taking the FEFAD Bank, Albania, as an example.[21] FEFAD Bank was chosen here partly because this institution has been operating for four years, and partly because the structure of the Albanian banking system is relatively simple and straightforward. This is so because, in contrast to other transition economies, there has been no period of *laissez-faire* financial sector policies which allowed large numbers of unstable local private banks to be set up, most of them operating as agent banks for their respective owners. As a consequence, the Albanian banking sector, aside from the two remaining state banks, consists of only two banks that were set up as joint ventures between an Albanian state bank and one or several foreign financial institutions, and only nine private banks with foreign capital, most of which comes from the neighbouring countries that are simultaneously Albania's main trade partners.

As they have in the past, the state-owned banks continue to dominate the financial sector, accounting for 81.4 per cent of total assets, 84.8 per cent of total deposits and almost 70 per cent of total loans in the banking system at the end of 1999 (see Table 8.5). However, as the state banks have long since been barred from issuing new loans on account of the notoriously poor quality of their existing portfolios,[22] the supply of credit to the private sector comes, *de facto*, exclusively from the joint-venture and private banks.

Table 8.5   The Albanian banking system: market shares by bank type

	1994	1995	1996	1997	1998	1999
Share of total assets (%)						
– state-owned banks	97.8	95.4	93.9	89.9	85.6	81.4
– joint-venture banks	1.9	4.3	6.5	6.5	5.1	5.8
– private banks	0.3	0.3	1.3	3.6	9.3	12.8
Share of total deposits (%)						
– state-owned banks	96.3	96.8	96.6	92.4	91.3	84.8
– joint-venture banks	3.0	2.5	2.3	4.5	3.5	4.5
– private banks	0.7	0.7	1.1	3.1	5.2	10.6
Share of total loans (%)						
– state-owned banks	97.2	96.0	91.3	82.3	79.3	68.7
– joint-venture banks	1.2	1.9	6.6	15.2	14.7	16.4
– private banks	1.6	2.1	2.1	2.5	6.0	15.0
Total Number of banks	6	6	7	9	10	13
Of which						
– state-owned banks	3	3	3	3	2	2
– joint-venture banks	2	2	2	2	2	2
– private banks	1	1	3	4	6	9

Sources: Bank of Albania; author's calculations.

Therefore, in order to appreciate the significance of the FEFAD Bank as a source of credit for the private sector, the institution's market share of lending by these two groups is the relevant indicator. As Table 8.6 shows, at the end of 1999, the FEFAD Bank accounted for 11.5 per cent of the volume of non-state banks' lending to the private sector, and 24.6 per cent of the private banks' lending.

Table 8.6   Outstanding private sector credit: the importance of the FEFAD Bank in the Albanian banking system, 1999

	April 99
Percentage of total private sector credit	9.2
Percentage of total private sector credit (non state-owned banks)*	11.5
Percentage of total private sector credit (private banks)	24.6

* Joint-venture and private banks.

Sources: Bank of Albania, FEFAD Bank; author's calculations.

The FEFAD Bank's market presence is particularly strong in medium-term lending.[23] In short-term lending, the other private banks are also very active, especially those with capital from the neighbouring countries. Much of their short-term lending takes the form of (cross-border) trade financing for large companies. Accordingly, the FEFAD Bank's share of the market for short-term loans issued by the private banks is only 14 per cent, whereas, thanks to its policy of lending to local service and production enterprises, its share of medium and long-term loans is as high as 37.5 per cent. And even in comparison to the private and joint-venture banks, the quality of the FEFAD Bank's portfolio stands out as being exceptionally good: at the end of 1999 non-performing loans accounted for only 1.3 per cent of its portfolio; and a mere 0.8 per cent of the outstanding volume was classified as loan loss.[24]

Conclusions and a tentative assessment

'Directors also noted that the establishment of a sound and modern financial sector should be a priority. They urged the authorities to close insolvent banks and place sound private banks at the core of the financial system.'[25] The results achieved with the greenfield approach in the countries chosen as examples show that ways to act on this advice do indeed exist. Financial institution-building can make a significant contribution to the development of local financial systems in both quantitative and qualitative terms.

Yet despite, or perhaps precisely because of these successes, critical questions about the approach are increasingly being raised. Therefore I would like to conclude by addressing at least two of the arguments that are frequently put forward in order to play down the significance of the results, or even to imply that the approach is counterproductive for the development of local financial systems.

Argument (a)

The approach relies, to a greater or lesser degree, on subsidies. On the one hand, the new financial institutions receive technical assistance financed by the donors; on the other, they are funded with soft loans. Therefore, the FEFAD Bank, the MEB and the MBG are artificial structures whose sustainability and viability are questionable.

Undeniably, all three micro banks were founded with technical and financial assistance packages. However, it should also be remembered that the scale of support has been significantly reduced over time, and this trend continues. Furthermore, the institutions are becoming increasingly self-sufficient, in terms of both employing local management staff and mobilizing their own loanable funds. In Albania, for example, all of the positions at the bank, apart from that of the General Manager, are held by local experts that have been trained within the project. In the Albanian private banking sector, which is exclusively foreign-controlled, this is an absolute exception to the rule.

As far as funding is concerned, the oldest of the institutions under consideration here, the FEFAD Bank, has now reached the point where it would be able to finance its entire loan portfolio with funds mobilized in the local financial market (see Table 8.3, row 10). Although it still makes use of subsidized funds, these no longer dictate the bank's level of activity.

Moreover, the profitability of all three microfinance institutions is increasing over time, so that the fact that they are financing an increasing proportion of their activities at market rates does not pose a threat to their financial viability.[26] Therefore, there is no justification for predicting that they will remain permanently tied to the donors' 'umbilical cord'. This success is increasingly coming to the notice of local and foreign investors. Enquiries have already started to come in from parties interested in acquiring an equity stake in these institutions. Thus, the medium-term exit strategy of some of their co-founders is unlikely to fail due to lack of demand, a fact which suggests that, from this point of view too, the state of the market confirms the viability of these institutions.

Argument (b)
The success of the target group-oriented banks is achieved at the expense of the development of local, private banks which are having to compete for the business of creditworthy enterprises without the benefit of subsidies.

The figures presented earlier provided no evidence to support the claim that the micro banks take borrowers away from other banks;[27] in other words, their impact is additive rather than substitutive. If such a claim were true, there would have to have been a trend towards increased lending to the private sector which was reversed when the micro banks entered the local banking markets; or alternatively, the total volume of outstanding credit to the private sector would have to have stagnated despite the entry of the micro banks. Yet the empirical evidence suggests that neither was in fact the case. Furthermore, 99 per cent (90 per cent and more) of the micro banks' outstanding loans have a balance of less than US$50 000 (US$10 000). In terms of portfolio volume, at least 90 per cent (at least 45 per cent) is accounted for by loans under US$50 000 (US$10 000). This means not only that the target group – micro, small and medium-sized enterprises – are being reached, but also that the micro banks are filling precisely the supply gap identified by the preparatory financial sector studies, and not only by them.[28]

The argument that subsidies going to micro banks are distorting competition is also unsustainable. For one thing, the subsidies are not being passed on to the target group in the form of lower interest rates. On the contrary, as a matter of principle, the interest rates are set on the basis of market conditions;[29] indeed, rather than complain about subsidies from the international donor community crowding out the local banks, observers, e.g. representatives of the international financial institutions, are much more likely to urge the management of the micro banks to lower their interest rates in order to increase still further the volume of lending by the banking system to the private sector.

Therefore, the competition represented by the micro banks in the local banking markets can itself be regarded as one of the factors boosting financial sector development. After all, they are doing precisely what the international financial institutions and the national central banks have repeatedly urged the local banks to do.[30] Indeed, instead of a crowding out effect, the micro banks can be seen to be having a demonstration effect. This manifests itself, for example, in the fact that the Bank of Albania recommends the FEFAD Bank as an example to other banks that, using the appropriate credit technology, loan operations can be conducted successfully, even in Albania's difficult lending environment.

Another reflection of this demonstration effect is the fact that other banks try to poach employees, and particularly loan officers, who were trained at the micro banks.

And finally it should be noted that, particularly in Albania, Bosnia-Herzegovina and Georgia, the micro banks are not the only subsidized intervention by the international donor community in the local financial system. Many millions of dollars have gone into these financial systems and the institutions that comprise them – i.e. state-owned and private commercial banks – in the form of technical assistance grants and soft loans with a view to contributing to the development of the financial sectors and particularly to encouraging lending to the private sector.[31] Thus, unless they are advocating a radical free-market solution that totally dispenses with all forms of external intervention, which would render donors and international financial institutions superfluous, at least in this field, those who raise the subsidy issue should be debating the merits of subsidies not in terms of competition and *Ordnungspolitik*, but rather in terms of whether or not the subsidies are being put to efficient use.[32] The greenfield approach has nothing to fear from such a debate. On the contrary, the figures presented in the foregoing analysis demonstrate clearly that in the three countries highlighted here, with their extremely underdeveloped financial systems, its contribution has been far more than the proverbial drop in the ocean.

Notes

1. See for example McKinnon (1973), King and Levine (1993) and Levine (1996).
2. An overview is provided in World Bank (1989); for a current perspective, see Long (1999).
3. This may sound like an obvious point, but for a long time development practitioners failed to recognize its importance; for a detailed analysis see Krahnen and Schmidt (1994).
4. This is confirmed by an analysis of the historical development of financial systems in Western Europe and the US, and also by observations of financial systems in developing countries; for a detailed analysis of this point, see Winkler (1999).
5. See for example Diamond (1984).
6. See also the overview of financial sector development in transition economies in EBRD (1998, pp. 92ff.).
7. As with other transition indicators, here too there is a gap between the Western and the Eastern/South-eastern transition economies, i.e. the institutional and technological deficiencies in the states of South-eastern Europe

and the CIS are significantly greater than in the countries of Central and Eastern Europe; see EBRD (1999).

8. The World Bank (1993) called these institutions 'agent banks'.

9. On appropriate lending technologies, see Schmidt and Zeitinger (1998, p. 29).

10. As a consequence, these credit lines often achieve disappointing results; see, for example, Webster et al. (1996).

11. On these two approaches, see Schmidt and Zeitinger (1998, pp. 40ff.) and Schmidt and Winkler (2000).

12. On this point, see Neuhauss (this volume). For a detailed description and analysis of the EBRD's Russia Small Business Fund, the largest downscaling project in the region, focusing on its design, its prospects and the problems associated with it, see Wallace (1996) and Zeitinger (1996).

13. See, with reference to the example of Russia, Graham et al. (1999).

14. See Zeitinger (1998).

15. Schmidt and Zeitinger (1996) discuss this set of problems in detail. In the context of the transition economies, there are additional grounds for arguing that credit-granting NGOs are not sustainable in the medium-to-long term. In contrast to Latin America, there is significant demand in the transition economies for non-credit financial services, such as current, term and savings accounts, international and domestic money transfers and various types of bank guarantees, not only among small enterprises, but even among the larger microenterprises; yet NGOs are not permitted to offer these services. That this is a fundamental problem facing NGOs was already emphasized by Otero (1994).

16. See also Buch (1996).

17. In particular, IFC, KfW, DEG, the EBRD, FMO and DOEN. In Georgia, the shareholders of the new microfinance institution also included four local banks.

18. In Albania, which in a sense acted as a pilot project for the others, the first step was to establish, within the framework of German–Albanian development cooperation, the credit-granting NGO Foundation for Enterprise Finance and Development (FEFAD). As long ago as mid-1997 FEFAD applied to the Central Bank, the Bank of Albania, for a licence to found FEFAD Bank. The full licence was finally issued in March 1999, and since 15 March 1999, FEFAD Bank has operated as a fully-licensed bank in the Albanian market. A detailed analysis of the making of FEFAD is provided by Reitemeier and Winkler (1997).

19. IPC has been active in the building of all three institutions, generally in the role of management consultants. Another link between the institutions is the fact that Internationale Micro Investitionen (IMI), an investment company co-founded by IPC, holds shares in each of them. Therefore, readers wishing to trace the subsequent development of the three banks can obtain updated figures for most of the indicators included in Table 8.3 from the websites of these two organizations (<www.ipcgmbh.de> and <www.imi-ag.de>).

20. In Bulgaria the Bulgarian National Bank estimated that roughly 13 500 non-financial private enterprises had a loan outstanding to the banking system as of the end of 1999. Given that in Bulgaria the ratio of private sector credit to GDP stands at approximately 12 per cent, i.e. significantly higher than in

Albania and Georgia, it is reasonable to assume that the total number of borrowers in these latter two economies is no larger and is in fact probably smaller.

21. See also the exhaustive assessment by Winkler (2000).

22. Lack of corporate governance and continuous political interference have led to a situation in which over 80 per cent of the loans in the overall portfolio of these banks are non-performing. The Bank of Albania prohibits banks from issuing new loans if more than 20 per cent of their portfolio consists of loans that are more than 30 days in arrears (see Baleta 1999, p. 21).

23. The Bank of Albania defines short-term lending as loans with a maturity of less than one year, medium-term lending as loans with a maturity between one and five years and long-term lending as loans with a maturity of more than five years.

24. The corresponding figures for the private banks as a group (including FEFAD Bank) are 9.5 per cent (non-performing loans) and 3.3 per cent (loan loss).

25. IMF (2000), IMF Concludes Article IV Consultation with Bosnia and Herzegovina, Public Information Notice (PIN) No. 00/22: <http://www.imf.org/external/np/sec/pn/2000/PN0022.htm> [p. 3].

26. See Calmeadow (1999) and also, in general terms, Schmidt and Zeitinger (1999, pp. 24ff.).

27. The level of activity of the micro banks in non-credit lines of business, such as payment transactions and deposit taking, is so low that the accusation that they are crowding out other banks in these markets is too absurd even to merit a response here.

28. For example, an SME strategy paper issued by the Albanian government at the end of 1999 reports that loan amounts up to US$120 000 are in short supply.

29. Compare, for example, the lending interest rates charged by all Bosnian commercial banks, as enumerated in Central Bank of Bosnia and Herzegovina, *Bulletin No. 4/1999*, Sarajevo, p. 118. The sole exception to this rule is the rate charged by MBG on its gold pawn loans. In Georgia, MBG's entry has lowered the going 'market interest rate' from 6–8 per cent per month to 3–4 per cent. As the inverted commas indicate, the previously prevailing interest rate can hardly be regarded as the result of market processes, but rather as the price controlled by a supply-side oligopoly whose dominance has been broken by MBG's market entry.

30. For example Baleta (1999, p. 24) argues that the presence of the foreign banks in a country, particularly in transition economies, ensures long-term benefits in the form of additional pressure exercised on the national (domestic) banks regarding the undertaking of the appropriate risks, the expertise and technology transfer, the promotion of competition, etc.

31. The Georgian National Bank publishes data on the volume of credit lines granted by non-residents to commercial banks for small and medium-sized enterprise development. At the end of 1999 the total volume of these lines amounted to almost US$23 million. This means that roughly 16 per cent of the total private sector lending by the Georgian commercial banks has been refinanced by these funds. In Albania, bilateral and international donors are said to have committed a total of US$177 million in the years 1992–8.

32. On this point, see also Murdoch (1999).

References

Baleta, T. (1999) 'Briefly the Albanian Banking System in 1998', Bank of Albania, *Economic Bulletin*, Vol. 2, No. 3: 13–25.

Buch, C. (1996) 'Opening up for Foreign Banks – Why Central and Eastern Europe Can Benefit', Kiel Working Paper No. 763, Kiel Institute of World Economics.

Calmeadow (1999) *Financial Performance Report* prepared for FEFAD, Albania, A Report of the Micro Banking Bulleting Project, Washington DC.

Central Bank of Bosnia and Herzegovina (1999) *Bulletin No. 4*, Sarajevo.

Diamond, D. W. (1984) 'Financial Intermediation as Delegated Monitoring', *Review of Economic Studies*, Vol. 51: 393–414.

EBRD (1998) *Transition Report* 1998, London.

EBRD (1999) *Transition Report* 1999, London.

Graham, D. H., Hartarska, V., Nadoluyak, D. and Safavian, M. (1999) 'The Legal and Regulatory Framework Shaping the World of Microfinance', Paper presented at the Third Annual Seminar on New Development Finance, Frankfurt, Germany.

IMF (2000) 'IMF Concludes Article IV Consultation with Bosnia and Herzegovina', Public Information Notice (PIN) No. 00/22: <http://www.imf.org/external/np/sec/pn/2000/PN0022.htm>

King, R. G. and Levine, R. (1993) 'Finance, Entrepreneurship, and Growth', *Journal of Monetary Economics*, Vol. 32: 513–42.

Krahnen, J. P. and Schmidt, R. H. (1994) *Development Finance as Institution Building*, Boulder, San Francisco, Oxford.

Levine, R. (1996) *Financial Development and Economic Growth – Views and Agenda*, World Bank Policy Research Paper 1678, World Bank, Washington DC.

Long, M. (1999) 'A 1999 Perspective on Finance and Development: World Development Report 1999', Paper for the Third Annual Seminar on New Development Finance, Frankfurt, Germany, 27 September.

McKinnon, R. I. (1973), *Money and Capital in Economic Development*, The Brookings Institution, Washington DC.

Murdoch, J. (1999) 'The Microfinance Promise', *Journal of Economic Literature*, Vol. XXXVII, No. 4: 1569–614.

Otero, M. (1994) 'The Evolution of Nongovernmental Organizations Toward Financial Intermediation', in M. Otero and E. Rhyne (eds), *The New World of Microenterprise Finance, Building Healthy Financial Institutions For the Poor*, Kumarian Press, West Hartford, CT, pp. 94–104.

Reitemeier, R. and Winkler, A. (1997) 'The Making of FEFAD', Paper presented at the First Annual Seminar on New Development Finance, Frankfurt, Germany.

Schmidt, R. H. and Winkler, A. (2000) 'Financial Institution Building in Developing Countries', *Journal für Entwicklungspolitik*, Vol. XVI, No. 3.

Schmidt, R. H. and Zeitinger, C.-P. (1996) 'The Efficiency of Credit-Granting NGOs in Latin America', *Savings and Development*, Vol. 20: 353–84.

Schmidt, R. H. and Zeitinger, C.-P. (1998) 'Critical Issues in Microbusiness Finance and the Role of Donors', in M. S. Kimenyi, R. C. Wieland and J. D. Von Pischke (eds), *Strategic Issues in Microfinance*, Aldershot: Ashgate pp. 27–51.

Wallace, E. (1996) 'Financial Institutional Development – The Case of the Russia Small Business Fund', in J. Levitsky (ed.), *Small Business in Transition Economies*, London, pp. 76–84.

Webster, L. M., Riopelle, R. and Chidzero, A.-M. (1996) *World Bank Lending for Small Enterprises 1989–1993*, World Bank Technical Paper Number 311, Washington DC.

Winkler, A. (1999) *Wirtschaftswachstum und Finanzsystementwicklung*, Habilitationsschrift, Universität Würzburg.

Winkler, A. (2000) 'Financial Development and Financial Institution Building in Albania', Frankfurt am Main, mimeo.

World Bank (1989) *World Development Report*, Washington DC.

World Bank (1993) *Russia – The Banking System in Transition*, Washington DC.

Zeitinger, C.-P. (1996) 'Micro-lending in the Russian Federation', in J. Levitsky (ed.), *Small Business in Transition Economies*, London, pp. 85–94.

Zeitinger, C.-P. (1998) 'New Development Finance – Lessons from Experience', Presentation at the Second Annual Seminar on New Development Finance, Frankfurt, Germany.

9
The Development of the Banking Sector in Eastern Europe: The Next Decade

Christa Hainz and Monika Schnitzer[1]

Introduction

The first decade of transition has seen tremendous changes in Eastern European economies. While in the first decade the focus of politicians was primarily on privatizing firms and setting up institutions necessary for a market economy, the focus of the second decade will need to be on developing the financial sector and making the financial institutions work. In this chapter we look more closely at the banking sector in Eastern Europe and we discuss three main questions. Below, we ask what the banking sector should look like; in particular, how competitive we would wish the banking sector to be. Next, we investigate how the initial conditions and the reforms strategies chosen in different countries have shaped the banking sector in Eastern Europe. We then contrast this picture of the banking sector as it is today with the desired market structure discussed below. Finally, we discuss what needs to be done in order to achieve the banking sector as we would like to see it.

What the banking sector should look like

It has been argued that some of the desired features of a banking sector, like efficiency, can clash with others, such as stability.[2] This suggests that there is a fundamental trade-off between efficiency and stability that policymakers face when designing and regulating the banking sector.

And more often than not the advice is to put more emphasis on stability than on efficiency, due to the systemic risk that is inherent to the banking sector. Competition, so the argument goes, may be good for efficiency but is bad for stability. Thus, competition in the banking sector should be limited. Here, we discuss and question the theoretical foundations of this alleged relationship between competition and stability and between competition and efficiency.

Motivated by recent financial market liberalizations in Western economies, the existing theoretical literature on bank competition is mainly concerned with the question of what impact this liberalization has on the stability of the banking sector. Matutes and Vives (1996) study a model where banks compete for deposits. They find that the probability of bank failure increases with the degree of competition. The reason is that more intensive competition has a negative impact on the profit margins a bank can obtain. Since bank failures have a negative impact on social welfare this means that bank competition has a negative impact on social welfare. Similarly, in Hellmann, Murdock and Stiglitz (1998), competition for deposits erodes profits and promotes gambling in the banking sector. This is because the ongoing concern value of the bank is lower. The problem here is that an increase in competition has little impact on the total amount of deposits but mainly increases market-stealing incentives. These two articles are examples of a theoretical literature that suggests that competition has a negative impact on the stability of the banking sector. Note that this argument takes the degree of competition as given, which means that it considers the short-run effect of competition on stability.

Consider next three papers that deal with the interaction of competition and efficiency in the banking sector. Efficiency here relates not only to the cost of credit and hence to the number of credits allocated, but also to the quality of projects financed. Broecker (1990) and Riordan (1993) study models where banks acquire information about potential customers before entering a relationship with them. Broecker analyses a competitive credit market where banks compete in prices and receive costless signals about the creditworthiness of potential borrowers. He shows that the number of bad loans provided increases with the number of banks operating, which has a negative impact on the average creditworthiness of borrowers who receive credit. This can reduce social welfare. Riordan emphasizes that more competition makes the 'winner's curse' problem more severe. Since banks are afraid to be too optimistic with their judgement about potential borrowers, more competition induces banks to be more conservative when approving loans. This greater conservativeness can also result in a significant welfare reduction.

The problem with the papers by Broecker and Riordan is that they assume that signals about potential clients are costlessly available to all banks. However, if one takes into account that information acquisition is costly, the interesting question is how competition affects the banks' incentive to invest in screening potential clients. This question is studied in Schnitzer (1999a), where we compare the screening incentives in two extreme scenarios; one with a monopolistic bank and one with Bertrand competition. What we find is that under Bertrand competition credit rates are lower than in the case of a monopolistic bank, but we also find that the credit allocation under Bertrand competition is less efficient because under competition not all banks have an incentive to acquire information when a monopolistic firm does and so it is more likely that bad loans are given. Thus, our second conclusion from the theoretical literature is that in a short-run framework, for a given degree of competition, competition can have a positive impact on efficiency because it reduces credit costs but it can also have a negative impact on the efficiency of credit allocation because it increases the number of bad credits given. Thus, we find that in a static framework there exists indeed a trade-off between lower credit costs in the case of more competition and fewer bad credits and more stability in the banking sector in the case of less competition.

However, the question is how robust this trade-off is if we take a long-run perspective. The articles discussed above are considering the short run only in so far as they take the degree of competition and the value of firms' investment projects as given. They neglect possible interactions of competition and the value of projects. However, the value of individual projects depends on the effort firm managers spend on restructuring their firms and designing good investment projects. How much effort managers spend on this activity depends on the profitability of their projects and thus on the credit costs they face. This in turn depends on competition in the banking sector.[3]

But there is also a reverse causation. In the long run, market entry and hence competition in the banking sector depends on the profitability of potential investment projects. The more the economy grows the more banks will find market entry attractive. Thus, in a long-run analysis the market structure in the banking sector and the value of firms' investment projects need to be determined endogenously and jointly because of their interaction.

In both Hainz (1999) and Schnitzer (1999b), we consider a dynamic framework which investigates the impact of bank competition on the firms' decision to restructure. The model of Hainz is about banks that use (firm-specific) collateral to extract rents from firms. The fact that banks have asymmetric information about the firms' asset endowment leads to adverse selection which is solved by credit rationing. More competition reduces the amount of collateral required for rent extraction and this in turn reduces credit rationing. Thus, more competition increases the availability of finance for restructuring purposes.

In Schnitzer (1999b), managers have to spend effort to restructure their firms and develop good investment projects. More competition reduces the credit costs and, by leaving a higher pay-off to the manager, increases the managers' incentives to restructure their firms. In this model, the market structure in the banking sector is determined endogenously. Market entry, as suggested above, depends positively on the profitability of the firms' investment projects. Thus, depending on the firms' expectations about future credit cost there exist two possible equilibria. If firms expect low credit costs they engage in restructuring. This encourages bank entry which leads indeed to low credit costs in the future. So the expectations of the firms were justified. If firms expect high credit costs instead, they do not engage in restructuring. This discourages bank entry which leads indeed to high credit costs. So again, the expectations of the firms were justified.

This leads us to our third conclusion from the theoretical literature. If we study the long run, we find that there is a positive interaction between bank competition and restructuring of firms.[4] Taking this line of argument one step further, our current research suggests that more restructuring, by reducing the likelihood of bad projects, also reduces the likelihood of bank failures and thus promotes banking stability. This suggests that in a long-run analysis competition could have a positive impact on stability in the bank sector after all.

Thus, we argue that in the long run, we do not find the same kind of trade-off between efficiency and stability in the banking sector that we observe in a short-run analysis. In contrast, intensive competition and low credit cost are the necessary preconditions to promote the development of good projects and growth in general – both of which are in fact necessary preconditions to guarantee the stability of the banking sector.

The current situation in the banking sector

Here we want to contrast the picture of what the banking sector should look like with what it does actually look like in transition economics today. The current banking sectors in Central and Eastern Europe have been characterized as being 'overbanked but underserviced'. It is argued that the number of banks exceeds the one that would make sense from an efficiency point of view if one considers potential economies of scale (Bonin and Wachtel 1999). These numerous banks can be split up in two major groups of players: the formerly state-owned commercial banks (SOCBs) and the new entrants. Former SOCBs have retained large stakes in the banking market and still have considerable market power. The new entrants have not changed the structure of the banking industry fundamentally, but they are responsible for a higher systemic risk which is due to their poor banking practices and undercapitalization. The current situation of the banking sector is determined by the initial conditions when the economies started transformation and the reform measures which have been undertaken so far. Below we briefly review this process.

Privatization

The state-owned banking sector inherited from central planning has been privatized, but the extent of privatization varies from country to country. Despite the formal privatization the state still keeps control in many respects. Countries used different methods of privatization. In the Czech Republic, banks were part of the mass privatization programme. The majority of vouchers is managed by the investment funds which were often founded by banks. Cross-ownership patterns among financial institutions and banks were established as well as between banks and firms. As owners of investment funds, the banks are represented in the management and supervisory boards of many firms. Thus, they have a dual role – as creditor and as equity holder – which can lead to incentive problems. In two of the largest banks the state still is the majority owner. The result of this privatization programme is a bifurcated ownership structure in which the state retains a core-investor stake (Bonin et al. 1998).

   Poland and Hungary chose a mixture of initial public offerings and selling ownership stakes to strategic foreign investors. Hungary in particular relied on foreign investors. Both countries experienced difficult negotiations with the strategic foreign investors which led to delays of the privatization process (Meyendorff and Synder 1997). In Poland the state retains a core-investor stake, combined with dispersed ownership. This allows bargaining between the state and the insiders to continue (Bonin et al. 1998). In Hungary, foreign banks are an integral part of the banking system; some of them acquired stakes in formerly state-owned banks. Before privatization the state-owned commercial banks were split up, along regional lines in Poland and along sectoral lines in Hungary (Bonin and Wachtel 1999). Due to this fragmentation the formerly state-owned banks in Poland can still exert monopoly power in their regions (Meyendorff and Snyder 1997).

In Russia, privatization could be described as an informal management-led process. Due to a lack of central control the managers together with local officials determined the banks' future ownership structure. This way of privatization gives neither the government nor outside investors a significant role in corporate control. In contrast to the Visegrad countries the state plays a much less important role in Russia, but control will continue to be exerted by insiders, especially bank managers (ibid.).

The initial results of privatization will influence the long-term structure and perspectives of the banking sector as changes of the ownership structure are difficult in a poorly developed institutional environment (ibid.).

Bad loans

To operate independently the banks need to have a sufficiently high capital endowment. In transition countries, however, they inherited loan portfolios with a high proportion of bad loans. The economies have chosen different approaches to solve this problem. In some countries the bad loans were transferred from the banks to a consolidation bank. In others a decentralized way was taken where the banks retain their bad loans and are responsible for the bad debt workout. Furthermore, the banks were recapitalized as the bad loans substantially reduced their capital endowment.

The Czech Republic used a combination of centralized and bank-based approaches. The consolidation bank took over all working capital loans and restructured them. The surprising result was that these loans were of better quality than the average loan portfolio of a Czech bank as all firms were granted such loans for working capital. In a second step, the major commercial bank transferred bad loans to the consolidation bank and was partially recapitalized with government bonds (Bonin and Wachtel 1999).

Poland addressed recapitalization and workout of problem loans at once. In this decentralized solution the banks had to classify the doubtful loans and transfer them to a workout unit within the bank. The workout unit has to reach an agreement with the firms on its financial restructuring. The drawback of this solution might be that the relationship between the banks and firms in trouble continue (Borish et al. 1997, Bonin and Wachtel 1999).

Hungary went through several rounds of recapitalization. In the beginning, more centralized reforms were used, then the government preferred a bank-based solution comparable to the Polish one. Hungary failed to design the recapitalization programme as a credible one-shot action and thus had to repeat the bail-outs. Therefore recapitalization was expensive for the government. In total, 8.5 per cent of GDP was spent between 1992 and 1994 to solve this problem (Borish et al. 1997, p. 67, Bonin and Wachtel 1999).

In Russia, politically very sensitive banks received government support to increase the capital endowment (Meyendorff and Synder 1997). In late 1998, after the crisis, an Agency for Restructuring Credit Organizations was founded which has a wide range of tasks, from taking control of banks to reversing previous asset stripping, but so far the restructuring has not been very successful (EBRD 1999).

These programmes were mainly used to solve the 'stock problem', the bad loans in the portfolio which the banks could not be made accountable for as they were inherited. However, the amount of recapitalization has not always been sufficiently high to create banks which are financially able to operate independently (Bonin and Wachtel 1999). What still has to be resolved is the 'flow problem'. If banks do not have appropriate incentives they continue to take excessive risks or neglect the selection of profitable projects and new bad debts accumulate.

Regulation

Early in the reform period the entry of 'de novo' banks was liberalized to create competitive pressure on the still existing or formerly state-owned banks. Little emphasis was placed on the quality of banks. The problem was that regulation of the banking sector and bank supervision were themselves in their infancy. The result was a massive entry of small banks which were weakly capitalized and ill-prepared for the banking business. This led to fraudulent behaviour which in turn increased the systemic risk of the banking sector. At the same time it was very difficult for the supervisory agencies to intervene as they have not been prepared for their monitoring tasks (EBRD 1998).

The whole banking sector is still undercapitalized. In some countries SOCBs have a higher ratio of capital to asset than private banks; in others the relationship is reversed. The relation depends on the entry regulations for new banks as well as on the extent of recapitalization. Many countries try hard to adopt the minimum capital requirements of the Basle agreement. However, these standards seem too low for transition economies since the macroeconomic environment is less stable and risk in general is higher than in established market economies (Bonin et al. 1998).

Foreign banks

Foreign banks contribute to the contestability of the market as long as formerly state-owned banks can still act as monopolists and new banks are not strong enough to create competitive pressure. The number and market share of foreign banks varies a lot in the region and depends on the legal framework, regulating their entry. The share of majority foreign-owned banks in total bank assets is highest in Hungary (more than 60 per cent in 1997). Hungary had already liberalized market entry in 1987 and foreign investors not only participate in privatization but also establish new banks (EBRD 1998).

The share is much lower in Poland and the Czech Republic (well above 10 per cent). Poland took a very liberal licensing policy in the beginning of the 1990s, but after two years became very reluctant. The situation changed again with the privatization of the state-owned banks where government was actively searching for strategic foreign investors (Bonin et al. 1998). In the Czech Republic, foreign banks did not participate in the first rounds of privatization. Thus foreign banks played a minor role in the beginning, but in the meantime they are catching up (ibid.). Currently, the state wants to sell some of its remaining stakes in the big banks to foreign banks. Poland as well as the Czech Republic prefer foreign capital to enter existing banks rather than to grant new licences (Buch 1997).

The market share of foreign banks is even lower in many successor states of the Soviet Union, e.g. 5–10 per cent in Russia (EBRD 1998). This reflects that a stable economic environment as well as a functioning payment system and interbank market are still lacking, both prerequisites for investments by foreign banks.

The benefits of foreign banks for transition countries include the influx of capital and know how, which are scarce factors. The introduction of modern banking practices, like for example loan evaluation, will lead to spillover effects. For foreign banks access to the credit market is much easier than to the deposit market as no extensive branch network is necessary. Thus they will increase interbank lending and thereby contribute to the development of financial markets.

But there are also critics who caution against the market entry of foreign banks. One of the major fears is that foreign banks gain too much influence on the domestic economy. Reality shows that foreign banks mainly serve their multinational customers (Bonin et al. 1998). Further objections concern the banks' contribution to increasing short-term portfolio flows which can adversely influence macroeconomic stabilization (ibid.). Another argument is that regulation might be less stringent in the foreign banks' home country. Thus these banks could easily be used, for example for money laundering activities. Authorities in the Baltics are therefore not very pleased with the market entry of Russian or Ukrainian banks (ibid.).

What conclusions can we draw for the current situation in the banking sector in Eastern Europe?

Competition

If we want to judge the competitiveness of the banking sector it turns out that the number of banks in the Central and Eastern European countries is not a proper indicator. Even though the number of banks may be quite large, competitive pressure is still rather low, for a number of reasons. As it is, banks are very heterogeneous and therefore do not offer homogeneous services for which competition would be intense. The basis for a low degree of competition was set when the state-owned banks were split up along sectors and – what is even more problematic – along regional lines. These measures supported the banks' market power. Furthermore, collusion among the banks is fostered as bank employees and bank managers from the former monobank know each other very well. The entry of 'de novo' banks could not break up the dominant position of the formerly state-owned banks. However, the market entry of foreign banks has significantly contributed to the contestability of the banking sector. Since they operate mainly on the credit market and to a lesser extent on the deposit market, they cannot exert enough pressure on domestic banks to develop market-oriented behaviour (Bonin and Wachtel 1999).

Stability

What about stability? All countries in Central and Eastern Europe experienced significant problems in the banking sector. The reason was a low capital endowment: new banks started with little equity and old banks often were not sufficiently recapitalized. Furthermore, the lack of good banking practices led the banks to take on excessive risks. The Visegrad countries faced significant problems; several banks became insolvent. A fully-fledged crisis occurred in Russia in 1998 as the whole banking sector was concerned and many banks were forced to close (Lindgren et al. 1996, Gorton and Winton 1998).

Efficiency

There are good reasons why, for efficiency, the number of banks should not be too large since there is a significant potential for economies of scale in transition countries. According to ERBD data, for each 1 per cent increase in scale the operating costs increase on average by 0.8 per cent (EBRD 1998). Therefore the proliferation of banks does not make sense from a social welfare perspective. As established banks, i.e. formerly state-owned banks, still have market power in the deposit market, the mobilization of savings suffers. The interest rate spreads are considerable. However credit demand is reduced due to high interest rates.

Empirical studies found that smaller banks expand their customer loans more rapidly than dominant banks (ibid.). This could be a sign for credit rationing by banks with market power. On an aggregate level credit rationing is expressed by a low share of credit to the private sector. But these figures are also influenced by the low amount of savings allocated to banks and the credits granted to the government or state-owned firms.

Finally, former state-owned banks are often huge and therefore 'too big to fail'. This means the government has to support them in cases with severe problems. With this expectation of future bail-outs the banks have little incentive to operate efficiently and prudently.

To summarize, transition countries find themselves in a very difficult situation. The economies cannot use the trade-off between competitive efficiency and stability which we found in the static context. Due to initial conditions and the reform process the large number of banks does not translate into a high degree of competition but leads to a high level of instability (Gorton and Winton 1998). Even worse is the dynamic perspective if the banking sectors continue to operate inefficiently and suffer from a high degree of instability. So the crucial question is, how can the situation be improved?

What needs to be done

We want to conclude this chapter with three suggestions on what should be done:

- The banking sector needs some consolidation, a shake-out of inefficiently small, undercapitalized and poorly trained banks. As banks get bigger and more diversified, the risk of bank failure and bank instability is reduced.

- The disadvantage of fewer banks may be less competition. But considering the current situation this risk seems relatively small, since there is rather little competitive pressure to start with. Regulation and bank supervision have to take a more active role to ensure competitive behaviour of the remaining banks.
- Competitive pressure is also provided by potential market entry by foreign banks. It is crucial to keep the banking sector open for foreign banks.

It is obvious that establishing a well-functioning banking sector needs time and not too much should be expected in the first decade. But it does not only need time; it also needs strong forces that work to this effect. It is likely that the pressure arising from the wish to join the European Union will prove very effective in this respect.

Notes

1. Financial support through DFG grant Schn 422/3–1 and through the EC's Phase ACE Programme, grant P98-1122-R, is gratefully acknowledged.
2. See for example Steinherr (1997).
3. See also Gorton and Winton (1998), who develop an asymmetric information model in which entry of new banks is necessary to finance entrepreneurial firms. They argue that the higher degree of instability that comes with this entry of new banks in the short run is justified because it promotes economic efficiency in the long run.
4. See also Rey and Rochet (1998), who develop a model of banking competition with moral hazard and adverse selection. In their model, competition among domestic banks alone cannot improve allocation of credit. Introducing foreign banks, however, with a better monitoring technology and a lower cost of funds, can improve the capital allocation and reduce the risk of failure of domestic banks.

References

Bonin, J. P., Miszei, K., Szekely, I. P. and Wachtel, P. (1998) *Banking in Transition Economies: Developing Market Oriented Banking Sectors in Eastern Europe*, Cheltenham and Northampton: Edward Elgar.

Bonin, J. P. and Wachtel, P. (1999) 'Toward Market-Oriented Banking in the Economies of Transition', in M. J. Brejer and M. Skreb (eds), *Financial Sector Transformation, Lessons from Economies in Transition*, Cambridge: Cambridge University Press, pp. 195–236.

Borish, M. S., Ding, W. and Noël, M. (1997) 'Restructuring the State-Owned Banking Sector: A Comparative Assessment of Approaches in Central Europe', *Most*, 7: 49–77.

Broecker, T. (1990) 'Creditworthiness Tests and Interbank Competition', *Econometrica*, 58: 429–52.

Buch, C. M. (1997) 'Opening up for Foreign Banks: How Central and Eastern Europe can Benefit', *Economics of Transition*, 5, 2: 339–66.

European Bank for Reconstruction and Development (EBRD) (1998) *Transition Report 1998: Financial Sector in Transition*, London: EBRD.

European Bank for Reconstruction and Development (EBRD) (1999) *Transition Report 1999: Ten Years of Transition*, London: EBRD.

Gorton, G. and Winton, A. (1998) 'Banking in Transition Economies: Does Efficiency Require Instability?', *Money, Credit and Banking*, 30, No. 3: 621–55.

Hainz, C. (1999) 'Credit Contracts and Restructuring in Transition Economics: On the Role of Bank Competition and Collateral', Muenchner Wirtschaftswissenschaftliche Beitraege (99–13), Discussion Paper, August, Munich.

Hellmann, T., Murdock, K. and Stiglitz, J. (1998) 'Liberalization, Moral Hazard in Banking, and Prudential Regulation: Are Capital Requirements Enough?', mimeo, Stanford University, California.

Lindgren, C.-J., Garcia, G. and Saal, M. I. (1996) *Bank Soundness and Macroeconomic Policy*, Washington DC: International Monetary Fund.

Meyendorff, A. and Synder, E.A. (1997) 'Transactional Structures of Bank Privatizations in Central Europe and Russia', *Journal of Comparative Economics* 25: 5–30.

Matutes, C. and Vives, X. (1996) 'Competition for Deposits, Fragility and Insurance', *Journal of Financial Intermediation*, 5: 184–216.

Rey, P. and Rochet, J.-C. (1998) 'Banking Competition, Stability and Innovation in Transition Economies', mimeo, Toulouse.

Riordan, M. H. (1993) 'Competition and Bank Performance: A Theoretical Perspective', pp. 328–43 in C. Mayer and X. Vives (eds) *Capital Markets and Financial Intermediation*, Cambridge: Cambridge University Press.

Schnitzer, M. (1999a) 'On the Role of Bank Competition for Corporate Governance and Corporate Control in Transition Economies', *Journal of Institutional and Theoretical Economics*, 155: 22–46.

Schnitzer, M. (1999b) 'Bank Competition and Enterprise Restructuring in Transition Economies', *Economics of Transition*, 7: 133–55.

Steinherr, A. (1997) 'Banking Reforms in Eastern European Countries', *Oxford Review of Economic Policy* 13, 2: 106–25.

Index

Compiled by Sue Carlton